# OWN *the* FUTURE

## 50 Ways to Win *from* The Boston Consulting Group

Edited by
Michael Deimler, Richard Lesser,
David Rhodes, and Janmejaya Sinha

WILEY

*Library of Congress Cataloging-in-Publication Data:*

Own the future : 50 ways to win from the Boston Consulting Group / edited by Michael
Deimler, Richard Lesser, David Rhodes, and Janmejaya Sinha.
    pages cm
  Includes index.
  ISBN 978-1-118-59170-3 (cloth); ISBN 978-1-118-65155-1 (ebk);
  ISBN 978-1-118-65176-6 (ebk); ISBN 978-1-118-65179-7 (ebk)
  1. Strategic planning. 2. Competition. I. Deimler, Michael S. II. Boston Consulting Group.
  HD30.28.O92 2013
  658.4'012–dc23

                                                                      2013004417

# Contents

# Acknowledgments

Our deepest debt is—as always—to the many clients of The Boston Consulting Group (BCG). The winning moves presented in these pages were begun and then evolved and matured during our close collaboration with them. We are gratified that so many outstanding leaders have found it beneficial to tackle some of their biggest challenges with BCG by their side. We are honored by their abiding trust in us and the work we do with them.

It all started in 1963, when Bruce D. Henderson founded BCG. Fifty years on, we publish this book to celebrate the anniversary and to renew our pledge to help clients face up to their toughest tests in an age of accelerating change.

We also publish this book to honor the individuals at BCG who have held up their ideas to the scrutiny of their peers in our proudly self-critical culture. We salute their commitment and thank them for broadening our horizons.

Everything you see here is the result of teamwork extending far beyond the authors of these 50 chapters. We thank the teams standing behind the authors—those who work late into the night collecting data, testing ideas, and presenting and honing the arguments.

We would also like to single out a few of our colleagues for specific acknowledgment. Hans-Paul Bürkner and Patrick Ducasse supported and encouraged us to celebrate our first 50 years with this book. Martin Reeves and David Michael were instrumental in developing and sharpening its character and content. Simon Targett, Katherine Andrews, Dan Coyne, Mark Voorhees, Harris Collingwood, Gerry Hill, Martha Craumer, Mickey Butts, Jeff Garigliano, Jon Gage, Amy Barrett, Pete Engardio, Catherine Cuddihee, and Bob Howard helped us and our coauthors to express ourselves clearly. Adam Whybrew, Matthew Clark, Eric Knight, Paul McNamara, and Tim Leach masterminded the process of creating this book.

—Michael Deimler, Richard Lesser, David Rhodes,
and Janmejaya Sinha

# Introduction

Own the future.

This is a statement of purpose. If leaders are to win, if they are to put their stamp on tomorrow, they must decide to do so today.

It is also a statement of priorities. To own the future, leaders must do two things.

First, and very fundamentally, they need to win in the marketplace. This is the competitive imperative. Simply put, they need to own—or control—more business than their rivals. In doing so, they will earn the right to wield greater economic power and gain access to more opportunities for growth and value creation.

Second, they need to be accountable for their actions. This is the social imperative. A core tenet of ownership is that with rights come responsibilities. In practice, this means that leaders can't carry out a slash-and-burn strategy in pursuit of a quick buck. Instead, they must commit to the long view, to building a sustainable business.

■ ■ ■

Resolving to "own the future" is one thing. Doing so is quite another—and altogether more challenging.

How can you own the future?

This question triggered the creation of our book. As part of the effort to mark the fiftieth anniversary of The Boston Consulting Group (BCG), we've gathered together 50 chapters on how to turn today's major challenges—many of which have been simmering for some time—into opportunities. This body of work is based not on ivory tower musings but on our close collaboration with clients across the private, public, and social sectors. BCG's guiding principle is "Shaping the Future. Together," and the chapters in this book testify to this.

Week in, week out, BCG's 800 partners, operating in 16 practice areas, work with leaders and their organizations to develop new ideas, new insights, and new ways to win and own the future. From these experiences, we've created a large portfolio of publications and multimedia content. In 2012, we produced more than 300 reports, articles, videos, podcasts, and interactive graphics, all of which are readily available on bcgperspectives.com.

For *Own the Future*, we have pulled together what we think are the best winning moves for leaders and their organizations today: most of these have been developed over the past decade in partnership with our clients, but some are classics that have been developed over the past 50 years and that have stood the test of time.

This book is the third in a series we've produced with John Wiley & Sons, a global publishing house, on groundbreaking business ideas. The two previous volumes were compendiums of BCG writings on strategy going back to the 1960s. This new volume is more contemporary and forward-looking. It has been put together for a very different purpose: to help business leaders navigate their way through a period of accelerating change.

At the book's core is a manifesto for radical transformation—something that has been BCG's underlying mission since its founding 50 years ago. The firm was born in convulsive times: the 1960s were a time of social ferment. Today, the world stands at a new crossroads, facing social, political, and economic turmoil on an unprecedented scale. Everywhere you look, things are changing.

Two things in particular are happening. First, we are experiencing the most radical restructuring of the global economy since the Industrial Revolution, when the countries of Western Europe surpassed China and India—until then, the world's largest markets. This is a seismic and secular shift. Second, as this process unfolds (which may take several decades), we are encountering striking levels of turbulence and volatility.

BCG is at the forefront of efforts to understand this dual phenomenon—and to help organizations stay one step ahead. We have produced some pioneering work on the reshaping of the global economy. In 2008, we wrote *Globality*, which described the competition between everyone from everywhere for everything. Two years later, we wrote *Accelerating out of the Great Recession*, which emerged from our Collateral Damage project and explained the contours of a two-speed world. Most recently, we wrote *The $10 Trillion Prize*, which calculated the likely impact of 1 billion Chinese and Indian middle-class consumers on the world economy by 2020.

We have also led the way in understanding the unprecedented nature of the turbulent conditions confronting business leaders today. Research and analysis by our Strategy Institute have shown that turbulence is striking more frequently than in the past (more than half of the most turbulent quarters over the past 30 years have occurred during the past decade), increasing in intensity (volatility in revenue growth, in revenue ranking, and in operating margins have all more than doubled since the 1960s), and persisting much longer than in preceding periods (the average duration of periods of high turbulence has quadrupled over the past three decades).

Amid all this change, it is not clear where the world is heading over the next 50 years. But one thing is clear: the game is changing. The old ways are rapidly becoming outdated, obsolete. New opportunities are opening up. Some see this transitional period in a gloomy, pessimistic way. By contrast, we at BCG are profoundly positive about the future. As Hans-Paul Bürkner, BCG's chairman and former CEO, says in his chapter, "Strategic Optimism: How to Shape the Future in Times of Crisis" (Chapter 49), "The fundamental drivers of growth are stronger than they have been at any point in human history.".

But to capitalize on these trends, and to really own the future, leaders must be proactive. They must challenge the status quo. In short, they must change the game or risk going out of business. This is not the time to tinker with reform. This is a time for large-scale transformation. In convulsive times, the stakes are higher—and the consequences of success or failure are greater.

■ ■ ■

The book's chapters, some of which have been abridged from longer reports, are arranged along 10 dimensions—each one an attribute of outstanding organizations and their leaders. In an age of accelerating change, foremost among these attributes is the need to be adaptive. This capacity to change—and, in particular, to turn each new challenge into an opportunity—is the secret of the most successful game-changing organizations.

BCG has long extolled the virtues of adaptive approaches. Bruce Henderson, BCG's founder and the architect of modern corporate strategy, wrote extensively on what he called strategic and natural competition, drawing on ideas about evolution and adaptation from Charles Darwin. In this book, we republish some of our latest thinking on this attribute, which has been featured in *Harvard Business Review*.

It is clear that leaders and their companies need to be more adaptive than they have been before, given the pace of change and the volatility of today's business climate. And they must be more global too.

We've been advising companies on the challenges and opportunities of globalization since our earliest days. We were among the first to explain the significance of Japan's rise, we were the first multinational consulting company to be authorized to conduct business in mainland China when we established an office in Shanghai in 1993, and today we have more than 75 offices in more than 40 countries around the world.

This gives us a privileged vantage point on the fast-globalizing world. What are we seeing? New sources of growth are continually appearing in far-flung cities and rural areas around the world. Also, new competitors are appearing. These include those that, driven by the cutthroat approach that has emerged in the wake of the Great Recession, are moving into adjacent sectors, product lines, or services. They also include those that, based in the emerging markets, are aggressively pursuing accelerated global strategies. Almost every year since 2006, BCG has identified 100 such global challengers that are vying for international leadership in their industries. Given this new competitive intensity, the ability to innovate has become increasingly critical. At the same time, companies must know how to find the new centers of growth and how to deal with the new competitors, which can be allies as well as adversaries.

Another feature of today's business environment is its extraordinary connectivity, even hyperconnectivity. Digitization has played a part, and so too have the spectacular advances of engineering, which have bridged the seemingly unbridgeable. As a result, organizations now need to be connected in the broadest sense with employees, customers, suppliers, shareholders, and a wide range of stakeholders.

Also, organizations need to be sustainable, and not only in the sense that they must be mindful of the environment. Creating a sustainable "business model," one that is built to last, is harder than ever. But there are organizations—we call them sustainability champions—that have found a way to square the circle: to do good and do well.

These four attributes—adaptable, global, connected, and sustainable—have come to the fore in this age of accelerating change. But although necessary, they are not sufficient to succeed. As well as these, organizations need to show what we call ambidexterity: an ability to be, on one hand, efficient and effective, and on the other hand, inventive and creative.

Let's take the first ability: to be effective and efficient. The attributes associated with this ability are timeless, immutable truths of business. They are not goals as such (profitable growth is a goal), but they are prerequisites for success—and they need to be held with ever greater tenacity in turbulent times.

One such timeless attribute is customer first. It is hard to imagine an organization not making its customers—the buyers of its products and services—a priority. But to really deliver on this commitment, executives must understand their customers in a deep and profound way—and even completely rethink how to connect with them.

Another attribute is what we call fit to win. There is no doubt that competition is intensifying: it is a Darwinian dog-eat-dog world out there. This means that organizations must be structured and led in a way that puts their ideas into action and gets things done.

A third such attribute is value-driven. The core objective of every organization is—or should be—to create value. How to do so has been a theme that BCG has returned to time and time again, ever since Bruce Henderson first opined on it in the 1960s. Without added value, there is no lasting business.

A fourth attribute, which has always been a feature of the most successful organizations down the ages, is "trusted." In fast-changing times, when the world is turned upside down, trust—always an essential attribute—becomes an invaluable source of competitive advantage. Leaders trusted by their employees can get things done amid great uncertainty; likewise, organizations trusted by their investors, suppliers, customers, and other stakeholders can leap ahead of their rivals. But trust is a precious commodity. It must be nurtured because, in today's global, connected, and transparent world, it can be so easily lost in an instant—with devastating consequences.

There are two more attributes that we think are critical to the success of organizations today—and they relate to the ability to be innovative and creative. In these testing times, the demands on leaders are especially high. In particular, the onus is on them to act and not to sit idly by in the hope of better times. This is why, in our view, leaders must be bold and inspiring.

Why bold? In our lexicon, the word *bold* describes the collection of characteristics needed to create growth opportunities: the readiness to innovate, to take calculated risks, to invest in alternative futures. This is not just about product innovation but fundamental business model innovation that can transform a company's prospects. Without boldness, it is hard to see how organizations can change the game.

Why inspiring? Simply put, leaders need to provide the spark, the story, the vision. This goes far beyond the more mechanical management skills required to run an organization. In some ways, inspiring leaders must energize and personify their organizations so that their organizations can inspire customers with their range of products and services.

Without these leadership characteristics, it is hard to see how organizations can ever hope to own the future.

■ ■ ■

Now more than ever, leaders need advice and guidance on their next steps. The decisions they make today and over the next 10 years will have an extraordinary and enduring impact on their own fortunes as well as those of their organizations, the global economy, and society at large.

By definition, the future is unknowable with certainty. But leaders can prepare by developing the capabilities needed to pivot one way or the other depending on circumstance and by putting themselves in the best position to win—to change the game and own the future.

We hope that these chapters, representing the collective wisdom of The Boston Consulting Group, will serve as a useful resource in that endeavor.

# Adaptive

The business environment has changed markedly over the past 30 years. Driven by a host of powerful forces—including digitization, connectivity, trade liberalization, global competition, and consumer activism—today's competitive terrain is more unsettled and less predictable than ever before. And the breadth of new conditions that companies face continues to grow. The effects on corporate performance have been dramatic. Turbulence within industries, measured by such metrics as volatility in revenue growth, revenue ranking, and operating margins, is demonstrably greater and more prevalent than ever. Industry leadership, once relatively stable, now changes rapidly.

To succeed, businesses must rethink how they generate competitive advantage. A critical element of this is understanding the competitive environment (or environments) in which the company operates—and choosing an appropriate *style* of strategy for that environment. Is the environment one that the company has the potential to shape, for example, or is it one over which the company has minimal influence? The two scenarios bear little resemblance and thus call for wholly different styles of strategy.

A second must-have for success is the ability to adapt to unpredictable and changing circumstances. Companies that can adjust and learn better, faster, and more economically than their rivals stand to gain a decisive advantage in the marketplace. Indeed, what we term *adaptive advantage* increasingly trumps classical, static sources of competitive advantage, such as scale and position.

The chapters featured here delve into these topics. Chapter 1, "Why Strategy Needs a Strategy," introduces the concept of strategic styles and explains how they should be deployed. We identify five distinct styles of strategy—classical, shaping, visionary, survival, and adaptive—and assert that executives will increasingly need to learn and manage a portfolio of different ones.

We believe that five capabilities are needed to be adaptive: the ability to read and act on signals of change; the ability to experiment rapidly, frequently, and economically; the ability to manage complex, multicompany systems; the ability to mobilize the organization; and the ability to generate value and achieve competitive advantage by sustainably aligning the company's business model with its broader social and ecological context. Chapter 2, "Adaptability: The New Competitive Advantage," discusses the first four of these and offers tips for large corporations seeking to become more adaptive. We discuss the fifth source of advantage in Chapter 34, "Social Advantage," which appears in Section 8 of this book.

Chapter 3, "Systems Advantage," focuses on a special case of adaptive advantage—gaining advantage through multiparty ecosystems. The article explains the rationale for such an approach and discusses principles for designing and managing advantaged and adaptive systems. Chapter 4, "Adaptive Leadership," argues that just as today's environment demands a different approach to strategy, it also calls for a different type of business leader. Increasingly, today's successful leaders eschew traditional command-and-control tactics. Rather, they focus on creating the conditions that enable dynamic networks of actors to achieve common goals against a backdrop of uncertainty.

Adaptability is an ability to develop new capabilities, but it wasn't always obvious that capabilities matter. In fact, when *Harvard Business Review* published our article "Competing on Capabilities" in 1992, the notion that capabilities are a critical source of strategic advantage was a novel one. At that time, managers were more focused on factors such as scale, position, and operational efficiency. Although those factors were and still are important, we argued that competition was a "war of movement" in which companies had to move quickly in and out of products, markets, and even entire businesses. We stand by that view. Today, the piece (a condensed version of which is published here in Chapter 5) is one of BCG's most well-read articles—and has redefined how executives think about competitive advantage.

# 1 Why Strategy Needs a Strategy

## Martin Reeves, Michael Deimler, Claire Love, and Philipp Tillmanns

The oil industry holds relatively few surprises for strategists. Things change, of course, sometimes dramatically, but in relatively predictable ways. Planners know, for instance, that global supply will rise and fall as geopolitical forces play out and new resources are discovered and exploited. They know that demand will rise and fall with gross domestic products (GDPs), weather conditions, and the like. Because these factors are outside companies' control, no one is really in a position to change the game much. A company carefully marshals its unique capabilities and resources to stake out and defend its competitive position in this fairly stable firmament.

The Internet software industry would be a nightmare for an oil industry strategist. Innovations and new companies pop up frequently, seemingly out of nowhere, and the pace at which companies can build—or lose—volume and market share is head-spinning. A player like Google or Facebook can, without much warning, introduce a new platform that fundamentally alters the basis of competition. In this environment, competitive advantage comes from reading and responding to signals faster than your rivals do, adapting quickly to change, or capitalizing on technological leadership to influence how demand and competition evolve.

Clearly, the kinds of strategies that would work in the oil industry have practically no hope of working in the far less predictable and far less settled arena of Internet software. And the skill sets that oil and software strategists need are worlds apart as well. Companies operating in such dissimilar competitive environments should be planning, developing, and deploying their strategies in markedly different ways. But all too often they are not.

What's stopping executives from making strategy in a way that fits their situation? We believe they lack a systematic way to go about it—a strategy for making strategy. Here we present a simple framework that divides strategy planning into four styles according to how predictable your environment is and how much power you have to change it. Using this framework, corporate leaders can match their strategic style to the particular conditions of their industry or geographic market.

## Finding the Right Strategic Style

Strategy usually begins with an assessment of your industry. Your choice of strategic style should begin there as well. Although many industry factors will play into the strategy you actually formulate, you can narrow down your options by considering just two critical factors: *predictability* (how far into the future and how accurately can you confidently forecast demand, corporate performance, competitive dynamics, and market expectations?) and *malleability* (to what extent can you or your competitors influence those factors?).

Put these two variables into a matrix, and four broad strategic styles—which we label *classical, adaptive, shaping,* and *visionary*—emerge (Figure 1.1). Each style is associated with distinct planning practices and is best suited to one environment.

Let's look at each style in turn.

### Classical

When you operate in an industry whose environment is predictable but hard for your company to change, a classical strategic style has the best chance of success. This is the style familiar to most managers and business school graduates—five forces, blue ocean, and growth-share matrix analyses are

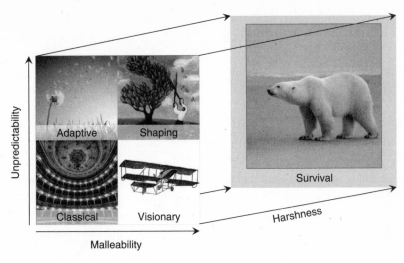

**FIGURE 1.1** Environment Determines the Most Appropriate Strategic Style
Source: BCG analysis.

all manifestations of it. A company sets a goal, targeting the most favorable market position it can attain by capitalizing on its particular capabilities and resources, and then tries to build and fortify that position through orderly, successive rounds of planning, using quantitative predictive methods that allow it to project well into the future. Once such plans are set, they tend to stay in place for several years. Classical strategic planning can work well as a stand-alone function because it requires special analytic and quantitative skills, and things move slowly enough to allow for information to pass between departments.

Oil company strategists, like those in many other mature industries, effectively employ the classical style. At a major oil company such as ExxonMobil or Shell, for instance, highly trained analysts in the corporate strategic planning office spend their days developing detailed perspectives on the long-term economic factors relating to demand and the technological factors relating to supply. These analyses allow them to devise upstream oil extraction plans that may stretch 10 years into the future and downstream production capacity plans up to 5 years out. These plans, in turn, inform multiyear financial forecasts, which determine annual targets that are focused on honing the efficiencies required to maintain and bolster the company's market position and performance. Only in the face of something extraordinary—an extended Gulf war, for instance, or a series of major oil refinery shutdowns—would plans be seriously revisited more frequently than once a year.

## Adaptive

The classical approach works for oil companies because their strategists operate in an environment in which the most attractive positions and the most rewarded capabilities today will, in all likelihood, remain the same tomorrow. But that has never been true for some industries, and it's becoming less and less true where global competition, technological innovation, social feedback loops, and economic uncertainty combine to make the environment radically and persistently unpredictable. In such an environment, a carefully crafted classical strategy may become obsolete within months or even weeks.

Companies in this situation need a more adaptive approach, whereby they can constantly refine goals and tactics and shift, acquire, or divest resources smoothly and promptly. In such a fast-moving, reactive environment, when predictions are likely to be wrong and long-term plans are essentially useless, the goal cannot be to optimize efficiency; rather, it must be to engineer flexibility. Accordingly, planning cycles may shrink to less than a year or even become continual. Plans take the form not of carefully specified blueprints but of rough hypotheses based on the best available data. In testing out those hypotheses, strategy must be tightly linked with or embedded in operations to best capture change signals and minimize information loss and time lags.

Specialty fashion retailing is a good example of this. Tastes change quickly. Brands become hot (or not) overnight. The Spanish retailer Zara uses the adaptive approach. Zara does not rely heavily on a formal planning process; rather, its strategic style is baked into its flexible supply chain. Zara need not predict or make bets on which fashions will capture its customers' imaginations and wallets from month to month; instead, it can respond quickly to information from its retail stores, constantly experiment with various offerings, and smoothly adjust to events as they play out.

## Shaping

Exxon's strategists and Zara's designers have one critical thing in common: they take their competitive environment as a given. Some environments, as Internet software vendors well know, can't be taken as a given. For instance, in young high-growth industries where barriers to entry are low, innovation rates are high, demand is very hard to predict, and the relative positions of competitors are in flux, a company can often radically shift the course of industry development through some innovative move. A mature industry that's similarly fragmented and not dominated by a few powerful incumbents, or is stagnant and ripe for disruption, is also likely to be similarly malleable.

In such an environment, a company employing a classical or even an adaptive strategy to find the best possible market position runs the risk of selling itself short and missing opportunities to control its own fate. It would do better to employ a strategy in which the goal is to shape the unpredictable environment to its own advantage before someone else does—so that it benefits no matter how things play out.

Like an adaptive strategy, a shaping strategy embraces short or continual planning cycles. Flexibility is paramount, little reliance is placed on elaborate prediction mechanisms, and the strategy is most commonly implemented as a portfolio of experiments. But unlike adapters, shapers focus beyond the boundaries of their own company, often by rallying a formidable ecosystem of customers, suppliers, and/or complementors to their cause by defining attractive new markets, standards, technology platforms, and business practices.

That's essentially how Facebook overtook the incumbent MySpace in just a few years. One of Facebook's savviest strategic moves was to open its social networking platform to outside developers in 2007, thus attracting all manner of applications to its site. By 2008 it had attracted 33,000 applications; by 2010 that number had risen to more than 550,000. So as the industry developed and more than two-thirds of the successful social networking apps turned out to be games, it was not surprising that the most popular ones—created by Zynga, Playdom, and Playfish—were operating from, and enriching, Facebook's site.

## Visionary

Sometimes, not only does a company have the power to shape the future, but it's possible to know that future and to predict the path to realizing it. Those times call for bold strategies—the kind entrepreneurs use to create entirely new markets (as Edison did for electricity and Martine

Rothblatt did for XM satellite radio) or corporate leaders use to revitalize a company with a wholly new vision (as Ratan Tata is trying to do with the ultra-affordable Tata Nano automobile). These are the big bets, the build-it-and-they-will-come strategies.

Like a shaping strategist, the visionary considers the environment not as a given but as something that can be molded to advantage. Even so, the visionary style has more in common with a classical than with an adaptive approach. Because the goal is clear, the strategist can take deliberate steps to reach it without having to keep many options open. It's more important for the visionary to take the time and care needed to marshal resources, plan thoroughly, and implement correctly so that the vision doesn't fall victim to poor execution. The visionary strategist must have the courage to stay the course and the will to commit the necessary resources.

## When the Cold Winds Blow

There are circumstances in which none of our strategic styles will work well: when all access to capital or other critical resources is severely restricted, by either a sharp economic downturn or some other cataclysmic event. Such a harsh environment threatens the very viability of a company and demands a fifth strategic style: *survival*.

As its name implies, a survival strategy requires a company to focus defensively—reducing costs, preserving capital, and trimming business portfolios. It is a short-term strategy, intended to clear the way for the company to live another day. But it does not lead to long-term competitive advantage. Companies in survival mode should therefore look ahead, readying themselves to assess the conditions of the new environment and to adopt an appropriate growth strategy once the crisis ends.

## Operating in Many Modes

Matching your company's strategic style to the predictability and malleability of your industry will align overall strategy with the broad economic conditions in which the company operates. But various company units may well operate in differing industry segments or geographies that are more or less predictable and malleable than the industry at large. Strategists in these segments and markets can use the same process to select the most effective style for their particular circumstances, asking themselves the same initial questions: How predictable is the environment in which our unit operates? How much power do we have to change that environment? The answers may vary widely. We estimate, for example, that the Chinese business environment overall has been almost twice as malleable and unpredictable as that in the United States, making shaping strategies often more appropriate in China.

To apply the right strategy style, you must correctly analyze your environment, identify which strategic styles should be used, and take steps to prime your company's culture for those styles. Then, you will need to monitor your environment and be prepared to adjust as conditions change over time. Clearly that's no easy task. But we believe that companies that continually match their strategic style to their situation will enjoy a tremendous advantage—potentially as much as several percentage points in total shareholder return (TSR)—over their industry peers that don't.

# 2

# Adaptability: The New Competitive Advantage

## Martin Reeves and Michael Deimler

lobalization, new technologies, and greater transparency have combined to upend the business environment. Just look at the numbers. Since 1980 the volatility of business operating margins has more than doubled, as has the size of the gap between winners (companies with high operating margins) and losers (those with low ones). Market leadership is even more precarious. The percentage of companies falling out of the top three rankings in their industry increased from 2 percent in 1960 to 14 percent in 2008. Market leadership also is proving to be an increasingly dubious prize: the once strong correlation between profitability and industry share is now almost nonexistent in some sectors. And it has become virtually impossible for some executives even to clearly identify in what industry and with which companies they're competing.

All this uncertainty poses a tremendous challenge for strategy making. That's because traditional approaches to strategy actually assume a relatively stable and predictable world.

Think about it. The goal of most strategies is to build an enduring (and implicitly static) competitive advantage by establishing clever market positioning (dominant scale or an attractive niche) or assembling the right capabilities and competencies. Companies undertake periodic strategy reviews and set direction and organizational structure on the basis of an analysis of their industry and some forecast of how it will evolve.

But given the new level of uncertainty, many companies are starting to ask:

- How can we apply frameworks based on scale or position when we can go from market leader one year to follower the next?
- When it's unclear where one industry ends and another begins, how do we even measure position?
- When the environment is so unpredictable, how can we apply traditional forecasting and analysis?
- When we're overwhelmed with changing information, how can we detect the right signals to understand and harness change?
- When change is so rapid, how can a one-year—or, worse, five-year—planning cycle stay relevant?

The answers these companies are coming up with point in a consistent direction. Sustainable competitive advantage no longer arises exclusively from position, scale, and first-order capabilities in producing or delivering offerings. All those are essentially static. Instead, managers are finding that it stems from the "second-order" organizational capabilities that foster rapid adaptation. Instead of being really good at doing some particular thing, companies must be really good at learning how to do new things.

Those that thrive are quick to read and act on signals of change. They have determined how to experiment rapidly, frequently, and economically—not only with products and services but with business models, processes, and strategies. They have developed skills in managing complex multistakeholder systems in an increasingly interconnected world. Perhaps most important, they have learned to unlock their greatest resources: the people who work for them.

A pattern similar to that illustrated in Figure 2.1 can be observed in many other industries.

## The Ability to Read and Act on Signals

To adapt, a company must have its antennae tuned to signals of change from the external environment, decode them, and quickly refine or reinvent its business model and even reshape the industry's information landscape.

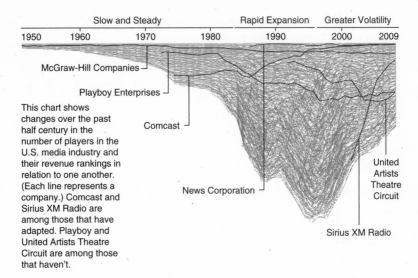

**FIGURE 2.1** Jockeying for Position—The Media Industry
Source: BCG analysis.

Think back to when Stirling Moss was winning Formula One car races: the car and driver determined who won. But today the sport is as much about processing complex signals and making adaptive decisions as about mechanics and driving prowess. Hundreds of sensors are built into the cars; race teams continually collect and process data on several thousand variables and feed them into dynamic simulation models that guide the drivers' decisions. A telemetric innovation by one team can instantly raise the bar for all.

In this information-saturated age, when complex, varying signals may be available simultaneously to all players, adaptive companies must similarly rely on sophisticated point-of-sale systems to ensure that they acquire the right information. And they must apply advanced data-mining technologies to recognize relevant patterns.

For example, a leading media company that was suffering from high customer churn revamped its analytic approach to customer data, applying "neural network" technologies to understand patterns of customer loss. The company found hidden relationships among the variables driving churn and launched retention campaigns targeting at-risk customers. The accuracy rate in predicting churn was an impressive 75 to

90 percent—a huge benefit, given that every percentage point in churn reduction added millions of dollars to profits.

Companies are also leveraging signal-reading capabilities to make operational interventions in real time, bypassing slow-moving decision hierarchies. At the time of writing, the U.K.-based grocery retailer Tesco continually performs detailed analyses of the purchase patterns of the more than 13 million members of its loyalty card program. Its findings enable Tesco to customize offerings for each store and customer segment and provide early warning of shifts in customer behavior. They also supported the development of Tesco's hugely successful online platform.

## The Ability to Experiment

That which cannot be deduced or forecast can often be discovered through experimentation. Of course, all companies use some form of experimentation to develop and test new products and services. Yet traditional approaches can be costly and time-consuming and can saddle the organization with an unreasonable burden of complexity. Furthermore, research based on consumers' perceptions is often a poor predictor of success. To overcome these barriers, many adaptive competitors are using an array of new approaches and technologies, especially in virtual environments, to generate, test, and replicate innovative ideas faster, at lower cost, and with less risk. Procter & Gamble (P&G) is a case in point. Through its current Connect + Develop model, it exploits open-innovation networks to solve technical design problems. It uses a walk-in, 3-D virtual store to run experiments that are quicker and cheaper than traditional market tests. And by employing Vocalpoint and other online user communities, it can introduce and test products with friendly audiences before a full launch. In 2008 alone, 10 highly skilled employees were able to generate some 10,000 design simulations, enabling the completion in hours of mock-ups that might once have taken weeks. More than 80 percent of P&G's new-business initiatives now make use of its growing virtual toolbox.

In addition to changing the way they experiment, companies need to broaden the scope of their experimentation. Traditionally, the focus has been on a company's offerings. But in an increasingly turbulent environment, business models, strategies, and routines can also become obsolete quickly and unpredictably. Adaptive companies therefore use experimentation far more broadly than their rivals do.

Adaptive companies are very tolerant of failure, even to the point of celebrating it. The software company Intuit, which has been extremely successful at using adaptive approaches to grow new businesses, launched a marketing campaign in 2005 to reach young tax filers through a website called rockyourrefund.com. The site offered discounts at Expedia and Best Buy and the opportunity to get tax refunds in the form of prepaid gift cards. The campaign was a flop, and practically no one used the site. But the marketing team documented what it had learned and won an award from company chairman Scott Cook, who said, "It is only a failure if we fail to get the learning."

# The Ability to Manage Complex Multicompany Systems

With an increasing amount of economic activity occurring beyond corporate boundaries—through outsourcing, value nets, and the like—companies need to think about strategies not only for themselves but for dynamic business systems. Increasingly, industry structure is better characterized as competing webs or ecosystems of codependent companies than as a handful of competitors producing similar goods and services and working on a stable, distant, and transactional basis with suppliers and customers.

In such an environment, advantage will flow to companies that create effective strategies at the network or system level. Adaptive companies are therefore learning how to push activities outside the company without benefiting competitors and how to design strategies for networks without necessarily being able to rely on strong control mechanisms.

Typically, adaptive companies manage their ecosystems by using common standards to foster interaction with minimal barriers. They generate trust among participants—for example, by enabling people to interact frequently and by providing transparency and rating systems that serve as "reputational currency." Toyota's automotive supply pyramids, with their *kanban* and *kaizen* feedback mechanisms, are early examples of adaptive systems. If the experience curve and the scale curve were the key indicators of success, Nokia would still be leading the smartphone market; it had the advantage of being an early mover and the market share leader with a strong cost position. But Nokia was attacked by an entirely different kind of competitor: Apple's adaptive system of suppliers, telecom partnerships, and numerous independent application developers created to support the iPhone. Google's Android operating system, too, capitalized on a broad array of hardware partners and application developers. The ability to bring together the capabilities of so many entities allowed these smartphone entrants to leapfrog the experience curve and become market leaders in record time.

## The Ability to Mobilize

Adaptation is necessarily local in nature—somebody experiments first at a particular place and time. It is also necessarily global in nature, because if the experiment succeeds, it will be communicated, selected, and refined. Organizations therefore need to create environments that encourage the knowledge flow, autonomy, risk taking, and flexibility on which adaptation thrives. A flexible structure and the dispersal of decision rights are powerful levers for increasing adaptability. Typically, adaptive companies have replaced permanent silos and functions with modular units that freely communicate and recombine. To reinforce this, it is helpful to have weak or competing power structures and a culture of constructive dissent. Cisco Systems is one company that has made this transformation. Early on, it relied on a hierarchical, customer-centric organization to become a leader in the market for network switches and routers. More recently, CEO John Chambers has created a novel management structure of cross-functional councils and boards to facilitate moves into developing countries and adjacent markets with greater agility than would previously have been possible.

As they create more fluid structures, adaptive companies drive decision making down to the front lines, allowing those most likely to detect changes in the environment to respond quickly and proactively. At Whole Foods, the basic organizational unit is the team, and each store has about eight teams. Team leaders—not national buyers—decide what to stock. Teams have veto power over new hires. They are encouraged to buy from local growers that meet the company's quality and sustainability standards. And they are rewarded for their performance with bonuses based on store profitability over the previous four weeks. .

Creating decentralized, fluid, and even competing organizational structures destroys the big advantage of a rigid hierarchy, which is that everyone knows precisely what he or she should be doing. An adaptive organization can't expect to succeed unless it provides people with some substitute for that certainty. The organization needs some simple, generative rules to facilitate interaction, help people make trade-offs, and set the boundaries for decision making.

For example, Netflix values nine core behaviors and skills in its employees: judgment, communication, impact, curiosity, innovation, courage, passion, honesty, and selflessness. Company executives believe that a great workplace is full of colleagues who embody these qualities; thus the Netflix model is to "increase employee freedom as we grow, rather than limit it, to continue to attract and nourish innovative people." Consistent with this philosophy, Netflix has only two types of rules: those designed to prevent irrevocable disaster and those designed to prevent moral, ethical, and legal issues. It has no vacation policy and does not track time—the company's focus is on what needs to get done, not how many hours or days are worked.

## The Challenge for Big Business

Becoming an adaptive competitor can be difficult, especially for large, established organizations. Typically, these companies are oriented toward managing scale and efficiency, and their hierarchical structures and fixed routines lack the flexibility needed for rapid learning and change. Such management paradigms die hard, especially when they have historically been the basis for success.

However, several tactics have proved effective at fostering adaptive advantage even in established companies. To the managers involved, they may look like nothing more than an extension of business as usual, but in fact they create a context in which adaptive capabilities can thrive. If you are the CEO of a large company that wants to be more adaptive, challenge your managers to:

- *Look at the mavericks.* Fast-changing industries are characterized by the presence of disruptive mavericks—often entirely new players, sometimes from other sectors. Ask your managers to shift their focus from traditional competitors' moves to what the new players are doing and to think of ways to insure your company against this new competition or neutralize its effect.

- *Identify and address the uncertainties.* Get your managers to put aside the traditional single-point business forecast and instead examine the risks and uncertainties that could significantly affect the company. This extension of the familiar long-range strategy exercise can force people to realize what they don't yet know and to address it.
- *Put an initiative on every risk.* Most companies have a portfolio of strategic initiatives. It should become the engine that drives your organization into adaptability—and it can, with a couple of enhancements. First, every significant source of uncertainty should be addressed with an initiative. Depending on the nature of the uncertainty, the goal of the initiative may be responding to a neglected business trend, creating options for responding to it, or simply learning more about it. In managing these initiatives, your company should be as disciplined with metrics, time frames, and responsibilities as it would be for the product portfolio or operating plan.
- *Examine multiple alternatives.* In a stable environment it is sufficient to improve what already exists or examine simple, infrequent change proposals. The simple step of requiring that every change proposal be accompanied by several alternatives not only surfaces a more varied and powerful set of moves but legitimizes and fosters cognitive diversity and organizational flexibility.
- *Increase the clock speed.* The speed of adaptation is a function of the cycle time of decision making. In a fast-moving environment, companies need to accelerate change by making annual planning processes lighter and more frequent and sometimes by making episodic processes continual.

■ ■ ■

The adaptive approach is no universal panacea. If your industry is stable and relatively predictable, you may be better off sticking to the traditional sources of advantage. But if your competitive reality is uncertain and rapidly changing, as is true in an increasing number of industries, you need a dynamic and sustainable way to stay ahead. Your survival may depend on building an organization that can exploit the four capabilities behind what we think of as adaptive advantage.

# 3

# Systems Advantage

## Martin Reeves
## and Alex Bernhardt

"**O**ur competitors aren't taking market share with devices; they are taking market share with an entire ecosystem." Stephen Elop, Nokia's president and CEO, offered that insight in 2011 to explain the rapid and disruptive rise of Apple's iPhone and Google's Android operating system in the global smartphone market.

According to traditional strategic paradigms, this swift and sizable competitive shift should not have happened. Nokia once had the advantages of being an early mover and market leader with a strong cost position. If the experience curve were the key driver of success, the company would have continued dominating the smartphone market. Yet Nokia was attacked by an entirely different kind of competitor: an adaptive business ecosystem. It was not simply Apple and Google, but their systems enlisting hundreds of component suppliers, multiple telecom partnerships, and innumerable independent application developers that proved so powerful. The ability to bring together the assets and capabilities of so many entities allowed these smartphone entrants to leapfrog the experience curve and become market leaders in record time.

Nokia's experience offers three lessons for today's managers. First, competitive shifts can occur with blistering speed. Second, when market and technology shifts accelerate, positional advantage becomes less durable, and the value of adaptiveness increases. Third, a multiplayer ecosystem can be a highly effective lever for addressing this adaptive imperative.

There's a reason why companies increasingly find themselves either part of—or competing against—loosely organized groups of players and partners. Advances in information technology and telecommunications—from cheap bandwidth and computing power to online collaboration platforms—have enabled diverse sets of individuals and companies to interact quickly, richly, and on a greater scale than ever before. Advances in shipping, such as the ease and efficiency that results from the universal standards of containerization—along with the steady erosion of trade barriers—have facilitated the exchange of physical goods within systems. Finally, the potential of a systems approach is increasingly being demonstrated by a growing number of examples from firms such as Apple, Procter & Gamble (P&G), and Toyota.

Yet most executives lack a structured way to think about and create an advantaged system of actors. Traditional approaches to strategy focus primarily on the individual firm or business unit. They are largely silent about managing a network of players beyond its boundaries.

But even if the broader playbook on "trans-corporate strategy" has yet to be written, it is possible to define some emerging guiding principles for companies seeking to use a systems approach in order to extend their adaptive capabilities.

## Properties of Adaptive Systems

An adaptive business system is formed by diverse players interacting in a semistructured fashion to achieve mutual business goals. Systems can take many familiar forms, including the following:

- Production systems orchestrated by a central player, aggregating diverse capabilities, such as the iPod/iTunes ecosystem
- Collaborative production communities, such as Wikipedia or Linux
- Innovation networks, such as P&G's extended ecosystem
- Marketplace platforms, such as eBay, Google AdSense, or the iPhone App Store

Although the technology sector has proved fertile ground for business systems, the systems approach is not limited to the digital world. Collaborative supply chains, such as Toyota's automotive supply pyramids, with their *kanban* and *kaizen* feedback mechanisms, are earlier examples of adaptive systems.

Systems exhibit several properties that enable them to deal effectively with adaptive challenges. They can mobilize an extremely broad range of capabilities and assets, innovate rapidly through parallel activity, and distribute risk across many players. Their modular structure facilitates responsiveness to changing needs through recombination, speedy scale-up, and broad-based signal detection.

The natural world of biology teems with adaptive systems that offer potential insights into how to structure, evolve, manage, and sustain advantaged and adaptive business systems. One example is the learning capability built into the human immune system, allowing it to cope with an unpredictable and virtually infinite set of diverse pathogens. Far from operating based on rigid design, the immune system "remembers" previous threats and adapts its tool kit to increase its effectiveness over time. Despite its sophistication, it can mobilize itself against threats by using "rules" and properties intrinsic to the system, rather than taking direction from the brain in a top-down manner.

Although no business is an island in today's globalized and hyperconnected world, not every business possesses *systems advantage*—the ability to build and maintain a system of companies whose high collective adaptability enables them to perform together more successfully and sustainably than their competitors.

# Guidelines for an Adaptive Systems Approach

In an increasing number of situations, traditional approaches to change taken by single enterprises acting alone are either too slow or too risky or lack sufficiently broad capabilities to enable successful adaptation. Although many situations might call for a systems approach, the following three are especially common across industries:

- To deal with high levels of product complexity or high demand for variety, a very diverse set of capabilities or assets is required.
- In periods of high uncertainty—which can occur whenever companies enter or create a new market—it is imperative to create a wide variety of options or to share risk.

- Situations of rapid or accelerating change in technology or customer demands call for the ability to conduct parallel experimentation with a diverse group of innovators.

Managing an adaptive system differs from managing a single company. For one thing, a system is more complex, with many more moving parts. Also, in a system there is less control over individual players—and a greater range of ambitions and motivations, some of which may conflict. As a result, the "instruction set" for systems is less detailed by design, and some aspects of the system emerge spontaneously from interactions among players over time.

We've studied adaptive systems in a range of contexts, from business to biology, to understand what makes them successful. Drawing on our analysis and from our own experience, we've developed nine guiding principles for creating and maintaining advantaged and adaptive business systems.

- *Establish common standards to enable frequent, low-cost interactions.* A good example of the power of standardization is the introduction of freight containers of standard sizes. Containerization enabled a dramatic decline in shipping costs and an order-of-magnitude increase in shipping traffic among diverse nations and companies as well as in modes of transport.
- *Foster trust among participants.* To work together effectively, actors in a system need to trust one another. Trust can be nurtured by enabling players to interact frequently and transparently in a "repeated game" that relies on shared norms and that is often facilitated by an explicit reputational "currency." One factor in eBay's success was the company's ability to accelerate trust among its members by enabling photos of products to be uploaded and by creating a mechanism for rating sellers—a scalable, visible form of trust.
- *Ensure minimal barriers to entry and sufficient rewards for participation.* Systems will form and persist only if they offer a compelling value proposition to current and potential members. Both the costs and benefits of participation (which needn't be entirely monetary) must be managed.
- *Limit the portability of value beyond the system.* For a system to be adaptive, members must be able to access and build upon the knowledge

of others. But to prevent inadvertently benefiting competitors, companies must link the ability to extract value from intellectual property or other kinds of resources to participation in the system. For example, sellers with a high rating on eBay have a documented monetizable asset: their price realization is 6 to 8 percent higher than that of unrated or poorly rated sellers. Because that rating is specifically linked to the eBay community, however, it would be difficult for sellers to monetize that reputation outside the eBay system. Thus, these sellers have an interest in the continued success of eBay.

- *Preserve redundancy*. Adaptive systems typically have redundant communication pathways and multiple members capable of executing critical functions. These features ensure that the system cannot be crippled by the loss of any individual member or by changes in needs or roles.

- *Facilitate diversity*. Systems must have a diverse set of participants and capabilities so that they foster innovation and adaptation in times of change. Indeed, the diversity of contributors in open-source systems such as the iPhone application network and Linux has been central to those systems' continuing success. During stable periods, pressure from competition and the desire for efficiency can tend to reduce diversity as a system moves toward equilibrium. To sustain adaptive capacity, it is critical to maintain diversity within the system by continually seeking potential new members and enabling them to contribute their unique capabilities, assets, or insights to the system.

- *Cultivate flexibility*. As interactions become trusted relationships over time, the perceived cost of change increases. This shift can cause a system's structure to become rigid—inhibiting the recombination and introduction of new capabilities that are essential for innovation and adaptation. Firms can cultivate flexibility by building modularity and interchangeability into their products and business systems, by avoiding exclusive long-term contracts, and by constantly looking for new partnerships in response to change.

- *Ensure tight feedback loops*. To maintain the system's adaptability, participants must be able to readily identify and respond to internal or external changes. Walmart fosters such feedback by frequently sharing real-time sales data with its suppliers, which can then respond with appropriate changes in distribution and stocking.

- *Determine what to structure and when to relax control.* A good rule of thumb is to enforce the mechanisms that enable productive interaction among members while relaxing constraints on who interacts with whom, as well as on specific outcomes and activities.

## Moving toward an Adaptive System

If you are among the many business leaders who are concerned about rapidly rising product complexity and variety, market uncertainty, and accelerating change in technologies and markets—or if you are struggling to maximize the strategic value of your growing list of external partners—the following questions will help your team prepare to create a systems advantage:

- How could a systems approach benefit our business?
- Who might we want to participate in the system, and how could we motivate them to participate?
- What platforms do we need to build or establish for the system to emerge?
- Which elements of the system should we standardize or control?
- Which elements of the system should we leave flexible and open to creativity and innovation?
- What do we "give away," and what do we control to sustainably capture value from the system?
- Which mechanisms do we need to ensure and maintain the adaptive capacity of the system?

A cruel paradox of competition—observed in business as well as biology—is that the efficiency and specialization that enable a competitor to excel in one environment often inhibit successful adaptation when the environment changes. Thus, in highly demanding and dynamic environments, the challenge is to find a strategy that enables specialization without rigidity. Adaptive systems can help companies answer that challenge by bringing together a diverse set of specialized capabilities in a flexible fashion, thereby conferring competitive advantage on a sustained basis.

# 4 Adaptive Leadership

## Roselinde Torres, Martin Reeves, and Claire Love

We commonly think of leaders as strong personalities who imprint their will on compliant organizations. Increasingly, however, business executives are finding something lacking in this view of the leader as hero. As the former CEO of IBM, Sam Palmisano, wrote in "The Globally Integrated Enterprise," an essay in *Foreign Affairs*, "Hierarchical, command-and-control approaches simply do not work anymore. They impede information flows inside companies, hampering the fluid and collaborative nature of work today."

Our research and experience suggest that the fundamental shifts in today's business environment compel us to rethink the nature of strategy, organization, and, consequently, leadership. Consider the following trends:

- Turbulence and uncertainty have undermined the effectiveness of long-range forecasting and traditional strategic planning in many industries. *How can leaders chart a course when they cannot predict the outcomes of their choices?*
- Companies are increasingly organized into interdependent, multicompany ecosystems, a result of lower transaction costs and "deconstruction." *When boundaries are blurred, who leads whom?*
- The pervasiveness and economics of digital communication and computation have made every business an information business. *In such an*

*environment, how can leaders ensure that their organizations are reading the right signals and acting on them?*

- Society's increasing interest in the social and ecological impacts of business makes it imperative for companies to consider the broader value and overall cost of their strategies. *How can leaders ensure that social and economic vectors are aligned?*
- Trust in big business has steadily eroded. *How can leaders regain society's confidence? How can they harness the creativity and passion of the workforce in pursuit of advantage?*
- The nature of competition has become more diverse. Some environments are mature and predictable, whereas others are highly uncertain. *How do leaders ensure that they are taking the right approach—or the right mosaic of approaches—for the specific challenge at hand?*

These shifts in the business environment call for adaptive strategies and organizations, which in turn require adaptive approaches to leadership. Adaptive leaders create the conditions that enable dynamic networks of actors to achieve common goals in an environment of uncertainty.

# Dimensions of Adaptive Leadership

Adaptive leadership can be distinguished from more traditional models in at least four dimensions. Following we describe a number of actions companies can take to support each of those dimensions.

## Navigating the Business Environment

Adaptive leaders must embrace uncertainty and adopt new approaches if they are to chart a course amid today's turbulent conditions.

- *Manage the context in which actors interact, not the instruction set.* In an uncertain world, rigid rules are counterproductive. The best solution will arise through learning and adapting to change over time. Netflix CEO Reed Hastings advises in his firm's "Reference Guide on our Freedom & Responsibility Culture": "Avoid chaos as you grow with ever more highly performing people, not with rules."
- *Cultivate a diversity of perspectives to generate a multiplicity of options.* Whereas traditional models of leadership may emphasize alignment, some adaptive leaders make dissenting opinion *compulsory*. Perhaps the most famous example of embracing opposing views comes from

Abraham Lincoln, who deliberately named his rivals to his cabinet. Leaders are more likely to find a diversity of perspectives at lower levels in the organization, where employees confront external realities directly and are likely to raise critical questions. For this reason, adaptive leadership deemphasizes hierarchy.

- *Allow leadership to be shared and to emerge from the given context.* In a volatile world, no single person can lead at all times and in all situations. The role of leader therefore should be assumed by the person or group best positioned to guide a specific decision. An executive at W. L. Gore & Associates, the global technology manufacturer, was quoted in *The Future of Management* as saying: "We vote with our feet. If you call a meeting, and people show up, you're a leader."[1]

- *Constantly question the world around you.* Adaptive leaders are always looking outward and realigning their organizations with a shifting environment. They read between the lines to intuitively grasp patterns that may be masked by complexity. They test their own assumptions by running thought experiments. An example is highlighted in the biography of former Intel president Andy Grove, who asked the then CEO: "If we got kicked out and the board brought in a new CEO, what do you think he would do?"[2]

## Leading with Empathy

Adaptive leaders create a shared sense of purpose and manage through influence rather than command and control.

- *See the world through the eyes of others.* By understanding alternative perspectives, adaptive leaders cultivate and embrace the cognitive diversity that underpins adaptive organizations. Their ability to empathize with colleagues, competitors, and other stakeholders enables them to exert influence across functional and corporate boundaries. By seeing the world through the eyes of others, these leaders also extend their ability to see patterns in a complex environment. In an interview at strategy-business.com, Herb Kelleher, cofounder

---

[1] Gary Hamel with Bill Breen, "Building an Innovation Democracy: W. L. Gore," excerpted in *The Future of Management* (Cambridge: Harvard Business School Press, 2007).
[2] Richard Tedlow and Andy Grove, *The Life and Times of an American Business Icon* (New York: Penguin Group, 2007).

and former president and CEO of Southwest Airlines, advised, "Treat your people well and they'll treat you well. . . . It has to come from the heart, not the head."

- *Create a shared sense of purpose.* In an era that has become infamous for rewarding profit making above all else, employees are understandably skeptical when leaders talk about values. And it seems that the more that mission statements are circulated, the more skeptical they become. Yet because a complex and dynamic environment requires people to act autonomously and intuitively—often without explicit instructions or rules—a strong sense of shared purpose and values is more important than ever. Indra Nooyi, chairman and CEO of PepsiCo, has spoken frequently of performance with purpose. As she pointed out in a recent interview, "The most important part of performance with purpose is the use of the word *with*. It's performance with purpose, not performance and purpose, or performance or purpose. Unless you focus on purpose, you cannot deliver performance. And unless you deliver performance, you can't fund purpose."

- *Reward accomplishment with autonomy.* Adaptive leaders reward people for what they accomplish, rather than tracking hours or tasks. And instead of relying solely on financial incentives, they motivate employees by giving them time to pursue individual passions—from a few hours of slack time a week to yearlong fellowships. Adaptive leaders understand that real commitment comes from individual opportunities for autonomy, mastery, collaboration, and recognition. As Marissa Mayer, formerly of Google and recently appointed as CEO of Yahoo!, explained in a speech titled "Nine Lessons Learned about Creativity at Google," "It is that license to do whatever they want that really ultimately fuels a huge amount of creativity and a huge amount of innovation."

## Learning through Self-Correction

Adaptive leaders encourage—indeed insist on—experimentation. Of course, some experiments will fail, but that is how adaptive organizations learn.

- *Enable individuals and teams to learn through experimentation.* Randy Pond, executive vice president of operations, processes, and systems at Cisco Systems, tells his organization on his blog at the company's site, "We'll continue to evolve as we learn what works, and as importantly, what doesn't." Adaptive leaders need to develop platforms that enable experimentation and learning, including opportunities to reflect on successes and failures. Leaders should also align rewards with experimentation in a way that doesn't punish "failure."

- *Develop your organization's "signal advantage."* In a changing environment, organizations have to detect, filter, and decode signals in order to anticipate and respond to what's coming next. Leaders should ensure that their organizations are constantly looking outward and staying close to their customers. As Sir Terry Leahy, the outgoing CEO of Tesco, advised, "The best place to find the truth is to listen to your customers. They'll tell you what's good about your business and what's wrong. And if you keep listening, they'll give you a strategy."[3]

- *Increase the agility with which the organization is able to correct itself.* Adaptive leaders allow decisions to be made at lower levels in the organization, and—to reduce the time between stimulus and response—they minimize the number of layers between the field and the CEO. As retired general Stanley McChrystal told the *Atlantic*, "Any complex task is best approached by flattening hierarchies. It gets everybody feeling like they're in the inner circle, so that they develop a sense of ownership."

## Creating Win-Win Solutions

Adaptive leaders focus on sustainable success for both the company as well as its external network of stakeholders.

- *Build platforms for collaboration.* In many industries, the success of a company depends on the engagement of its extended ecosystem of suppliers and collaborators. Technology now makes it possible for large groups to collaborate on complex tasks, such as product innovation, across functional and corporate boundaries. As Cristóbal Conde, former president and CEO of SunGard, the global software and services company, told the *New York Times*, "A CEO needs to focus

---

[3] Taken from "How Leadership, Loyalty, and Transparency Fuel Growth," a speech given at the National Retail Federation's 99th Annual Convention & Expo, January 2010.

more on the platform that enables collaboration, because employees already have all the data."

- *Deploy leadership influence beyond the boundaries of the firm.* In the absence of formal authority, leaders looking to mobilize a company's extended ecosystem must structure the game for win-win outcomes and also use "soft power" such as vision, charisma, networking, and collaboration to exert influence. In an interview posted on bcgperspectives.com, Red Hat CEO Jim Whitehurst told BCG that the success of the open-source technology company comes from the fact that it was able "to bring a huge ecosystem to bear that has been difficult for others to duplicate."
- *Align the business model with its broader social and ecological context to create "social advantage" and strengthen the business's sustainability.* Leaders must do more than maximize profitability. They must ensure the sustainability of their companies' business models and look for opportunities to align economic and social vectors for sustainable advantage. As John Mackey, the CEO of Whole Foods, recently told Darden School of Business professor R. Edward Freeman (in an interview posted on Whole Foods' site), "The leadership's job is to manage the business in such a way as to create value simultaneously for all of these interdependent stakeholders. It is a better strategy for [maximizing long-term profits]."

## Modulating the Leadership Model

Unpredictable environments will require leadership styles characterized by the four dimensions outlined in this chapter. Not all environments or challenges are alike, however. Just as different organizational models are necessary for different environments, so too are different leadership styles. Over time, an organization might move from one leadership archetype to another—for example, when a stable industry is disrupted, a shift to a more experimental style might be required. Or when an industry matures and becomes more stable, then a more deliberate, analytical style may be optimal. When an organization is not yet adaptive, but needs to become more so, strong individual leadership may be required initially to disrupt the status quo—but might later give way to a more collective style.

There is no universal checklist for becoming an adaptive leader, but by focusing on the four dimensions we've described, leaders can better equip themselves for a turbulent and unpredictable business environment. To gauge how adaptive your leadership model is, ask yourself and your leadership teams just three questions about what you are doing and how you are thinking as leaders:

- How many of the adaptive leadership practices cited in this chapter do we currently employ?
- Do we have the right leadership model for our specific business environment?
- What changes could we make to develop a more adaptive leadership model?

We conclude with a quote from John Clarkeson, former CEO of BCG, who presciently and vividly sketched this new model of leadership 20 years ago:

Leadership will flow to those whose vision can inspire the members of the team to put their best abilities at the service of the team. These leaders will create rather than demand loyalty; the best people will want to work with them. They will communicate effectively with a variety of people and use the conflict among diverse points of view to reach new insights. They will exert influence by the values they choose to reinforce. They will make leaders of their team members.

# 5

# Competing
# on Capabilities

## George Stalk, Jr., Philip Evans,
## and Lawrence E. Shulman

*This article was first published in 1992 and represented a significant extension in strategic thinking—going beyond scale, position, and operational efficiency to introduce a broader view of competitive advantage.*

Companies that compete effectively on time—speeding new products to market, manufacturing just in time, or responding promptly to customer complaints—tend to be good at other things as well: for instance, the consistency of their product quality; the acuity of their insight into evolving customer needs; the ability to exploit emerging markets, enter new businesses, or generate new ideas. But all these qualities are mere reflections of a more fundamental characteristic: a new conception of corporate strategy that we call capabilities-based competition.

For a glimpse of the new world of capabilities-based competition, consider the astonishing reversal of fortunes represented by Kmart and Walmart.

In 1979, Kmart was king of the discount retailing industry, an industry it had virtually created. With 1,891 stores and average revenue per store of $7.25 million, Kmart enjoyed economies of scale in purchasing,

---

distribution, and marketing that, according to just about any management textbook, are crucial to competitive success in a mature and low-growth industry. By contrast, Walmart was a niche retailer in the South with only 229 stores and average revenue about half that of Kmart stores—hardly a serious competitor.

And yet, only 10 years later, Walmart had transformed itself and the discount retailing industry. Growing nearly 25 percent a year, the company achieved the highest sales per square foot, inventory turns, and operating profit of any discount retailer. Its 1989 pretax return on sales was 8 percent, nearly double that of Kmart.

What accounts for Walmart's remarkable success? Most explanations focus on a few familiar and highly visible factors: the genius of founder Sam Walton, inspiring his employees and building a culture of service excellence; the "greeters" who welcome customers at the door; the motivational power of allowing employees to own part of the business; the strategy of "everyday low prices." Economists also point to Walmart's big stores, which offer economies of scale and a wider choice of merchandise.

But such explanations only redefine the question. *Why* was Walmart able to justify building bigger stores? Why did Walmart alone have a cost structure low enough to accommodate everyday low prices and greeters? And what enabled the company to continue to grow far beyond the direct reach of Sam Walton's magnetic personality? The real secret of Walmart's success lies deeper, in a set of strategic business decisions that transformed the company into a capabilities-based competitor.

The starting point was a relentless focus on satisfying customer needs. Walmart's goals were simple to define but hard to execute: to provide customers access to quality goods, to make these goods available when and where customers want them, to develop a cost structure that enabled competitive pricing, and to build and maintain a reputation for absolute trustworthiness. The key to achieving these goals was to make the way the company replenished inventory the centerpiece of its competitive strategy.

This strategic vision reached its fullest expression in a logistics technique known as cross-docking. In this system, goods are continuously delivered to Walmart's warehouses, where they are selected, repacked, and then dispatched to stores, often without ever sitting in inventory. Instead of spending valuable time in the warehouse, goods just cross from one loading dock to another in 48 hours or less.

Cross-docking enabled Walmart to achieve the economies that come with purchasing full truckloads of goods while avoiding the usual inventory and handling costs. This reduced Walmart's cost of sales by 2 to 3 percent compared with the industry average. That cost difference made possible the everyday low prices. Low prices in turn meant that Walmart could eliminate the expense of frequent promotions. Stable prices also make sales more predictable, thus reducing stock-outs and excess inventory. Finally, everyday low prices bring in the customers.

With such obvious benefits, why didn't all retailers use cross-docking? The reason: it is extremely difficult to manage. For example, cross-docking requires continuous contact among Walmart's distribution centers, suppliers, and every point of sale in every store to ensure that orders can flow in and be consolidated and executed within a matter of hours. So Walmart established a private satellite communication system that sent daily point-of-sale data directly to its 4,000 vendors.

Another key component of Walmart's advantage was the company's transportation system. The company's dedicated truck fleet made it possible to ship goods from warehouse to store in less than 48 hours and to replenish store shelves twice a week on average. By contrast, the industry norm was once every two weeks.

To gain the full benefits of cross-docking, Walmart had to transform its approach to managerial control. Traditionally in the retail industry, decisions about merchandising, pricing, and promotions were made at the corporate level. Cross-docking, however, turns this command-and-control logic on its head. Instead of the retailer pushing products into the system, customers "pull" products when and where they need them.

The job of senior management at Walmart, then, is not to tell individual store managers what to do but to create an environment where they can learn from the market. Accordingly, the company's information systems provide store managers with detailed information about customer behavior.

The final piece of this capabilities mosaic is Walmart's human resources system. The company set out to enhance its organizational capability with programs such as stock ownership and profit sharing geared toward making its personnel more responsive to customers.

In contrast, Kmart did not see its business this way. While Walmart was fine-tuning its business processes and organizational practices, Kmart was focusing on a few product-centered strategic business units, each a profit center under strong centralized line management. While Walmart was building its ground transportation fleet, Kmart was moving out of trucking because a subcontracted fleet was cheaper. While Walmart was building close relationships with its suppliers, Kmart was constantly switching suppliers in search of price improvements.

This is not to say that Kmart managers did not care about their business processes. After all, they had quality programs too. Nor was it that Walmart managers ignored the structural dimension of strategy: they focused on the same consumer segments as Kmart. The difference is that Walmart emphasized behavior—the organizational practices and business processes in which capabilities are rooted—as the primary object of strategy and therefore focused its managerial attention on the infrastructure that supported capabilities. This subtle distinction made all the difference between exceptional and average performance.

In industry after industry, established competitors have been outmaneuvered by more dynamic rivals.

- In the years after the Second World War, Honda was a modest manufacturer of a 50-cc engine designed to be attached to a bicycle. Today its scale in the global automobile industry is on a par with that of General Motors and Ford.
- Xerox invented xerography and the office copier market. But between 1976 and 1982, Canon introduced more than 90 new models, cutting Xerox's share of the mid-range copier market in half and going on to become a competitor not only in mid-range copiers but also in high-end color copiers.
- In the 1980s department store giants like Macy's saw their greatest challenge coming neither from other large department stores nor from small boutiques but from The Limited, a multibillion-dollar design, procurement, delivery, and retailing machine exploiting dozens of consumer segments with the agility of many small boutiques.

These examples represent more than just the triumph of individual companies. They signaled a fundamental shift in the logic of competition, a revolution in corporate strategy.

When the economy was relatively static, strategy could afford to be static. In a world characterized by durable products, stable customer needs, well-defined national and regional markets, and clearly identified competitors, competition was a "war of position" in which companies occupied competitive space like squares on a chessboard, building and defending market share in clearly defined product or market segments. The key to competitive advantage was *where* a company chose to compete. *How* it chose to compete was also important but secondary, a matter of execution.

Competition is now a "war of movement" in which success depends on anticipation of market trends and quick response to changing customer needs. Successful competitors move quickly in and out of products, markets, and sometimes even entire businesses.

A capability is a set of business processes strategically understood. Every company has business processes that deliver value to the customer. But few think of them as the primary object of strategy. Capabilities-based competitors identify their key business processes, manage them centrally, and invest in them heavily, looking for a long-term payback.

Take the example of cross-docking at Walmart. Cross-docking is not the cheapest or the easiest way to run a warehouse. But seen in the broader context of Walmart's inventory replenishment capability, it is an essential part of the overall process of keeping retail shelves filled while also minimizing inventory and purchasing truckload quantities.

What transforms a set of individual business processes like cross-docking into a strategic capability? The key is to connect them to real customer needs. A capability is strategic only when it begins and ends with the customer. Capabilities-driven competitors conceive of the organization as a giant feedback loop that begins with identifying the needs of the customer and ends with satisfying them.

As managers have grasped the importance of time-based competition, for example, they have increasingly focused on the speed of new product development. But as a unit of analysis, new product *development* is too narrow. It is only part of what is necessary to satisfy a customer and, therefore, to build an organizational capability. Better to think in terms of new product *realization*, a capability that includes the way a product is not only developed but also marketed and serviced. The longer and more complex the string of business processes, the harder it is to transform them into a capability—but the greater the value of that capability once built because competitors have more difficulty imitating it.

Weaving business processes together into organizational capabilities in this way also mandates a new logic of vertical integration. At a time when cost pressures are pushing many companies to outsource more and more activities, capabilities-based competitors are integrating vertically to ensure that they, not a supplier or distributor, control the performance of key business processes.

Even when a company doesn't actually own every link of the capability chain, the capabilities-based competitor works to tie these parts into its own business systems. Consider Walmart's relationships with its suppliers. In order for Walmart's inventory replenishment capability to work, vendors have to change their own business processes to be more responsive to the Walmart system. In exchange, they get better payment terms from Walmart than they do from other discount retailers.

Another attribute of capabilities is that they are collective and cross-functional—a small part of many people's jobs, not a large part of a few. This helps explain why most companies underexploit capabilities-based competition. Because a capability is "everywhere and nowhere," no one executive controls it entirely. For these reasons, building strategic capabilities cannot be treated as an operating matter and left to operating managers, to corporate staff, or still less to strategic business unit (SBU) heads. It is the primary agenda of the CEO.

Only the CEO can focus the entire company's attention on creating capabilities that serve customers. Only the CEO can identify and authorize the infrastructure investments on which strategic capabilities depend. Only the CEO can insulate individual managers from any short-term penalties to the profit and loss statements (P&Ls) of their operating units that such investments might bring about.

Indeed, a CEO's success in building and managing capabilities will be the chief test of management skill in the 1990s. The prize will be companies that combine scale and flexibility to outperform the competition along five dimensions:

- *Speed.* The ability to respond quickly to customer or market demands and to incorporate new ideas and technologies quickly into products.
- *Consistency.* The ability to produce a product that unfailingly satisfies customers' expectations.
- *Acuity.* The ability to see the competitive environment clearly and thus to anticipate and respond to customers' evolving needs and wants.

- *Agility*. The ability to adapt simultaneously to many different business environments.
- *Innovativeness*. The ability to generate new ideas and to combine existing elements to create new sources of value.

# Becoming a Capabilities-Based Competitor

Few companies are fortunate enough to begin as capabilities-based competitors. For most, the challenge is to become one.

The starting point is for senior managers to undergo the fundamental shift in perception that allows them to see their business in terms of strategic capabilities. Then they can begin to identify and link together essential business processes to serve customer needs. Finally, they can reshape the organization—including managerial roles and responsibilities—to encourage the new kind of behavior necessary to make capabilities-based competition work.

The experience of a medical-equipment company we'll call Medprod illustrates this change process. Medprod managers became aware that at accounts where Medprod had placed one or more full-time service representatives on-site, the company renewed its highly profitable service contracts at three times the rate of its other accounts. When these accounts needed new equipment, they chose Medprod twice as often as other accounts did and tended to buy the broadest mix of Medprod products as well.

The reason was simple. Medprod's on-site service representatives had become expert in the operations of their customers. They knew what equipment mix best suited the customer and what additional equipment the customer needed. So they had teamed up informally with Medprod's salespeople to become part of the selling process. Medprod then made a dramatic commitment—to place at least one service rep on-site with selected customers—no matter how little business each account currently represented.

Next Medprod combined its sales, service, and order-entry organizations into cross-functional teams that concentrated almost exclusively on the needs of the targeted accounts. The company trained service reps in sales techniques, which freed up the sales staff to focus on the more strategic role of understanding the long-term needs of the customer's business. Finally, the company even taught its service reps how to fix competitors' equipment.

The result: the company increased its market share by almost 50 percent. This story suggests four steps by which any company can transform itself into a capabilities-based competitor:

- *Shift the strategic framework to achieve aggressive goals.* Medprod managers abandoned the company's traditional internal profit center orientation, instead identifying and managing the capabilities that linked customer need to customer satisfaction. The chief expression of this new capabilities-based strategy was the decision to provide on-site service reps to targeted accounts and to create cross-functional sales and service teams.

- *Organize around the chosen capability and make sure employees have the skills and resources to achieve it.* Rather than retaining the existing functional structure and trying to encourage coordination through some kind of matrix, Medprod managers created a new organization— Customer Sales and Service—and divided it into "cells" with overall responsibility for specific customers. The company also provided the necessary training and created systems to support employees in their new roles.

- *Make progress visible and bring measurements and reward into alignment.* The company had to develop a whole new set of measures—for example, Medprod's "share-by-customer-by-product," the amount of money the company invested in servicing a particular customer, and the customer's current and estimated lifetime profitability. Team members' compensation was calculated according to these new measures.

- *Do not delegate the leadership of the transformation.* Because capabilities are cross-functional, the change process requires the hands-on guidance of the CEO and the active involvement of top-line managers. At Medprod, it was the CEO who oversaw the change process, evaluated proposals from functional heads, and made the final decision.

# A New Logic of Growth:
# The Capabilities Predator

Once managers reshape the company in terms of its underlying capabilities, they can use these capabilities to define a growth path for the corporation. At the center of capabilities-based competition is a new logic of growth.

In the 1960s, most managers assumed that when growth in a company's basic business slowed, the company should turn to diversification. This was the age of the multibusiness conglomerate. In the 1970s and 1980s, however, it became clear that growth through diversification was difficult. And so, the pendulum of management thinking swung once again. Companies were urged to "stick to their knitting"—that is, to focus on their core business, identify where the profit was, and get rid of everything else. Competing on capabilities provides a way for companies to gain the benefits of both focus and diversification—a company that focuses on its strategic capabilities can compete coherently in a remarkable diversity of regions, products, and businesses. Such a company is a "capabilities predator"—able to come out of nowhere and move rapidly from nonparticipant to major player and even to industry leader.

Capabilities-based companies grow by transferring their essential business processes—first to new geographic areas and then to new businesses.

Strategic advantages built on capabilities are easier to transfer geographically than more traditional competitive advantages. Honda, for example, became a manufacturer in Europe and the United States with relatively few problems. Walmart's move from small towns in the South to large, urban, northern cities also spanned a cultural gap. And Walmart did it with barely a hiccup. Although the stores were much bigger and the product lines different, the capabilities were exactly the same.

But the big payoff for capabilities-led growth comes not through geographic expansion but through rapid entry into whole new businesses. Capabilities-based companies do this in at least two ways. The first is by "cloning" their key business processes. Again, Honda is a typical example.

For example, a big part of Honda's original success in motorcycles was due to the company's less visible capability in "dealer management." Typically, local dealers were motorcycle enthusiasts who were more concerned with finding a way to support their hobby than with marketing, parts inventory management, or other business systems.

Honda, by contrast, managed its dealers to ensure that they would become successful businesspeople. The company provided operating procedures and policies for merchandising, selling, floor planning, and service management. It trained all its dealers and their entire staff. The part-time dealers of competitors were no match for the better prepared Honda dealers.

Honda's move into new businesses, including lawn mowers, outboard motors, and automobiles, depended on recreating this same dealer management capability in each new sector.

But the ultimate form of growth in the capabilities-based company may not be cloning business processes so much as creating processes so flexible and robust that the same set can serve many different businesses. This was the case with Walmart. The company used the same inventory replenishment system that made its discount stores so successful to propel itself into deep-discount warehouse clubs, pharmacies, European-style hypermarkets, and large, no-frills grocery stores known as superstores. Its Sam's Club warehouse business took only four years from its establishment in 1983 to surpass all its competitors' sales.

While Walmart was growing quickly by entering new businesses, Kmart tried to grow by acquisition, with mixed success. It bought and sold a number of companies in unrelated businesses such as restaurants and insurance—an indication the company had difficulty adding value.

This is not to suggest that growth by acquisition is necessarily doomed to failure. Indeed, the company that is focused on its capabilities is often better able to target sensible acquisitions and then integrate them successfully.

In conclusion, the essence of strategy is *not* the structure of a company's products and markets but the dynamics of its behavior. And the goal is to identify and develop the hard-to-imitate organizational capabilities that distinguish a company from its competitors in the eyes of customers:

- The building blocks of corporate strategy are not products and markets but business processes.
- Competitive success depends on transforming a company's key processes into strategic capabilities that consistently provide superior value to the customer.

- Companies create these capabilities by making strategic investments in a support infrastructure that links together and transcends traditional SBUs and functions.
- Because capabilities necessarily cross functions, the champion of a capabilities-based strategy is the CEO.

Capabilities-based companies have the advantage of competing against rivals still locked into the old way of seeing the competitive environment. As more companies transition to capabilities-based competition, the simple fact of competing on capabilities will become less important than the specific capabilities a company has chosen to build. Given the necessary long-term investments, the strategic choices managers make will end up determining a company's fate. Capabilities are often mutually exclusive. Choosing the right ones is the essence of strategy.

# Global

Tip O'Neill, a prominent Irish American politician of the twentieth century, once quipped that "all politics is local." This century's corollary might be that "all business is global." Almost any sizable business needs to be global to succeed.

However, many business leaders in mature markets are unprepared for the demands of creating global businesses. The growth markets of today and tomorrow—China and India, but also parts of Southeast Asia and Africa—take many leaders outside their comfort zone: they demand new business models, new products and services, and new mind-sets. What worked in Munich is unlikely to work in Mumbai.

We now live in a world in which everyone from everywhere is competing for everything: customers, capital, talent, raw materials, intellectual property, and brand loyalty. Chapter 6, "Globality: The World beyond Globalization," describes how multinationals are going up against nimble competitors from new economies that understand what it takes to succeed in these new markets.

We call these competitors global challengers when they are both fast growing and fast globalizing. Global challengers understand how to create products and services for consumers who have lower incomes than consumers in the West but similar aspirations and optimism about the future. They know how to overcome the distribution and infrastructure bottlenecks that can frustrate multinationals accustomed to smooth roads and steady utility service. In Chapter 7, "The New Global Challengers," we predict that multinationals will not just be competing with global challengers but also cooperating with them in joint ventures and partnerships that make use of their complementary skills.

Western executives who visit only Beijing, Shanghai, Mumbai, New Delhi, and Jakarta on their swing through Asia are missing the most promising urban areas. More than 700 cities in emerging markets have populations exceeding 500,000, and most of them are growing fast. Competition is frequently less intense in many of these places because they are off the beaten track. As Chapter 8, "Winning in Emerging-Market Cities," points out, companies that want to win in emerging markets need to be present in these places.

Although the largest and best known emerging market, China is still not well understood by executives of multinationals, who frequently fail to grasp how quickly it is growing and how rapidly products are adopted. The world's most populous country is already the largest market for automobiles, consumer electronics, and home appliances. One of the central points of Chapter 9, "What the West Doesn't Get about China," is that being late to market can mean losing the market.

Africa is not yet on the agenda in many corporate boardrooms, but it should be. The per capita GDP of the top African nations—Algeria, Botswana, Egypt, Libya, Mauritius, Morocco, South Africa, and Tunisia—exceeds that of the BRIC nations of Brazil, Russia, India, and China. Life expectancy, literacy, education, and the standard of living in those countries are comparable to those in the BRICs and in other rapidly growing Asian nations as well. Moreover, Africa's ambitious local companies, profiled in Chapter 10, "The African Challengers," have started to make their mark in worldwide markets. It is not too late to take a fresh look at a continent often overshadowed by Asia and South America.

The opportunities in these markets are as unbounded as the optimism of the new consumers who inhabit them. There has never been a more exciting time to run a global business.

# 6

# Globality: The World beyond Globalization

## Harold L. Sirkin, Jim Hemerling, and Arindam K. Bhattacharya

There is a new era of global business competition emerging that we call *globality*. Globality is not simply a new word for globalization; it is a fundamentally different phenomenon.

Globalization was an activity largely conducted by a set of multinational companies—based in the United States, Europe, and Japan—known as incumbents. They were driven by the quest for low-cost production and the desire to enter promising new markets in developing countries.

Globality is not an activity so much as it is an environment, a state of being. It is mainly fueled by a set of business competitors that are based not in the developed world but in the rapidly developing economies (RDEs). These are the *global challengers*.

In this environment, incumbents find themselves dealing with a range of new management issues—concerning costs, human resources, supply chains, innovation, and more—that we call the seven struggles of globality.

Globality presents both threats and opportunities to all players. Incumbents face tough new challenges, but these can be met and turned to advantage. Challengers stand at the brink of huge opportunities but still face barriers to seizing them.

Based on the authors' 2008 book, *Globality—Competing with Everyone from Everywhere for Everything*, published by Business Plus.

# Competing with Everyone from Everywhere for Everything

During globalization, incumbents competed primarily with other incumbents in markets around the world. In the new era of globality, however, incumbents suddenly (or so it seems) find themselves competing with everyone from everywhere for everything.

"Everyone" includes many types of companies. A large number of today's challengers once served as suppliers and vendors to the incumbents. Others were state-owned entities; some still are. Many challengers did not even exist when the incumbents first entered their markets. Some operated in one industry and then switched to another.

These global challengers have emerged from everywhere. As one would expect, many are based in the large cities of the RDEs, but plenty more have grown up in secondary and tertiary cities and even in rural areas. They hail not only from the high-profile BRIC countries—Brazil, Russia, India, and China—but also from Argentina, Chile, Egypt, Hungary, Indonesia, Malaysia, Mexico, Poland, Thailand, and Turkey.

And globality's players are competing for everything: capital, talent, raw materials, intellectual property, real estate, brand awareness, partners, suppliers, advisors, customers, press coverage, and brand loyalty.

Almost everything is up for grabs. Almost nothing can be locked up.

# The Seven Struggles

To survive, compete, and succeed in the age of globality, every incumbent will have to work its way through the seven struggles. These are often difficult and complex issues that rarely have simple, one-off solutions, and they need to be constantly revisited.

## Struggle 1: Minding the Cost Gap

Incumbents went global primarily to reduce the cost of goods that they were selling back "home" in developed markets. But they still had (and still do have) very high cost structures compared with those of companies based in RDEs, where all the essential ingredients of business are far less expensive than in developed countries.

So for incumbents, the first struggle is to carefully mind the cost gap—the differential between their product and service costs and those of the challengers—keeping the gap small enough that it's insignificant to large segments of consumers. Alternatively, they can add an optimal mix of distinguishing features and incremental benefits to justify a premium.

## Struggle 2: Growing People

During globalization, managing human resources was largely a matter of attracting (or poaching) people to fill the essential boxes on the org chart and then motivating and retaining them. Top talent could be scarce, vying for people could get rancorous, and loyalty often seemed like an antiquated notion, but the rules of the game were at least fairly well defined.

Globality presents a very different human resources challenge. Many an incumbent has established an operation in a low-cost country only to find that there are not enough workers available to make a go of it. Or they discover that a significant percentage of the huge pool of available skilled workers is not as skilled as it first appeared. Or the incumbent's senior managers simply don't want to live and work in certain locations.

As a result, companies are finding it necessary to grow employees "from scratch," which involves entirely new approaches to recruiting, training, and retaining people at every level.

## Struggle 3: Reaching Deep into Markets

Incumbents, understandably, have their eyes on the very large prize contained in the markets of RDEs. Not only are these markets huge, they are increasingly wealthy and sophisticated.

The struggle is to do whatever it takes—including adapting products and go-to-market approaches—to move beyond the relatively small, affluent urban markets, where most incumbents have been operating for the past two decades, in order to reach the hundreds of millions of potential buyers who live in the smaller cities, towns, and villages. This is made all the more complicated by a dearth of consumer information and the complex and arcane nature of distribution systems.

## Struggle 4: Pinpointing

Over the years, incumbents have offshored various elements of their operations, primarily to reduce costs, but these moves have not necessarily been part of a strategic rethinking of the entire value chain.

The challengers—smaller, nimbler, and with fewer (if any) legacy assets to consider—have shown themselves to be adept at configuring their value chains with no home-market or executive favoritism. They locate each element of the operation where it will make the greatest contribution to the entire system—whether because of low costs, access to talent, proximity to major customers or markets, or other considerations. Then they design their business processes so that location and value chain configuration are highly transparent and virtually irrelevant.

## Struggle 5: Thinking Big, Acting Fast, Going Outside

Challengers have often favored the external path to growth through mergers, acquisitions, alliances, and partnerships. These activities have enabled tiny companies, sluggish bureaucracies, and firms with gaps in capabilities to rapidly learn, quickly gain new strengths, and, almost overnight, make giant leaps forward.

This is not to say that incumbents have failed to master the art of the deal. It's just that the challengers seem able to make their moves more quickly, with less deliberation, and to take advantage of the new arrangements with greater ease. Increasingly, incumbents will find themselves bidding against challengers for important worldwide assets—and may even themselves be targeted for acquisition by a challenger.

## Struggle 6: Innovating with Ingenuity

The challengers have generally been known as expert copiers, interpreters, simplifiers, and adapters—rather than as great inventors, large-scale innovators, or major creators of intellectual property.

But they have tremendous ingenuity: the ability to spot a customer need or a market opportunity in its early stages, seize upon whatever talents and resources fall most readily to hand, come up with a multitude of possible solutions, choose one or more for rapid commercialization, get those products into the market quickly, and, if necessary, adapt and refine them just as rapidly. They're also able to scrap new products altogether, without remorse or recrimination. Incumbents will need to increase both the pace and the quantity of their innovation efforts.

### Struggle 7: Embracing Manyness

*Globality* means "manyness": a remarkable diversity of countries, economies, markets, locations, facilities, employees, customers, products, languages, attitudes, and beliefs. It means organizations that are polycentric rather than monolithic.

Manyness can be an uncomfortable concept for incumbents that have long believed in the company way, the single global strategy, the seamless worldwide organization, the optimal profile of the high-potential achiever, the heroic leadership style.

In the era of globality, companies discover that the world may look flat when observed from a distance but can be decidedly lumpy when experienced on the ground. The struggle is to resist the temptation to homogenize and regularize and to figure out how to take advantage of the richness and vigor that can come from manyness.

# The Way Forward

For most companies, success in the era of globality will require a global transformation. There are a number of steps to take in achieving that goal.

- *Change your mind-set.* Many executives are in denial about the emerging reality. Some see only the threats; others think there is plenty of time to prepare for the new competitive environment. Not so. Now is the time to listen to people inside and outside your organization, engage in conversation, honestly examine your attitudes and behaviors, and rethink what you do and how you do it.
- *Assess your company's situation.* Before deciding on any action, take careful stock of your company's situation. What is your current strategy? How well are you implementing it? What does your global footprint look like now? Do you have the right people in the right places? What are the strengths and weaknesses of your organization?
- *Try more things.* Challenger companies try things without engaging in a complicated process of analysis and decision making. They'll put into play a new idea or approach in a way that seems almost haphazard to incumbents. If the new idea doesn't work, it's scrapped.

Incumbents must loosen up a little, accept smaller gains, and tolerate a little more failure.

- *Challenge yourself.* Before your worst-nightmare competitor emerges from one of the RDEs, become your own challenger. Develop a product or service that will top your current best seller. Establish relationships with key partners that can't be shaken. Spin off a unit that has the potential to grow faster and larger than your core. Attack your competitors as a challenger would.
- *Shift into hyperdrive.* Enlist the best people and enable them to operate globally. Have people who have transitioned into the era of globality motivate and encourage those who have not. Educate and push yourself: read material that mystifies you, travel to new places, converse with people outside your regular circles. Don't wait. Don't look back. Don't equivocate.

Above all, remain positive. The era of globality is as full of opportunities as it is loaded with threats. There are 3 billion new customers out there—huge pools of interesting talent, new partners to collaborate with, intriguing business practices to be studied and adapted.

The era of globality will be challenging, risky, exciting, provocative, and rewarding.

It will be, in short, what you make of it.

# 7

# The New Global Challengers

**Marcos Aguiar, Arindam K. Bhattacharya, Thomas Bradtke, David C. Michael, Tenbite Ermias, Whitney Haring-Smith, David Lee, Michael Meyer, Andrew Tratz, Masao Ukon, and Bernd Waltermann**

Emerging markets have become the world's economic engines. They are large and becoming larger, thanks to annual GDP growth exceeding 6 percent and a rapidly growing class of consumers with disposable income.

These markets have become highly prized by companies everywhere, not just for their growth, but also as sources of talent, capital, and companies. Over the past five years, nearly 1,000 public companies headquartered in emerging markets have reached at least $1 billion in annual sales.

Many of these companies are content to focus on their home market, while others are expanding abroad; many of those going overseas aspire to be global leaders in their industries. These are the global challengers. They are the companies that will shape the global economy over the next decade.

The 2013 BCG global challengers have moved far beyond the low-cost position that placed many of them on the original 2006 list. These 100 companies are winning with a broad range of strategies and capabilities. In doing so, they are fundamentally altering industries ranging from aircraft manufacturing and medical devices to e-commerce and mobile telephony.

Not just competitors of multinationals, global challengers can be attractive potential customers. In 2011, the 2013 BCG global challengers purchased about $1.7 trillion of goods and services and invested more than $330 billion in capital expenditures.

Finally, with the global marketplace becoming more demanding, global challengers are potential partners of multinationals, as they often have complementary skills.

We have entered the era of allies and adversaries.

# Global Challengers

Let's examine some of the highlights of the newest class of global challengers.

### Growth

From 2008 through 2011, the revenues of global challengers grew by 16 percent annually. Global challengers had higher average revenue in 2011 than the average nonfinancial S&P 500 company did. During that time, earnings of the global challengers expanded by 10 percent and total shareholder return (TSR) grew by 20 percent annually.

Job growth has been equally impressive. From 2006 through 2011, the 2013 BCG global challengers added 1.4 million jobs, while employment at nonfinancial S&P 500 companies remained constant. Even more striking, revenue per employee of the global challengers now exceeds that of the nonfinancial S&P 500.

### From Diverse Lands

Our 2006 list was dominated by China, where 44 global challengers were based. But newcomers from other countries have pushed some former challengers off the list—there are now just 30 Chinese companies—followed by 20 from India and 13 from Brazil. The number of home countries is steadily increasing with challengers emerging from Egypt, Colombia, Qatar, Saudi Arabia, and South Africa.

### Focus on New Consumers

From 2010 through 2020, emerging markets will add 270 million households with discretionary income that makes them attractive to consumer-facing companies. Global challengers stand to benefit from this shift since nearly one-third of them are consumer products or consumer services companies.

Many of these companies have embarked on an acquisition spree. For instance, in mobile telecom, VimpelCom—based in Amsterdam but founded in Russia, its largest market—bought Wind Telecom and control of Orascom Telecom Holding for $6 billion in 2011. In travel, the merger between Chile's LAN Airlines and Brazil's TAM Airlines created the largest South American airline, Latam Airlines Group. In fast-moving consumer goods, India's Godrej bought Indonesia's Megasari Makmur Group.

Through such deals, some challengers have risen quickly. But no challenger has a guarantee of success. Challengers are more likely to fall off the list than to rise above it. Since 2006 only seven companies have achieved "graduate" status, our designation for onetime challengers that have achieved sustained industry leadership.

One of the key ways that the global challengers have evolved is in the degree of state ownership or control. The number of state-controlled challengers has dropped from 36 to 26.

Although the state is still the "visible hand" in the economies of these markets, many companies under state ownership or control have either chosen not to go global or stumbled when they tried. Since 2011, 12 state-owned or state-controlled companies—most of them Chinese—have fallen off the list. Only 9 state-owned or state-controlled companies were added.

At least five factors explain the setbacks of state-owned and state-operated enterprises on the global stage. First, their relative competitive advantage often resides in domestic markets, where the state tends to encourage them to focus. Second, private-sector companies have generally had more success than state enterprises in meeting the needs of consumers. Third, state-sector people practices tend to be less flexible than those of private enterprises, limiting their ability to engage overseas talent. Fourth, state shareholders are often more conservative in putting capital at risk in large overseas mergers and acquisitions (M&A) transactions. Finally, they can face resistance from stakeholders in other countries as they seek to expand. Although many state companies have overcome these challenges, others are at risk of falling behind globally.

To succeed outside of their home countries, state-controlled enterprises will need to attract talent, take risks, develop successful business models, and appease the concerns of key stakeholders in their target markets.

All of the 2013 BCG global challengers are at a turning point. The cost advantage they once enjoyed over their competitors from mature markets is eroding. But they have also been building new capabilities—manufacturing higher-quality products, harnessing their cash resources, and investing in research and development (R&D).

## High-Quality Products

Many challengers are still low cost, but this description is more likely to describe their business models than their product offerings. The Middle Eastern airlines—Etihad Airways, Qatar Airways, and Turkish Airlines—have low-cost structures while winning global awards for exceptional service and quality. Huawei's Ascend D1 Quad is among the fastest smartphones in the world.

## Capital Availability

Despite spending on aggressive globalization and growth plans, the challengers are still well financed. Many challengers have the capital to make significant strategic investments. During the 2008 to 2010 period, they put their capital to work to take advantage of low equity prices by completing hundreds of cross-border acquisitions that provided access to international assets and management.

## Innovation

Global challengers increasingly see the need to become more innovative and are rapidly increasing their research spending. They boosted their annual spending on R&D by 34 percent annually from 2007 through 2011. Mindray, a medical equipment supplier based in China, generates more U.S. patents per dollar of revenue than many global leaders. About 46 percent of Huawei's 150,000 employees are in R&D. Tigre, a Brazilian PVC pipe and fitting company, launches about 500 new products a year.

Many innovations are aimed at creating new business models rather than tangible products. For example, the Fung Group, formerly known as the Li & Fung Group, has pioneered an innovative role acting as an intermediary between designers in developed markets and Chinese manufacturers.

# Competition and Cooperation

Increasingly, challengers and multinationals are competing head to head. Multinationals have modified their cost structures and product portfolios to pursue opportunities in emerging markets, where they face challengers on their home turf. And some challengers, such as conglomerate Alfa and baker Grupo Bimbo, both from Mexico, are expanding into the home markets of multinationals.

Over the next several years, global challengers and multinationals will heatedly compete on several fronts. They will be vying to develop products and services that appeal to the new consumer class in emerging markets. As these consumers venture online, generally on a mobile device, global challengers will also compete on the digital frontier. Finally, they will be fighting for position in such growth spots as Africa and Southeast Asia.

Paradoxically, as competition between multinationals and challengers has become more cutthroat, these companies are also more likely to face scenarios where partnerships make sense. Bargaining power is more balanced, so partnerships no longer need to be reached solely on the basis of the low costs of challengers or the high gloss of Western brands but rather on a wide range of complementary skills.

Challengers and multinationals will increasingly come together to develop new products, exchange—rather than transfer—technology, and enter new markets. India's Bajaj Auto and Japan's Kawasaki, a manufacturer of motorcycles and other vehicles, for example, have created an alliance to jointly market products in the Philippines and Indonesia. Meanwhile, Dr. Reddy's, an Indian pharmaceutical company, is teaming with Merck to develop generic cancer treatments. In a twist, Dr. Reddy's, known for generic manufacturing, is conducting product development, while Merck is handling manufacturing.

# The Game Has Changed

The global challengers are constantly evolving. Only half of the companies selected in 2006 made the cut in 2013. To reach the next level of global expansion, challengers require even greater capabilities and greater engagement with both private and public entities.

Meanwhile, the success of the challengers raises the stakes for multinationals. They need to be entering and building positions in emerging markets with localized strategies, partnering with challengers when it will help them get ahead.

Finally, governments, especially those in mature markets, should recognize challengers as a positive force for growth in jobs and income. Rather than imposing restrictions, governments should be actively encouraging acquisitions and investments, developing regional hubs to entice overseas investment, and avoiding excessive nationalism and protectionism.

The BCG global challengers are game changers in their global industries. They are meeting the needs of customers in the world's high-growth markets and bringing greater choice to customers everywhere. Established multinationals must both compete and partner with these challengers to thrive. We are just at the dawn of a major new era of global competition— of challengers and multinationals, of allies and adversaries.

# 8 Winning in Emerging-Market Cities

## David Jin, David C. Michael, Paul Foo, José Guevara, Ignacio Peña, Andrew Tratz, and Sharad Verma

**M**ore than one-third of the world's population lives in cities that are located in the emerging markets. By 2030, the number of emerging-market urban dwellers is expected to increase by 1.3 billion. In contrast, cities in developed markets are expected to add only 100 million new residents in the next 20 years.

This massive growth will fundamentally change the competitive landscape in many ways. Consumer demand will rapidly increase as the middle class in these markets expands, new infrastructure will be required as cities grow, and those companies that are best positioned to capture the opportunity will tap into larger profit pools, grow faster, and use emerging-market cities as a catalyst for innovation.

Just consider this: at the time of writing in 2010, emerging-market cities drive more than 60 percent of world GDP growth. There are already 717 emerging-market cities with populations of more than 500,000, and another 371 such cities are expected to reach this size by 2030. There are only 240 cities of equal size in the developed world.

Income levels in emerging-market cities are reaching an inflection point, with the middle-class population expected to rise dramatically. The leap in the number and size of emerging-market cities, alongside the burgeoning number of middle-class households and the infrastructure required to support them, is creating unprecedented new growth opportunities for companies—and significant new complexities. Companies wishing to grow in emerging markets must rapidly increase the number of cities served, and they must improve their ability to win in a range of urban market segments. This will require that they develop new business models and channels to serve these markets profitably. Dramatic organizational change may be required. A "cities strategy" is key to growth in emerging markets, and successful companies will be those that embrace this challenge.

Beneath the headline figure of 1.3 billion new residents of emerging-market cities are countless individual stories of change and mobility. Mr. Yang exemplifies the unique situations in which such consumers find themselves.

A few years ago, Mr. Yang moved from the Chinese countryside to nearby Xiaochang, a fast-growing city in landlocked Hubei province approximately 700 kilometers west of Shanghai.

He and his wife took out a mortgage on a sparsely furnished one-room restaurant next to a hospital, with sleeping quarters in the back. Since then, Mr. Yang has used his earnings from the restaurant to buy a range of "middle class" goods, including two TV sets, a mobile phone, a refrigerator, a washing machine, an air conditioner, a DVD player, a computer, and a small mini-van that he uses to drive his daughter to the city's best private kindergarten.

Mr. Yang now worries about the rising cost of his child's education, whether to buy a new car and a separate apartment, the poor quality of local health care, and what rapid housing and infrastructure construction in the area mean for his business. Mr. Yang has never used a credit card, and although he has Internet access, he has never shopped online because of security concerns.

Few executives are likely even aware of this city's existence. Indeed, the consumers we spoke with in Xiaochang owned only Chinese branded goods. But given that fast-growing smaller cities like Xiaochang are at the forefront of emerging-market-city growth, companies without a strategy for determining in which and in how many of these cities to compete risk overlooking a huge opportunity.

## The Rise of the Cities

The same phenomena that created Xiaochang have built up scores of cities like it in China—and hundreds more in other emerging markets—creating wealth beyond such megacities as Mexico City, Mumbai, and Shanghai. The development process itself is familiar, being driven by both rural migration and urban population growth. But what is different in the emerging markets is the scale and speed at which it is occurring.

Cities with fewer than 5 million inhabitants already represent 83 percent of the urban residents in emerging markets and are growing more rapidly than the megacities. Because many of these cities have characteristics quite different from those of the larger cities, the strategies that companies use when they enter these markets must be refined accordingly.

One of the first steps in making the decision about whether or not to become active in an emerging-market city and in developing an appropriate strategy is to understand the nature of the various cities involved by segmenting them into distinct groups. This can provide a lens for prioritization as well as highlight the need for different go-to-market approaches to address different types of cities. There are four major groups that are relevant for nearly all businesses.

- *Megacities.* Megacities are defined here as those with populations of 10 million or more. They are critical markets now and will remain important for decades to come. Their role as financial and trade capitals allows them to act as international gateways for their countries or regions. They are characterized by high population density, which lowers the barrier to reaching consumers, and they are key markets for higher-end offerings such as complex financial products and luxury goods. Because megacities often represent the leading edge for consumption habits and high-end brands within a country, they can be important stepping-stones for companies to reach deeper into national markets. Perhaps most important, megacities tend to attract young, highly motivated individuals in their regions in search of a better education and a better future.
- *Cluster capitals (and satellite cities).* Cluster capitals are trade hubs that are surrounded by smaller satellite cities. There are nearly 150 cluster capitals (with populations of 5 to 10 million), including Changsha (China), Joinville (Brazil), and Veracruz (Mexico). Cluster capitals are large, of course, but another reason for their strategic importance is their proximity to a significant number of nearby satellite cities (of which there are 500 to 1,000). As a result, cluster cities can function

as regional hubs within a country, and their strategic importance should not be underestimated.

- *Specialist hubs.* There are already more than 100 specialist hubs— midsize cities (with populations of 1 to 5 million) whose growth is often closely linked to the development of local natural resources or industrial hubs. These cities are experiencing higher growth rates than others in the emerging markets, with recent real GDP growth of more than 3 percent. Examples include Aguascalientes (Mexico), Ahmedabad (India), Hyderabad (India), Recife (Brazil), and Wenling (China).

  Specialist hubs are overlooked by many multinational competitors. However, the middle-class and affluent populations in these cities are rapidly expanding and driving significant changes in the consumption mix.

- *Horizon towns.* There are hundreds of small, geographically dispersed emerging-market cities that we call horizon towns. These cities are often characterized by less developed infrastructure and lower GDP per capita growth than other emerging-market cities. Examples include Calkiní (Mexico), Macapá (Brazil), Moradabad (India), and Yinchuan (China).

  Horizon towns tend to be the most challenging cities to address in a comprehensive way because of their small size and geographic dispersion. Most multinational companies have not invested heavily in covering horizon towns, which are consequently dominated by local competitors.

# Capturing the Consumer Opportunity

Not only is the population of emerging-market cities increasing, but growing numbers of residents are seeing their incomes rise markedly. By 2015, 125 million households representing 460 million residents of cities in Brazil, China, India, Indonesia, Mexico, Russia, South Africa, and Turkey are expected to have graduated to the middle class.

This change in income levels is currently reaching an inflection point, with many products previously unattainable by average residents starting to become necessities. Once households enter the middle class, consumption of categories such as luxury goods and home decor increases rapidly. The car market provides a preview of what will occur in many other categories. In 2000, emerging-market cities accounted for 8 percent of total car sales. A decade later, more than 37 percent of the world's cars, including a significant share of luxury cars, were purchased in these markets.

Basic consumer products may be experiencing this increased demand ahead of other goods and services, but rapid growth will undoubtedly be seen in other categories as well. By 2015, emerging-market cities are expected to account for approximately 30 percent—or $2.6 trillion—of the total global consumption of clothing and household items. And these cities are already some of the fastest-growing markets for luxury goods in the world.

Education is a high priority—in some cases, even the single largest expenditure—for many emerging-market city dwellers. Many of the emerging-market urban residents we spoke with also identified improved health care and financial services as priorities.

# Capturing the
# Infrastructure Opportunity

Emerging-market cities will need better housing and infrastructure—including transportation, water, sanitation, and electricity. We anticipate that emerging markets will need $5.3 trillion worth of investment in electricity infrastructure from 2010 to 2030, for example, approximately 60 percent of the global generating capacity. Emerging markets will require an estimated $13.8 trillion in housing investment from 2010 to 2030, with a huge portion of the demand coming from Brazil, China, India, and Mexico. There are many ways for companies to play a role in meeting the infrastructure needs of emerging-market cities: through city planning, financing and investment, the construction and management of new infrastructure, the operation and maintenance of existing infrastructure, or the supply of raw materials, components, and innovative technologies.

The shortfall between needed infrastructure in emerging-market cities and available public funds is estimated to be in the neighborhood of $11 trillion to $14 trillion through 2030. This creates an opportunity for private investors to help governments raise funds to bridge the financing gap or for private construction firms and asset managers to take a financial stake in their contracts. Although the emerging markets have different financing capabilities and different degrees of openness to privatization, the sheer size of this gap has encouraged many governments to embrace private financing in the form of public-private partnerships (PPPs). The amount invested in greenfield projects involving private participation was $62 billion in 2007 for the six largest emerging-market countries, compared with $25 billion in 2003.

# The New Agenda for Emerging-Market Growth

Capturing the tremendous growth opportunity presented by the emerging-market cities will require a new management agenda for the emerging markets, with cities as its focal point. This agenda requires executives to tackle the following imperatives:

- *Define growth plans on the basis of specific target cities—the portfolio of emerging-market cities to be served now and in the future.* Most companies will find that they are serving far fewer cities than they should be and that they need to be much more ambitious and specific.
- *Specify the necessary go-to-market models to enable profitable expansion into more and smaller cities.* Multiple go-to-market models are imperative, and they will be fundamentally different from those required for megacities.
- *Develop true expertise and insight regarding consumer needs across a range of city environments in emerging markets.* Consumers in emerging-market cities have a great variety of unique needs and behaviors. Most companies fail to invest properly in gaining direct insights into these consumers and translating those insights into products and services.
- *Forge a game plan to profit from the infrastructure boom.* Infrastructure-related companies need to grasp the magnitude and speed of the infrastructure growth taking place in emerging-market cities. While new local champions are rising up on the crest of this wave, many companies in developed markets are missing out.
- *Develop talent and organization plans at a city-by-city level over a 5- to 10-year time frame.* As the number of commercially important cities skyrockets, the need for companies to have talent based in all these locations also grows.

- *Upgrade capabilities for managing complexity and risk.* As demand unfolds across a massive number of emerging-market cities, every company that takes this growth challenge seriously will experience a higher level of complexity and risk.

The rise of emerging-market cities represents the world's single largest commercial growth opportunity for decades to come. While the promise is vast, the complexities are also daunting. Never before in history have companies been faced with the challenge of doing business simultaneously in thousands of cities around the globe. Growth for many companies requires taking up this challenge. Those that do so and succeed will become true global winners.

# 9

# What the West Doesn't Get about China

## George Stalk, Jr. and David C. Michael

When many managers think about China, they imagine a container ship whose hold and deck are brimming with cartons of toys, clothing, iPhones, and other goods bound for the world's consumer markets, whose populations power China's economic engine.

That view couldn't be more wrong.

Despite the Chinese government's well-publicized program to encourage domestic consumption, few Westerners grasp just how much progress the country is making on this front. Although millions of peasants live on subsistence wages, millions more Chinese are moving to urban centers and achieving a recognizably middle-class lifestyle. Consider just a few data points that give evidence of China's unexpectedly fast-paced move toward a more balanced, consumer-driven economy:

- In a variety of consumer categories—including such items as automobiles, consumer electronics, and jewelry—China already ranks as the number one market in the world (Figure 9.1).
- The combined flow of shipping containers between Asia and North America and between Asia and Europe is already less than the flow

China is already the world's largest consumer of a variety of products and services:

| Sector | Compound Annual Growth (2007-2012) |
| --- | --- |
| Automobiles | 19% |
| Consumer Electronics | 17% |
| Home Appliances | 14% |
| Internet Use | 22% |
| Jewelry | 20% |
| Mobile Phones | 22% |

**FIGURE 9.1** An "Emerging" Market? Not in These Categories
Source: BCG analysis.

among Asian nations—with much of the latter consisting of goods imported to China.

- Domestic demand accounts for most sales of Chinese-produced air conditioners, motorcycles, trucks, and steel.
- Adoption rates of new technologies among the rising middle class exceed those of nearly every other developing country. Today China has 400 million Internet users, most with broadband access. Mobile telephony is ubiquitous in urban areas, and most of its consumers have leapfrogged landlines.
- China's cities are growing so quickly that the country now has more urban centers than most Western nations do. For instance, China currently has about 90 cities with a middle-class population of 250,000 or more; the United States and Canada together have fewer than 70. According to projections, by 2020 China will have 400 cities with at least 250,000 middle-class inhabitants—and 50 of those cities will have more than 1 million middle-class inhabitants. And by then it is expected to have 800 cities whose residents' real disposable incomes are greater, on average, than those of Shanghai's residents today.

- Looking beyond consumer markets, we find that Chinese companies are already recognized as among the world leaders in numerous business-to-business (B2B) technologies, including wind-turbine blades, solar panels, high-speed rail equipment, steam boilers, port terminal cranes, and electric-transmission equipment.

Few Western managers who visit China get a realistic picture of its economic development. They typically go to Beijing or Shanghai. They stay in five-star hotels—often Hiltons and Hyatts. There's apt to be a Starbucks in the lobby. The familiar atmosphere leads them to think that China's market will someday resemble a typical Western economy, full of Western-made products. But, in fact, cities far from Beijing and Shanghai are teeming with goods and services from domestic companies—and if Western companies don't get to those cities soon, they'll be left out.

To be sure, despite its rapid progress China is still far from self-sufficient in a number of areas. It remains dependent on foreign multinationals for market access—many Chinese companies lack the ability to generate significant export trade on their own. The country can provide a college education for a growing share of the population but still relies largely on foreign universities for top-flight graduate education. Its only traditional energy resource is coal, and its demand for imported oil has been a major factor in rising prices over the past decade. China is also a net importer of food. Finally, it lacks the innovative pharmaceutical and health care sectors of Western economies, and as its consumers become increasingly upscale, they will demand more of the pills and procedures that Westerners take for granted.

## How Multinationals Should Navigate the Emerging China

Although every multinational has a China strategy, most companies aren't moving quickly enough for their strategies to succeed. To better position themselves, they need to be aware of these trends:

1. The rise of domestic competitors will happen faster than most multinational corporations expect. Local companies in some high-growth markets—for example, Xizi in elevators, 7 Days Inn in budget hotels,

and Midea in consumer appliances—have already become leaders. Multinationals that hope to have strong market share a few years down the road need to establish themselves now.

2. Whether or not they are currently selling in China, companies looking to capitalize on the opportunities there need to be ready to do business in hundreds of locations, not just in a handful of the current megacities. This has dramatic implications for organizational structure, distribution infrastructure, choice of business partners, and the amount of capital needed.

3. Companies must prepare for extraordinary growth in demand. Some Western companies today are struggling to handle 35 percent annual sales growth in China—but the markets they're playing in are growing at 60 percent. Despite their enormous investments in human and capital resources, these companies are already ceding share to competitors—and their competitors will increasingly be Chinese companies. In a market growing this quickly, it can be worthwhile to build excess capacity, and it's smart to take a hard look at whether your present forecasts may be overly conservative.

4. Western companies need to understand that Chinese consumers have very different needs than consumers in their home markets. Chinese households don't want cappuccino machines; they want water filters, air filters, and soy milk makers (at the moment, one of the hotter consumer categories in China—and one with no foreign competition). The classic example involves automakers, which had to learn that many Chinese who can afford cars like to employ drivers, so backseat features are very important to them.

5. Multinationals must realize that product adoption rates will be higher in China than in most markets they've experienced, meaning that in some categories, the competitive landscape will be settled quickly. Companies that don't strive to be number one at the outset won't have the luxury of entering and being competitive later.

6. As Chinese companies gain prowess in their home market, more will expand abroad. They are likely to move into Africa and South America before they enter North America and Europe. Whether they realize it or not, Western companies aren't fighting just for a position in the Chinese market—they're also fighting to forestall potential competitors in other emerging markets and eventually

on their own turf. Multinational corporations may not be inclined to pay much attention to small local companies in China today, but they should.

7. Western companies will increasingly be on their own when dealing with many of the politically based difficulties of doing business in China. The power of Western governments to impose their will on the Chinese is diminishing rapidly—if it was ever really there at all—as the rise of China's own markets makes the country less dependent on Western companies. Competing in China will have less to do with government policy and more to do with offering the right products and services to the right customers at the right price.

Some Western companies are showing adroitness in exploiting the new opportunities in China. Among them are Volkswagen, Yum! Brands, General Electric, and Procter & Gamble (Figure 9.2). But these are exceptions. Most Western companies underestimate how quickly the Chinese market is developing and how little time they have to establish a competitive foothold—particularly in cities other than Beijing and Shanghai.

| | |
|---|---|
| **Volkswagen** | The German multinational was the first Western automaker to enter China, establishing its initial joint venture there in the 1980s, when other car manufacturers considered the country too risky. By the 1990s it had captured up to 90 percent of the market for passenger cars. Although it has since lost share to other overseas companies, it sold 2.3 million vehicles in 2011. |
| **Yum! Brands** | The parent company of KFC, the first fast-food chain to open in China, Yum! is the largest and fastest-growing restaurant chain in the country. It currently operates nearly 4,100 restaurants (more than 500 of which opened in 2010) in 700 cities across China. |
| **General Electric** | GE has operated in China for many decades in sectors including energy, aviation, health care, and transportation. It plans to extend its Chinese operations even further and recently announced five new deals expected to generate $2 billion in revenue. |
| **Procter & Gamble** | The consumer goods giant has several brands that hold the top spot in the Chinese market, including Rejoice, Safeguard, Olay, Pampers, Tide, and Gillette. Fully 97 percent of its employees are Chinese, including many in top management positions. P&G recently opened the Beijing Innovation Center, which will provide global research and development support, and plans to invest at least $1 billion in China through 2015. |

**FIGURE 9.2** How Four Multinationals Figured China Out
Source: Company websites.

In many ways China today is what the United States was to Great Britain in the late 1800s. British managers couldn't imagine or execute the strategies necessary to do business in a geographic landscape far more vast than their home market. The same challenges now face Western managers in China, but on an even greater scale: never before have businesses had to deal with market opportunities spread across such a wide geography, with so many different languages and ethnic populations. These are challenges that require aggressive action—and ones few companies are currently prepared to meet.

# 10 The African Challengers

Lionel Aré, Sami Chabenne, Patrick Dupoux, Lisa Ivers, David C. Michael, and Yves Morieux

The African economy is overshadowed by Asia to the east and, to a lesser degree, by South America to the west. Over the past decade, however, Africa has begun to emerge. Hidden in plain view, scores of African companies have been competing and rapidly expanding in the global economy. Their ambitions may be larger than their revenues, but collectively they are making a mark.

To spotlight the economic awakening of Africa, we have identified 40 fast-growing African companies with global aspirations—the African challengers—in order to understand their specific strategies and challenges and the evolution of African capitalism.

## A Fresh Perspective

The conventional view is that Africa in the year 2010—with 20 percent of the world's land and 15 percent of its population, but just 4 percent of global GDP—has been down so long it will be hard for it to ever rebound. This view is understandable—but out of date. While the Great Recession shrank most economies, Africa's was able to grow. In 2009, the continent's GDP expanded by 2 percent, while GDP dropped 4 percent in the United States, 2.8 percent in the European Union, and 1.5 percent in Latin America.

Seven countries (Algeria, Angola, Egypt, Libya, Morocco, Nigeria, and South Africa) account for 75 percent of the continent's GDP. In 2008, GDP per capita ranged from $330 in the Democratic Republic of the Congo to almost $15,000 in Botswana. These contrasts reflect the realities of a continent that is rich in natural resources but also rife with poverty, health problems, geopolitical risk, and the lingering effects of colonialism.

But despite these challenges, the top African economies—which we call the African Lions—display GDP per capita comparable to that of the so-called BRIC nations of Brazil, Russia, India, and China. The Lions comprise Algeria, Botswana, Egypt, Libya, Mauritius, Morocco, South Africa, and Tunisia. Great diversity exists among both the African Lions and the BRIC nations. But life expectancy, literacy, education, and standard of living within the African Lions are comparable to those of the BRIC countries and the Asian Tigers (Indonesia, the Philippines, Thailand, and Vietnam). Beyond these lions, several other highly populated sub-Saharan countries such as Angola, Nigeria, Kenya, Tanzania, and Ghana are now enjoying very high growth rates and the progressive emergence of a consuming class.

African companies have been able to take advantage of these positive trends. Between 1998 and 2008, the revenues of the 500 largest African companies outside of the banking sector have grown by 8.3 percent annually. Exports have helped power this increase, surging from 3 percent annual growth during the 1990s to 18 percent annual growth during the 2000s. Direct foreign investments by African companies have risen even more sharply.

# African Contenders

The 40 African challengers range in size from $350 million to $80 billion in annual sales in 2010; they all display strong growth, an international footprint, and ambitious plans to further expand overseas. Three countries of origin dominate the list: South Africa (with 18 companies), Egypt (with 7 companies), and Morocco (with 6 companies).

Several industries are well represented on the list: financial services (10 companies); mining and natural resources (8 companies); technology, media, and telecommunications (6 companies); logistics services (5 companies); and industrial goods (5 companies).

On the basis of their export sales and foreign assets, we divided the 40 challengers into five groups:

- *Big local players.* These three companies—ONA-SNI Group, the largest Moroccan conglomerate; CIB, an Egyptian bank; and Cevital, an Algerian food company—have reached critical mass in domestic markets and have started international campaigns. Their assets and sales remain more than 90 percent domestic, but international activity is picking up.
- *Exporters.* The vast majority of the sales of these five companies are exports, but their assets are largely local. They tend to be mining and oil companies, such as Sonatrach, the Algerian government-owned oil company; OCP Group, a Moroccan mining company and the largest global exporter of phosphates; and Sonangol, a government-owned oil company in Angola.
- *Regional players.* At least 10 percent of the assets of these 12 companies are located outside of their home country but within Africa. The regional players understand local markets but also have scale. This group includes such companies as Maroc Telecom, the main Moroccan telecom operator, with operations in Mauritania, Burkina Faso, Mali, and Gabon; Ecobank, a bank based in Togo that serves western and central Africa; and Shoprite, a South African food retailer with stores in 17 African countries.
- *Multicontinental players.* These 17 companies have at least 10 percent of their assets outside of Africa. Many were originally regional players that expanded overseas, but others, especially those based in South Africa, never built a continental business. Banco Africano de Investimentos, the leading Angolan bank, has expanded into Europe and, more recently, Brazil. Orascom Telecom, based in Egypt, has farflung operations. Aspen Pharmacare, based in South Africa, has become the largest generic drug maker in the southern hemisphere.
- *Global players.* The three global players have more than half their assets outside of the continent and are a global sales presence. Anglo American, a natural-resource company, is the world's largest producer of platinum. SABMiller is the world's largest brewer, and Old Mutual is a financial company that reaches into more than 30 countries.

# Keys to Success

The African challengers share several characteristics that have allowed them to prosper.

## Native Advantages

African challengers benefit from doing business in a place with many native advantages, including natural resources, cheap labor, and a fast-growing population that is unencumbered by legacy technology and systems. The continent has 82 percent of global reserves of platinum, 55 percent of diamond reserves, and more than 50 percent of phosphate reserves.

Labor is much less expensive in Africa than in other developing markets. The average wages of a worker in Egypt are half those of a worker in China and one-sixth those of a Brazilian worker.

Africa's large population creates a ready-made market for the African challengers. Although most Africans are poor, the collective purchasing power of the continent is rising. Between 2000 and 2008, GDP per capita increased by 51 percent (adjusted for purchasing power parity).

Finally, many African companies are unencumbered by legacy assets and business models. With so few landlines on the continent, telecom operators are offering mobile-only services. Many banks are jumping into electronic banking without ever having built large branch networks.

## A Beneficial Business Environment

For most of the past decade, rising commodity prices have helped the performance of mining and natural resources companies. Other African challengers have taken advantage of deregulation, especially in banking and telecommunications. For example, MTN Group, a South African telecom operator, has built a mobile network and captured a 50 percent share in Nigeria, a market that is doubling annually.

Several countries have undertaken active economic development programs, such as Morocco's Emergence Plan, beneficial to the challengers. Morocco has also retooled its educational system to better meet the needs of business, signed several bilateral free trade agreements, and privatized several government-owned companies.

## The Challenger Mind-Set

Not all African companies have the mind-set required to achieve global stature. The following are two important components of the challenger mind-set:

- *Long-term vision.* Many of the African challengers were not looking for quick profits when they expanded overseas. Fifteen percent of them are family-owned companies without the short-term pressures typical of public companies. Similarly, government-owned companies, which account for 30 percent of the challengers, are able to look beyond short-term shareholder return and make strategic bets overseas.
- *Creativity.* The African challengers have consistently displayed resourcefulness in building businesses under challenging conditions. SABMiller, for example, developed a new beer in Uganda, called Eagle Lager, using locally grown sorghum rather than more expensive imported malt. Likewise, MTN developed a solar pay phone in Uganda to serve fishermen on Lake Victoria.

# The Global Challenge

The African challengers must continue to move up the globalization ladder. Fortunately, they can draw on lessons learned from challenger companies in India, China, and Latin America that have created global operations.

## Managing Volatility

One of the keys to succeeding in global expansion is the ability to cope with the volatility of business and economies. Many companies have helped themselves by pursuing the following strategies:

- *Expanded geographic reach.* By moving their operations closer to their global customers, companies can lower transportation costs and protect themselves from currency fluctuations.
- *Supply chain optimization and integration.* Companies can lower their costs and exposure to changing raw material prices by maintaining a tight supply chain.

- *Government support.* Many companies from developing markets are able to use government support to assist their expansion plans.
- *Raising productivity.* Increases in productivity can counterbalance the effects of rising labor costs. To date, productivity increases have allowed African companies to stay competitive, but the continent's growth in productivity lags behind that of Brazil, China, and India.

  Although education and technology are the keys to improved productivity, flexible and adaptable organizational structures can help, too. The African challengers can avoid proliferating structures, processes, and systems—and the cumbersome command-and-control models that still dictate how many companies operate—by building organizations based on cooperation, leadership, and engagement.

- *Expanding outside of Africa.* The African challengers have already sharply increased their levels of cross-border mergers and acquisitions, but most of the activity is contained within the continent. The challengers can broaden the markets they serve, start to build a global workforce, acquire global brands, and diversify risk.

  Cross-border deals are difficult to master because of the potential geopolitical, cultural, and security risks. African challengers that decide to expand through acquisition must diligently manage their selection of targets and consolidation of operations.

- *Boosting human capital.* In Africa, with its low levels of education, attracting and retaining talent is especially daunting. The proportion of the high school–age population attending school has been steadily rising but is still woefully low. Although public investment in education is in line with global averages in Africa, private investment is lacking. In China, for example, private funds represent 80 percent of total education spending. Beyond fulfilling their corporate social responsibility, African challengers that invest in education can help shape course work and programs designed to produce qualified job candidates.

  Creating a global workforce should be another part of a long-term plan to boost talent and human capital. Only 21 percent of the top executives at African challenger companies are foreign, compared with 45 percent at multinational companies. Foreign executives can provide African companies with capabilities that may be difficult to find in the local job market.

- *Creating global brands.* Few African challengers may create strong brands outside of the continent. Acquisitions can give African challengers global recognition. SAB followed this playbook when it acquired the Miller beer brand in 2002. Likewise, Royal Air Maroc offers maintenance services through a joint venture with Snecma, the well-known French aviation manufacturer.

- *Benefiting from state support.* Beyond ensuring political stability and legal protections, governments can assist in several other ways. They can promote regional economic blocs, such as the Maghreb of Morocco, Algeria, and Tunisia, to combat the subscale size of individual country markets. State support should not, however, be a crutch. Companies need to show independence and take responsibility for defining their own strategies and growth models.

# Looking Ahead

The African challengers represent the growing strength of African capitalism. Capitalism produces winners and losers, and there will certainly be rough spots along the way for African companies. But as the success of our challengers suggests, the future is bright for a continent only now starting to fully flex its capitalist muscles.

# Connected

It has been nearly 50 years since the song "It's a Small World After All" was unveiled at the 1964 World's Fair in New York, a year after the founding of BCG. Since then, the Internet has emerged as a force to bring the globe together. In the next few years, nearly half the world's population will likely be online, with the majority of those users living in emerging markets.

This connectivity is radically changing the business landscape and the traditional bases of competitive advantage. The Internet has disrupted many industries, including recorded music, newspapers, and travel; altered the dynamics of many other sectors; and enabled new online businesses.

As discussed in Chapter 11, "The Digital Manifesto," digital technology and social media offer companies new ways to connect with customers, suppliers, and partners. In many cases, this ubiquitous connectivity makes it possible to create new business models, such as Tesco's virtual stores in subway stations in Seoul: a commuter can order products on her phone and have them delivered to her home that day.

With this connectivity comes an unprecedented volume of potentially valuable data that companies can translate into precious information and insight. As Walter Wriston, the legendary leader of Citibank, said in the 1980s, "Information about money has become almost as important as money itself." Chapter 12, "Data to Die For," gives companies a way to think about the implications of big data for their business.

One company that has successfully exploited the connectivity, mobility, and data patterns of consumers is Apple—with its iPod, iPhone, iPad, and iTunes ecosystem. Steve Jobs recognized that computing was moving from a paradigm of power to one of portability. He designed products that allowed access to media and information in a convenient, easy-to-carry, and personalized fashion, when most hardware manufacturers were building more powerful, feature-laden computers. Chapter 13, "The Collision of Power and Portability," examines the evolution of computing through this lens of connectivity.

The nature of connectivity varies by nation. In China, where television programming is tightly controlled and many people live in rural regions, the Internet is wildly popular as a form of entertainment. Between 2008 and 2011, the average time online per person increased from 2.8 to 3.6 hours per day—about an hour a day more than Internet users in the United States.

The Chinese have also gravitated toward weibos, Twitter-like microblogging services that give people an opportunity to express themselves in a nation where expression is tightly controlled. Sina Weibo attracted more than 300 million users in its first three years of operation. As detailed in Chapter 14, "China's Digital Generations 3.0: The Online Empire," these developments have vast implications for how to reach and connect with customers. To date, however, few companies have shifted much of their advertising and marketing dollars to online channels.

So, the bottom line is that connectivity is changing everything. Companies in a connected world must rethink their strategies, organizations, and operations and how they engage with customers. The challenges are immense, but so are the opportunities.

# 11 The Digital Manifesto

## David Dean, Sebastian DiGrande, Dominic Field, and Paul Zwillenberg

Every business needs to "go digital." Data about customers, competitors, suppliers, and employees are exploding. Ninety percent of all data were created in the past two years. By 2016, there will be 3 billion Internet users globally, and the Internet economy will reach $4.2 trillion in the G20 nations.

No company or country can afford to ignore this phenomenon. We have entered the "second half of the chessboard," where the scale and speed of change are indelibly altering industry structures and the way that companies do business.[1] Farsighted companies have a once-in-a-lifetime opportunity to reinvent everything about the way they do business.

## A Shifting Center of Gravity

Twenty years ago, at its commercial birth, the Internet was a novelty. Today, residents of many villages around the world are more familiar with Internet content than with indoor plumbing or air-conditioning. By 2016,

---

[1] The second half of the chessboard is a metaphor for the point at which exponential growth begins to have a fundamental economic impact on an organization's overall business strategy. If one grain of rice is placed on the first square of a chessboard, two grains on the second, four on the third, and so on, the sixty-fourth square would have 2 billion times more rice than the first half of the chessboard.

almost 3.5 billion consumers, or 45 percent of the world's population, will use the Internet.

This shift is one of just several changes under way as the Internet matures and becomes fully embedded in everyday life.

- *From fixed to ubiquitous access.* Increasingly, the Internet is everywhere—not just on mobile phones but also in cars, refrigerators, and watches. By 2016, mobile devices will account for over 80 percent of all broadband connections in the G20 nations.
- *From developed to emerging nations.* Emerging markets have become a major engine of online commercial activity. By 2016, the Internet economy of China will approach the size of the U.S. Internet economy and emerging nations will be responsible for about 34 percent of the overall Internet economy of the G20 nations and for 48 percent of their growth.
- *From passive to participatory.* Social media have taken hold everywhere, especially in emerging markets. More than 90 percent of Internet users in Argentina, Brazil, and Mexico participate in social media, a higher percentage than in any developed nation. The shift to an interactive Web fundamentally changes the nature of companies' interactions with customers.

## The Internet Meets Main Street

As the Internet becomes ubiquitous, it naturally takes on the contours of the particular nation's economy, reflecting its structure and norms. Just as the ocean looks very different depending on whether you are at the coast of Maine, Mexico, Morocco, or Malaysia, so too does the Internet.

### The Evolving Local Experience

The Internet can help enhance the strengths and overcome the structural weaknesses of the traditional economy. The United Kingdom, for example, has become a nation of digital shopkeepers, but the Netherlands has not, even though the fixed-broadband infrastructure is much stronger there. The reason: the Dutch are light credit card users. The Czech Republic has a relatively strong e-commerce market, reflecting the poor retail experience in its physical stores.

It is easier to make a payment using a mobile phone in Kenya than in Kansas. Kenya is unencumbered by the infrastructure, regulations, and inertia that hamper mobile payments in developed markets, and consumers are eager to access banking services.

In China, the shortage of television programming and weak enforcement of intellectual property laws have made the Internet a prime vehicle for entertainment. The nation's one-child policy encourages the use of chat rooms and social networking among young people with no siblings at home.

## The Retail Experience

Online purchases will account for more than 20 percent of retailing in the United Kingdom and between 8 and 12 percent in other leading economies by 2016. Even in nations without a large e-commerce footprint, online research is creating better-informed shoppers and improving the offline shopping experience. For example, the online tools at Ikea's website allow shoppers to see how a piece of furniture will actually look in their home.

# A Digital Future

The world is rapidly becoming populated by companies that have the Internet in their DNA. They are Main Street's version of Amazon.com. For example, Wiggly Wigglers, a U.K. organic garden supply shop, and Hiwave Dry Seafood, a Hong Kong vendor, were founded prior to the creation of the commercial Internet and figured out how to thrive on it. Open English, a company "born in the cloud," teaches English to Latin Americans. All three are companies that are comfortable seeing the world as their marketplace, creating an online brand and presence, analyzing data patterns, and using apps in the cloud.

## Small Is Beautiful

Small and medium enterprises (SMEs), historically the growth engine of national economies, are also becoming Internet successes. During 2010 and 2011, BCG surveyed employees at more than 15,000 SMEs. We divided the survey respondents into four groups: (1) high-Web companies, which use a wide range of Internet tools to market to, sell to, and support customers;

interact with suppliers; and empower employees; (2) no-Web businesses, which do not have a website; and (3) medium- and (4) low-Web businesses, which are in between.

In the United Kingdom, sales of high- and medium-Web businesses grew by 4.1 percent annually from 2007 through 2010—about seven times faster than sales of low- and no-Web businesses. In countries as different as China, Brazil, Germany, and the United States, those SMEs that embraced the Internet grew significantly faster than those that didn't, often by a significant factor.

SMEs are rapidly adopting social media tools to increase the richness of their interactions with customers. More than 40 percent of these businesses in the United States and the United Kingdom report using social media tools. Among high-Web businesses, 60 percent use social media as a source of new ideas from customers.

## Digital Champions

Some large companies have also figured out how to thrive in the digital world. In many of its markets, Tesco is the leading retailer, but not in South Korea, where it was trailing E-mart. Tesco responded by creating virtual shops in subway stations—billboards designed to replicate the look of store shelves, down to the arrangement of products. With their mobile phone, commuters can scan the QR code of any item on display and have it delivered to their homes that day. These virtual displays enabled Tesco to turn the time spent waiting for a train into shopping time—and become South Korea's number one online supermarket.

Many companies not under immediate threat are nonetheless taking steps to use the Internet to their advantage. In emerging markets, traditional companies wanting to build their online retail presence are creatively overcoming constraints. In Mexico, for example, 7-Eleven stores allow offline payment for online purchases. In China and India, cash on delivery is becoming a standard form of payment in online transactions. In Argentina, where poor roads and heavy congestion make home delivery difficult, Walmart encourages store pickup of online purchases.

Burberry, a British fashion house founded in 1856, broadcasts live 3-D video streams of fashion shows in its stores and to smartphones and tablets. Online shoppers can order clothes before they are available on store shelves.

## Industry Disruption

Disruption creates both challenges and opportunities. Over time and to varying degrees, music labels have discovered how to live in the digital world. Universal Music, the largest label, has diversified away from recorded music. A material portion of its revenue now comes from merchandising, licensing, ticketing, touring, e-commerce, and digital music partnerships.

Health care could be ready to experience the disruptive force of the Internet. It took $300 million and 13 years to map the first human genome. In 2011, it cost only $3,000, and every five months the cost was being cut in half. Unlocking the causes of illness and developing cures depend not just on falling per unit costs but on the ability of the health care industry—or attackers—to mine and combine genomic data with medical records and data about costs and patient outcomes.

In financial services, the proliferation of smart cards, debit cards, and mobile payments is creating rich veins of intelligence about consumer behavior that are waiting to be tapped, by banks or nonfinancial competitors. Likewise in the utility industry, smart meters and connectivity between the grid and the Internet are creating an environment in which information about energy usage is almost as important as energy itself.

# The CEO's Agenda: Building the Digital Balance Sheet

Companies need to start strengthening their digital assets:

- Information and analytics about customers, suppliers, employees, and competitors
- Connectivity and feedback loops that lubricate the digital enterprise
- Intellectual property that provides a digital edge
- The people, culture, and capabilities needed to execute and deliver digital successes

At the same time, companies should actively address their digital liabilities—ways of working that handicap the ability to exploit their digital assets:

- Organizational structures, incentives, and cultures that collectively discourage adaptability and risk taking
- IT systems, processes, and tools that limit flexibility and focus
- Rigid strategies unsuited to a volatile business environment

By understanding their digital balance sheets, executives will acquire a solid sense of what needs to be done. The following three levers will help companies build their digital equity.

## Take an Adaptive Approach to Strategy

Although the strategic concepts of scale, segmentation, and cost position remain valid, the traditional way of looking at those concepts—in terms of three- to five-year planning cycles—is out of date. There is a better way to think about and create strategy in the digital age.

Companies need to recognize the unpredictability of today's environment and devise a strategic approach that values real-time data analysis and experimentation. They need to recognize relevant patterns in the data and use these insights to continuously adjust and reinvent their business model. They also need to be able to quickly enter, scale up, or scale down new businesses in diverse industries when opportunities emerge or when experiments do not pan out.

## Run Forward and Walk Backward

Traditional companies will need to run forward into the future while walking backward away from their traditional businesses. Executives need to simultaneously manage their legacy businesses and build the foundations for the future in wholly new areas.

## Develop Capabilities, an Organization, and a Culture Aimed at Building Digital Equity

Given the complete change in business model, skill sets, and risk profile that is required, digital transformations require focus, commitment, and engagement throughout the organization. Leaders must change the mind-set of the senior leadership team—and possibly the composition of the team itself—if they want to change the organization. It also may be necessary to establish partnerships, alliances, and collaborations with suppliers, customers, and even competitors. Leaders need to create a culture of experimentation so that employees feel comfortable rapidly testing ideas that challenge orthodox approaches to innovation.

## The Policy Maker's Agenda: Keeping the Internet Moving

The growth of the Internet economy is not a foregone conclusion. In setting policies, governments should be guided by what is needed to encourage growth, innovation, and consumer choice rather than by dogma. In most areas, governments should let the market sort out the winners and losers, but they do have a constructive role to play:

- Promoting investment in expanded coverage, high-speed infrastructure, and affordable mobile Internet access
- Putting a priority on education and skills building
- Encouraging innovation and entrepreneurial activity
- Facilitating global talent mobility so that the most valuable employees can go where their skills can be put to the best use
- Keeping a vigilant eye on emerging chokepoints that hinder innovation and the adoption of new technologies

We are still only at the beginning of realizing the benefits of the Internet for consumers, businesses, and society. These benefits are built on competition, consumer choice, and access. In an age of mobile capital and talent, the countries that foster these policies will see the fastest growth and greatest payback.

# 12 Data to Die For

## Simon Kennedy
## and David Matheson

Using information to make one's name or fortune is hardly a new concept. In 1978, Fred Smith, founder of FedEx, famously said that "the information about the package is as important as the package itself" and applied this insight to develop the real-time tracking tools that gave his company a huge advantage in the marketplace.

What is powering the efforts of the Googles of today's business world is the rapidly increasing amount of information—about everything from stock trades to hip replacements—that exists in digital form. Inexpensive to search and relatively easy to manipulate, the digital format is creating manifold opportunities for companies to more easily take advantage of the information that they have, and that others don't, for competitive advantage. The information asymmetries that result will increasingly shape markets and decide who wins, who loses, and even who gets to play. In short, in a world awash with information, some companies find ways to know more than others, and the difference can allow them to devise and drive whole new business models.

In some circumstances, shortcomings in collecting or understanding information have more than commercial ramifications: they can determine who lives or dies. Automakers, airlines, food service companies, and health care providers, among others, can put consumers at risk if data flows go awry. Indeed, perhaps tens of thousands of preventable patient deaths occur every year in U.S. hospitals, according to a number of studies. These deaths often result from a breakdown in the transmission of information from those who have it to those who need it, a fatal form of asymmetry. For example, information about a patient's preexisting conditions or drug regimen may not get from one doctor to another.

Even though so much is at stake, many companies still find themselves on the wrong side of the information divide. Worse, some don't even know that that's where they are. But there are ways to narrow the gap—and even to cross the divide.

# Why Do Companies Come Up Short?

Why do information asymmetries occur? Given that this is the information age, why don't those who can benefit from existing data routinely have access to all the bits and bytes that they need?

Often the problem is that companies do have access but don't recognize or appreciate what is in their grasp. With so many facts at hand about so many things—products, customers, sales, and more—it's easy to fail to connect the dots. Simply put, many companies have a competency issue in this area: very few have an advanced data analytics capability or even a "home" for one. The operations side produces streams of data and IT ships them around, but no one has the time, tools, or ability to really take the data apart and try to find opportunities for advantage.

Of course, the problem can also stem from not having enough data. Privacy concerns are one factor inhibiting the flow. In the United States, the Health Insurance Portability and Accountability Act (HIPAA) is just one law that imposes privacy requirements on providers. Although the constraints are not absolute, many providers err on the side of caution and refuse to share or release *any* information about individuals.

Often the owners of other types of data also put the brakes on sharing—for competitive reasons, for reasons of convenience, or because they want to limit their liability. Clearly transparency does not benefit all players equally. Many companies depend on information asymmetries to lock in customers and maintain price levels—and until things change, they have little incentive to share data.

Then there is the cost issue. Information flows suffer from a variant of the "tragedy of the commons." In most supply chains, the *value* of digitized information is something that all players can share, but often a single player must bear all or most of the *cost* of capturing the data in the first place.

Finally, there is the problem of interoperability. Information not intended for sharing is not generally stored or used in formats that make it easy to share or combine—that is, to be interoperable.

All of these hurdles are being addressed in one way or another. But revisions in privacy policies and increased interoperability, among other changes, can't overcome the most basic hurdle of all: the need for imagination. Frequently it's a new question, insight, or view of the world that spells the difference between generating mounds of useless data and distilling information that actually confers an advantage. And when imagination, data, and new technology combine, the advantage is generally substantial.

## Strategies That Pay Off

Information asymmetries occur in all industries. Wherever there's a market, there's information, and, generally, wherever there's information, there are at least temporary asymmetries in who has it. Hedge funds are known for using complex mathematical models to identify and exploit subtle and short-lived pricing opportunities in the financial markets. But consumer goods companies are in the game, too, investing millions in systems to forecast when the latest crop of coffee beans, for example, will mature—information that can help shape production and pricing plans. And so are those industrial goods companies that build complex options models to reduce their exposure to commodity price swings. Those that win do a better job with the information that everyone has, or they get access to information that no one else has.

So how can a company become a winner? Obviously the answers vary widely by industry and situation, but here are some strategies that have paid off handsomely:

- *Leverage new information.* Google sells something it doesn't own: words. The company tracks people's searches to identify the most popular search terms and, through its AdWords program, prices these terms with extreme efficiency for sale to interested companies. Without search engines, however, there would be no market for search terms.
- *Invent new techniques for using existing information.* Orbitz's success in employing new technology to sift through millions of flight permutations to find the cheapest fares is well known. Similar magic is being

performed to create more efficient ways to operate, generate greater customer insight, and spark innovative business models.

- *Develop a "closed market" to create proprietary information.* Comdata, a unit of the business services company Ceridian, is the leading issuer of "fleet cards," the credit cards used by truckers to buy fuel and supplies as they crisscross the United States. One huge advantage Comdata brings to this market is a proprietary network of some 8,000 credit card terminals (as of 2007, the time of writing) at truck stops around the country that provide both customized transaction control (only diesel fuel and certain other supplies may be purchased) and location information (such as the fact that employee X just bought 200 gallons outside Chicago). By controlling the processing of those transactions on its private data "pipes," Comdata can offer information-based services that other fleet card issuers can't provide, because they use the "public" pipes owned by the big mainstream credit card companies.

- *Provide the leadership needed to get disparate, often competing, companies along the value chain to share information.* Walmart and General Motors have both built networks and shared information with their first-tier suppliers to enable all the companies in the supply chain to work more effectively and efficiently.

- *Simplify and integrate complex information flows.* In health care, many companies are seeking to build a more integrated, interoperable information platform that can be shared by all the relevant players. Such a platform would permit physicians in one part of the health care system to readily use data or images from another, improving decision making and saving time and money. This effort will require collaboration among many companies and sectors, the adoption of common standards, and substantial investment. An analogue from the retail world is the adoption of the universal bar code system.

## The Need for a Strategy

Not every company can hit the information jackpot as dramatically as Google. But finding a smart strategy to deal with data flows and information asymmetries is no longer optional. Databases are becoming bigger and faster, more distributed, more subject to manipulation, and increasingly interoperable. Fewer and fewer industries can be described today as "information light."

Consider the probable impact of the digital information revolution on just one industry: health care. The revolution will bring greater clarity about what works and what doesn't across all of medicine. It will reinforce competition and consequently improve performance, especially as increased interoperability raises standards of care.

It will also force a struggle over the ownership of data among patients, insurers, providers, and suppliers. That struggle may lead to another revolution by giving impetus to life cycle models of health care management. And it should clarify the value of investments in IT and in other innovations that can be measured.

All of this change in the health care industry will happen—if not spurred by the health care establishment itself, then by outside forces—because increasingly in this digital world, the battle in health care, and in other industries as well, is not just to control data but to monetize metadata, the data about the data. Potentially disruptive competitors surely see an untapped opportunity in managing health care information—and using metadata to fuel their growth. In this environment, the status quo is much less assured.

Similar waves of change are coming to every industry. That piece of information is clear—and is available to all companies. On that point, at least, there should no longer be any asymmetry.

# 13 The Collision of Power and Portability

## Philip Evans

Companies from opposite poles of technology's power-portability spectrum are colliding. This is not normal, day-to-day competition but a confrontation between business paradigms, with tablets at the fault line. The changes under way will affect everything from smartphones to notebooks, as well as the companies that make and sell these devices and their component parts and software. Google's acquisition of Motorola Mobility is an early consequence as companies start to adapt.

## The Power-Portability Spectrum

Intelligent devices at either end of the power-portability spectrum have very different business paradigms. At one extreme reside the largest, most powerful—and least mobile—machines: supercomputers, mainframes, and server-filled data centers. At the other are the smallest, least muscular, but most mobile devices; the wearable iPod Nano is perhaps the exemplar.

System architecture at the power end of the spectrum is mature and modular. The dominant device in 2011 is the personal computer (PC), and by far the largest share of PC industry value is being extracted by the two companies that control the layers where monopoly position is easiest to maintain—because of network effects, in the case of Microsoft, or scale economies, in the case of Intel.

Driving technological and industry development at the power end are what might be termed the big exponentials—the laws of progressive improvement. Best known is Moore's law: the number of transistors on an integrated chip doubles every 18 months (or did until recently). Equally important are Kryder's law (data density on a storage medium doubles every year) and Butters's law (the capacity of a fiber-optic cable doubles every nine months).

The big exponentials have three major consequences for how we use technology. The first (yet another law: Myhrvold's) is that the complexity of applications expands faster than the uses to which those applications are put. Microsoft Excel was a 1.2-megabyte program when it came out in 1987; by 2010, version 12.0 was 58 megabytes. The program expanded to fill the technology available—because it could.

The second major consequence is the evolution from integral to modular design. As each device or service matures, the locus of innovation shifts from architecture to components. Assemblers combine largely interchangeable components to meet the requirements of different user segments. Component suppliers compete on cost, speed, reliability, capacity, and so forth. The architecture remains fixed.

The evolution from integral architecture to modular design has been occurring for some six decades. Remember when a supercomputer required a colossally integrated design, mainly to stop it from melting? Today the same functionality is provided by racks of modular PCs running Linux, itself the most modular of operating systems. The computer industry made a big jump toward modularity with the launch of the IBM System/360 in 1964 and another with the introduction of the PC in the early 1980s. Likewise, the information superhighway evolved from a variant on cable television (Prodigy and AOL) to open interoperability between browsers and Web pages, mediated by the common standards of TCP/IP and HTML. The results have been layered, modular architectures, not just of products but of the industries that make the products.

The third major implication of the big exponentials is in the design of computers. In the earliest days of computing, the principal design constraint was the central processor's computing power. Systems were designed to use that asset as efficiently as possible. The central processing unit (CPU) was secreted in a refrigerated sanctum accessed by "dumb" terminals and guarded by a polyester-robed priesthood. Code was written in a language designed for run time efficiency; great code was code written in the fewest lines.

By the 1980s, CPUs had become so powerful that efficiency no longer mattered. The industry responded by building minicomputers and, eventually, microcomputers—PCs—that were grossly inefficient in their use of CPU cycles but that put computing power where the user sits. The movement of data among users became the new constraint.

Thanks to the Internet and broadband networks, transporting information is hardly a problem today, but two very different constraints now shape IT architectures. One is the cost of system maintenance: data integrity, error correction, backup, updating, debugging, and crash recovery. The pendulum has swung back: by centralizing services in data centers and providing software and data through the cloud, uptime can be managed more efficiently.

The other new constraint is input/output, or I/O: the ease with which we can access media and information in a convenient, portable, and personalized fashion. The big exponentials make new I/O interfaces possible; pent-up consumer demand makes it attractive. Single-purpose, analog devices (phones, music players, cameras) can be replaced by multipurpose, digital ones. This immense opportunity has lured computer makers from the power to the portability end of the spectrum, where, until recently, the greatest growth and profits lay in laptops and netbooks.

But computer companies were prisoners of their paradigm: they brought with them their layered, modular business model and the biases of their home turf. They tended to overprovision processing power and waste CPU cycles, thereby using batteries inefficiently. They underinvested in seamless interfaces because they did not recognize I/O as the new constraint. They mixed and matched features and functions in the expectation that the market would sort out which ones mattered to whom.

Then they ran into Apple.

## The Portability Paradigm

From its beginnings, Apple has pursued a different model, one based on a more integrated design and architecture. Because network effects are so powerful, this model confined the Mac to a small, premium niche in the computer business and almost bankrupted the company 15 years ago. However, the paradigm it represents, anomalous in the power segment, is perfect for portability.

In 2001, Apple took the plunge into mobility with the introduction of the iPod, a device apparently unrelated to its core computer business. Like the Mac, the iPod's integrated hardware and operating system had its own data format (AAC), its own particular method of uploading (iTunes), and, in the early days, a near-proprietary connector (Firewire). Apple's one critical concession to openness was iTunes for the Windows PC. The full significance of the iPod was not immediately apparent, since it was not a paradigm shift among portable devices; it was simply the best digital music player on the market. From the computer industry's point of view, it looked as if Apple, having lost the battle against Microsoft, had decided to take on Sony in an entirely different business.

The real significance became clear, though, as Apple undertook its own migration back across the spectrum toward the power-focused domain of the PC.

The first step was the extension of the iPod franchise with the creation in 2003 of the iTunes music store, which quickly undermined traditional retailers and forever changed how music is marketed. Apple has sold some 15 billion songs through the store, which it can run as a breakeven operation, monetizing the investment through hardware sales.

Apple repeated the cycle further along the spectrum with the iPhone, which combines a range of functions in another extraordinarily successful device of tightly integrated hardware and software. In stark contrast with device makers at the power end, Apple optimized the iPhone around I/O rather than a proliferation of feature combinations, resisting the temptation to add complexity simply because it could. Experts initially failed to grasp why it was such a significant innovation and competitive threat. Consumers, innocent of tech theology, grasped the point immediately. By 2011, Apple had sold about 200 million devices powered by its mobile iOS operating system and shifted the balance of power away from the telecommunications carriers that had dominated that industry.

Apple built on its portable hardware advantage by developing an ecosystem. The key steps were publishing application programming interfaces (APIs) so that developers could write for the iOS platform and expanding the iTunes Store from songs to apps. By 2011, Apple offered some 425,000 apps, and the number downloaded passed 14 billion. In the I/O-constrained context of a phone, apps (so far) provide a better experience than HTML and JavaScript through a browser.

The third step in Apple's migration along the spectrum, following exactly the same principles, came in April 2010 with the iPad. This breached territory traditionally dominated by the netbook—and, to an extent still to be determined at the time of writing, by the laptop. Again consumers got it right away. At the launch, Wall Street projected first-year sales of 1 million to 5 million units. Actual sales were about 25 million in the first 14 months. Netbook sales, previously the fastest-growing segment of the Windows PC industry, are plummeting.

Apple reinforced its success with its own version of "embrace and extend." Vertically, on the technology stack, the company codesigned and bundled the hardware and operating system. It extended the OS into key applications such as Mobile Safari, iPhoto, and the iPod music playing program, as well as into various retailing platforms: the iTunes Store, the App Store, and iBooks. At the same time, Apple moved down into components by developing deep and preemptive relationships with its suppliers. It also invested heavily in capabilities for designing custom hardware components, such as the A4 and A5 chips.

Meanwhile, Apple has successfully exploited synergies laterally across the power-portability spectrum. The Apple brand delivers a powerful halo effect for each new device that comes to market. The look and feel of iOS is converging, not only among iOS devices but also with the Mac OS. The company has created cloud services—MobileMe and now iCloud—that integrate data access across multiple devices. It has built these devices, from the smallest iPod to the most powerful Mac, on a common software foundation. Above all, Apple has established direct retailing relationships with its customers.

# The Power-Portability Collision

Technology has driven the fusion of devices and capabilities across the power-portability spectrum. Companies following the Windows PC paradigm exploited this trend. But true to their heritage, they overemphasized capabilities facilitated by modularity and underestimated the value of architectural integration. Apple, with its distinctive legacy, played the game differently and established a position at the portability end of the spectrum that will be difficult to dislodge. Tablets and netbooks are the intermediate case where things still hang in the balance.

It's easy to look at tablets versus netbooks as the manifestation of trade-offs between screen versus keyboard, Apple versus Microsoft, apps versus browser, Flash versus HTML5. To do so minimizes the conflict between two paradigms. Tablets are the tectonic fissure in the structure of the information devices industry. They are the point where two fundamentally different paradigms compete to provide similar services. The netbook is the least powerful edge of a modular paradigm rooted in the abundance of power. The iPad is the least portable edge of an integrated paradigm developed to enable portability.

There is a school of thought that holds that if the big exponentials keep working, this domain, too, should ultimately become commoditized. The value of codesign should decline and that of feature and component recombination should rise. Modular should supplant integrated. Open should replace closed. Android should supplant iOS. Google will inherit the Wintel paradigm, and the modular Android stack will eventually prevail. But collisions are messy and unpredictable. The evolution of technology industries is not preordained. It depends on individual genius as well as impersonal forces. For now, individual genius is winning.

# 14 China's Digital Generations 3.0: The Online Empire

## David C. Michael, Christoph Nettesheim, and Yvonne Zhou

China may still be classified as an emerging market, but on the Internet it has arrived. It already has one of the largest online retail markets in the world at the time of writing, with more online shoppers than any other market, including the United States.

Although China is a huge online market, it is not an easy one. Consumers are rapidly gaining sophistication, but they have their own patterns of online consumption and behavior that are different from those of consumers in the West. Companies that want to succeed in China's consumer market must understand both these new consumers and their rapidly evolving digital lifestyles. They also need to learn how to reach, sell to, and retain these consumers as they create the world's most important consumer market of the future.

## A Massive Mass Medium

Increasingly, the Internet is becoming a staple in the everyday life of Chinese consumers across a wide spectrum of lifestyles and incomes. In fact, the Internet has spread so widely and so quickly that two new groups can now be considered legitimate Internet market segments: seniors (defined as individuals aged 51 and older) and rural residents.

Rural residents have joined in the online world at an accelerating pace and are expected to join the urban senior segment as the fastest-growing segments in China's online world.

As of 2011, Chinese consumers spent 1.9 billion hours *a day* online—an increase of 60 percent from two years earlier. This surge was powered by both an expanding Internet user base and a greater online presence, as the average time online per person has increased by close to an hour over the past several years, and television viewing has declined. Chinese users average about an hour a day more online than U.S. Internet users.

The government, meanwhile, is encouraging the Internet's growth. During the current five-year plan, which runs through the end of 2015, the government has committed to spending $250 billion on broadband infrastructure. Moreover, in response to consumer demand for more and faster Internet, the government launched an antitrust probe of China Telecom and China Unicom that has prompted the two dominant carriers to agree to accelerate their broadband rollouts, lower prices by 35 percent, and increase speeds.

As the quality of infrastructure improves, the Chinese will be surfing the Web more often at home and at work and less often at Internet cafes. They will also be relying on their mobile phones. The share of hours spent accessing the Internet on mobile devices is rising rapidly among all age groups. In fact, the number of Internet hours that seniors spend on mobile devices has more than tripled in recent years, to approximately 30 percent. Mobile access will rise as 3G and later 4G penetration increases.

As the Internet becomes ubiquitous, it will play an even larger role in China. Half of Internet users currently say that the Internet is their most trusted source of information, followed by television at 30 percent and newspapers at 15 percent, according to BCG's research. Trust and familiarity go hand in hand. The more time consumers spend on the Internet, the more they trust it.

Young professionals and university students lead the pack in putting their faith in the Internet, with 70 percent and 63 percent, respectively, citing it as their most trustworthy information source in a 2011 survey, compared with only 27 percent of users aged 51 and older.

## Not Just Fun and Games

In the early days of the Internet in China, users gravitated to leisure pursuits such as watching videos and listening to music. Those activities are still highly popular, especially among younger users. China has local sites similar to YouTube, such as Tudou and Youku, which have agreed to merge, and similar to Hulu, where traditional programming is offered, such as iQiyi and LeTV.

As their comfort level and sophistication have grown, however, users have branched out from entertaining themselves to a more diverse mix of activities, including those they once avoided, notably e-commerce. Per capita online spending is currently expected to rise significantly, reflecting both the rising level of trust by consumers and the greater protections put in place by merchants.

Along with e-commerce, users are spending much more time on community-oriented and information activities. Community-oriented activities include e-mail, instant messaging (IM), and forms of social media.

Microblogging platforms (called "weibos") are generating both national and local conversations on important social issues that have historically been kept under wraps. In July 2011, for example, one of China's bullet trains crashed in Wenzhou, in the southeast of the country, killing 40 passengers. Sina Weibo (the most influential of the competing weibo platforms) quickly became, in the words of a *Wall Street Journal* columnist, "a conduit for inconvenient truths and cynical speculations about the accident."

The government has an uneasy relationship with this newfound passion for public discourse. In at least one case, Sina Weibo and Tencent Weibo, the two largest microblogging sites, temporarily disabled comments on blog posts as part of a government crackdown on social networking brought on by political unrest.

# A Nation of Avid Adopters

As the Internet in China becomes a home for digital shopkeepers and an instrument for public discourse and social change, it will also start to look and feel similar to the Internet of more developed nations. In fact, in some cases, Chinese consumers are more avid users of online services than U.S. consumers are—using their mobile devices to listen to music, read books online, or engage in social networking.

Chinese Internet users are also maturing. Between 2008 and 2011, the average age of Internet users rose from 24.7 to 28.9 and approached the average age of users in the United States (30.0) and Japan (30.4). The aging of the Internet reflects both new users and the general aging of the population.

Maturity means that future growth of the user base will slow.

However, opportunities will continue to expand, as new services appear and people become more willing to pay for them. Companies that acquire scale and customer loyalty in China's online market will have achieved a solid foothold, ensuring future growth.

## The Power of Digital Dialogue

The weibo posts about the train crash in Wenzhou are emblematic of the awakening of a national conversation about issues of public concern and private interest. Blogging and microblogging have higher penetration rates among Internet users in China than among those in the United States or Japan. Sina Weibo, the leading microblogging site, has generated 300 million users in less than three years.

Weibos have become a fast-moving stream of collective consciousness. Although controversy and complaints may receive the most attention, especially in the Western media, celebrity gossip is a more common form of currency. Users also post news stories, exchange photos with former classmates, and comment on recent purchases.

This wellspring of opinions is forcing companies to respond. Although the role of weibos in the overall marketing landscape is still evolving, companies at least need to be able to respond swiftly and decisively when their products and services are called into question on microblogging sites and elsewhere online.

Besides crisis control, companies ought to be examining how and when they can harness the power of online conversations to burnish their brands. Positive commentary about products and services, in other words, can go viral just as easily as gossip and news about catastrophes.

## A Call to Action

Even if companies never intend to sell online, they must embrace China's online world. It is currently consuming roughly 2 billion hours a day of people's attention. Young professionals, a highly desirable consumer segment, average nearly 5 hours a day online. The Internet may be more important to brand building and overall awareness in China than television was in the United States during its heyday.

The question, then, is what companies should be doing to reach and hold onto China's digital generations. All companies with ambitions in China should have a strong Internet presence and strategy. They need to meet their customers in the places where they spend time, and increasingly that is online. The Internet is not just another channel. A few key challenges confront companies as they sell to engage with China's digital generations:

- *New business models.* Companies cannot necessarily rely on what has worked in other markets, as the stumbles of many Western companies have amply demonstrated. But they can tap into the current fascination of the Chinese people with the online experience to experiment with new ways to build relationships with Chinese consumers. In particular, the popularity of weibos and online videos presents opportunities to both engage with customers and develop new revenue streams through innovative online business models.
- *Consumer insight.* Companies need to develop a deep understanding of digital consumers in China. The market is moving too swiftly and is sufficiently different from any other market to rely on old or imported segmentation strategies.
- *Digital marketing.* In the online world, brands are built by well-managed conversations with consumers, rather than through the simple broadcast of messages. Companies need to create an integrated digital marketing plan that emphasizes online presence and dialogue with consumers. They will have to regularly review the alignment between marketing mix and consumer trends. They must monitor and respond to online conversations about their products and services, engaging and building relationships with consumers. They should also review and select the right professional services partners that understand and can guide them through these choices.
- *Digital transformation.* Companies will have to build new capabilities and a new organization and culture to manage their online presence and multiple channels.
- *Business development and partnership.* Although they certainly should build their internal capabilities, companies will not be able to do it alone. Sooner or later, they will have to partner with other players to fill in gaps in their capabilities, distribution, or technology. The sooner

they start educating themselves on their needs and the field of potential partners, the stronger their negotiating stance will be.

The most important step is the first one. Companies cannot win in China unless they understand and embrace China's digital generations. They are the future of the largest consumer market in the world.

# IV Sustainable

S ustainability is now mainstream. Most companies view the need to develop sustainability strategies as a core goal rather than a sideline undertaken primarily to silence potential critics. This shift reflects the continued growth in the global population and of emerging economies— two forces that are compelling business and political leaders to find ways to make more efficient use of limited natural resources. At the same time, consumers and investors are increasingly favoring companies that feature a low environmental impact, positive social impact, and a proven commitment to sustainability.

Sustainability can also be a source of cost reductions, revenue growth, and competitive advantage. These assertions are borne out by hard data. According to our analysis, companies that are leaders in sustainability outperform those that take less aggressive measures. That's the case we make in Chapter 15, "The Benefits of Sustainability-Driven Innovation."

Making sustainability a source of revenue growth is far from easy, of course. Although many consumers express interest in buying green products, they don't always purchase them—particularly if the price tag is higher. In Chapter 16, "Creating Practical Consumer Value from Sustainability," we zero in on how one sector—the home improvement industry—has made sustainability a profit generator by moving beyond marketing green products as a way to help the planet. Instead, successful companies combine the feel-good message with a clear business case for how going green can deliver material benefits to consumers. With that approach, sustainability and profitability can go hand in hand.

However, the sustainability strategies that work in the developed world cannot always be transferred to emerging economies, where concerns such as fighting poverty often take precedence. Chapter 17, "Potential Impacts of the New Sustainability Champions," explores how companies in rapidly developing economies have used technology and operating creativity to make major strides toward social and ecological sustainability. One is a cement manufacturer in India that slashed energy consumption. Another is a Kenyan bank that helped farmers adopt more sustainable farming practices. These innovators show how on-the-ground ingenuity can pave the way for cost-effective gains in sustainability. If adapted to other emerging markets, these approaches could literally change the world.

But the drive for sustainability is just beginning. Significant obstacles remain—not the least of which is the lack of global consensus on how to address climate change. It is clear, however, that a business topic once considered the narrow province of do-gooders is now at the very heart of how visionary corporate leaders craft a winning strategy.

# 15 The Benefits of Sustainability-Driven Innovation

## David Kiron, Nina Kruschwitz, Martin Reeves, Knut Haanaes, and Eugene Goh

What connects corporate sustainability with business profits? Global executives say an important factor is business model innovation. Greif, a 135-year-old leading manufacturer of industrial packaging headquartered in Columbus, Ohio, is one company whose commitment to sustainability is expressed in its business model, which has evolved as part of Greif's sustainability agenda.

Scott Griffin is chief sustainability officer at Greif, which had net sales of $4.2 billion in 2011. He told us there are four keys to Greif's sustainability agenda, which has become central to the company's overall business operations and strategy. One is top management attention to sustainability. "One reason sustainability works here at Greif is high-level, strong executive commitment," says Griffin. Unlike many chief sustainability officers, Griffin reports directly to the CEO and is a member of the company's executive strategy team.

Another key to Greif's approach to sustainability is collaboration. In the past three years, Greif has collaborated more with customers and nongovernmental organizations because of sustainability-related

This chapter is based on and adapted with permission from an article titled "Sustainability: The Benefits of Sustainability-driven Innovation" published in *MIT Sloan Management Review* in winter 2013.

issues. These collaborations not only have helped the company establish sustainability-related goals, such as reductions in greenhouse gas emissions, but also have provided new opportunities for customer engagement and the development of new corporate capabilities.

Collaboration with customers ties into the third element of Greif's sustainability program: business model innovation. For instance, Greif worked with customers to analyze the life cycles of several of its products. The collaboration identified new business opportunities connected with reconditioning and extending the life of a major product line, steel and plastic drums. Greif now owns the largest global industrial packaging reconditioner, EarthMinded Life Cycle Services.

New internal organizational structures are the fourth key to Greif's sustainability agenda. Greif created a global energy team composed of business unit representatives in charge of achieving multiyear sustainability goals connected with energy reduction goals. Team members have access to a pool of capital that they can allocate for sustainability projects that they believe will help meet their sustainability objectives. "Having the global energy team use the capital as they see fit is one of the most effective things we have done," Griffin said. In 2011, the global energy team helped cut Greif's greenhouse gas emissions per unit of production by 10 percent from 2008 levels. Greif now has similar teams for sustainability goals connected with energy, waste, and water.

Greif's story highlights several key findings from our four annual executive surveys to which thousands of managers and executives in dozens of industries have responded. Our findings suggest that business model change, top management support, the existence of a business case, and collaboration with customers are associated with creating economic value from sustainability activities and decisions. An overwhelming majority of managers who said their companies have all these characteristics also said that their sustainability activities add to their profits. Sustainability-driven innovators is our designation for companies that change their business model because of sustainability and also generate profits from their sustainability-related activities and decisions.

Our research suggests several ways in which companies can become more effective at connecting business model change with sustainability-based profits. Based on the behavior of sustainability-driven innovators, we conclude by discussing three recommendations for how managers can improve their odds of profiting from their sustainability activities.

The evidence suggests that certain combinations of sustainability-related business model change appear to have a bigger link to profitability than others. Companies that change both target segments and the value chain, for instance, appear more likely to add to profit than companies that change other combinations.

Sustainability-driven innovators often do more than just change their business model. They also tend to have a business case for sustainability, work closely with key stakeholder groups on sustainability issues, and have the attention of top management focused on their sustainability efforts. Having a business case for a company's sustainability efforts bolsters the influence of business model change on sustainability-based profitability.

Marks and Spencer's sustainability strategy, Plan A, which identified 100 activities and goals related to waste, supply chain, climate change, health, and sustainable raw materials to achieve by 2015, is a case in point. Introduced in 2007, Plan A reportedly created about $296 million in net economic benefit for Marks and Spencer. As Mike Barry, head of sustainability business at Marks and Spencer, told BusinessGreen.com, Plan A "is about making hard cash by doing the right thing."

## The Stakeholder Effect

In any company, customer demand for sustainable products can be a compelling force for organizational change. Just ask Lewis Fix. Fix is vice president of sustainable business and brand management for Montreal-based Domtar, whose main product line, uncoated free sheet—things like copy paper, envelopes, and check paper—is in a sector that has been contracting for the past several years.

Fix was an early proponent of making the company's mills compliant with the Forest Stewardship Council (FSC) certification and pursuing more FSC-certified fiber, which was more stringent than the standard certification offered by the industry's Sustainable Forestry Initiative. This approach was challenged when the company merged with Weyerhaeuser, according to Fix. Some executives resisted complying with FSC standards, claiming that FSC and its environmentalist supporters were "extreme" and the company should not waste energy or money to "appease" them.

Today, though, all of Domtar's mills are FSC-certified, and not solely because of Fix's efforts. In 2009, a new CEO came on board who actively supported a range of aggressive environmental goals. But it also took a significant customer to say that it wanted a majority of its paper suppliers to be FSC-compliant. "It actually didn't take long for our mills to 'get it,'" Fix told us. "If Staples says that's what they want, we're going to find a way to make sure we're doing business with Staples."

The combination of sustainability-oriented collaboration and business model change is strongly correlated with sustainability-based profits. Timberland, for example, worked closely with its supply chain for leather, a key material in many of its products, to improve efficiencies and reduce costs. "We were very involved in developing this industry standard for assessing tanneries," said Betsy Blaisdell, senior manager of environmental stewardship for Timberland. "Our supply chain leather team said that they want to have a target for only sourcing our leather from silver- or gold-rated tanneries, which, through the Leather Working Group assessment, demonstrate best practices related to energy, chemical, and water management."

## The Role of Top Management

Companies that change their business models because of sustainability and make sustainability a permanent part of top management's agenda appear more likely to profit from their sustainability efforts than companies that make sustainability-related changes without that level of top management support. Former Campbell Soup CEO Doug Conant, who led the company's corporate social responsibility efforts, explained why. "You can talk about making it a priority, but if you don't organize to do it in a priority way, it doesn't get done. It has to have a line that gets all the way up to the CEO in a compelling way," Conant said.

## Recommendations

Mustering an appetite for organizational change can be difficult. However, the three to four types of business model innovations that are most strongly correlated with a sustainability-related increase in profitability do not represent mere tweaks to business operations. Such changes are associated with a deeper understanding of customers, increased collaboration with outside groups, and, in some cases, a new perspective on how to compete through an organization's sustainability activities. Following are three recommendations for how companies can increase their odds of profiting from their sustainability efforts.

1. *Be prepared to change your business model.* Respondents to our surveys believe—by a wide margin—that sustainability is necessary to be competitive. And we have established that business model innovation is a key indicator of whether a company will profit from its sustainability activities. Because the business model innovations most strongly associated with increases in sustainability-based profits can involve significant corporate change, expectations that sustainability will add to profits should take into account both the need for and the speed of corporate change. Setting multiyear sustainability goals that matter may require consistent top management attention, especially if achieving them requires adding new capabilities and changing elements of your business model.

2. *Understand how your customers think about sustainability and what they are willing to pay for in connection with sustainable products or services.* Find out whether your customers are willing to pay a premium for sustainability and explore whether you need to charge a premium for a more sustainable product or service. Use this information to determine whether targeting current or new customers with a more sustainability-oriented brand is a viable option.

3. *Collaborate more with individuals, customers, businesses, and groups beyond the boundaries of your organization.* Many companies are forming outside advisory groups to help frame their sustainability agenda. This process can be an opportunity to get closer to customers, who, in turn, can be a useful resource for identifying appropriate members. Nongovernmental organizations (NGOs) have become much more constructive in their corporate engagements and can help your company identify credible and meaningful feasible sustainability objectives that lack the appearance of "green-washing." Participate in or help create an industry group; either approach can be an effective benchmarking tactic, as well as an opportunity to shape perceptions about your brand's connection with sustainability. In addition, participating in such groups gives your business an opportunity to shape what "doing good" means in your market.

# 16

# Creating Practical Consumer Value from Sustainability

## Knut Haanaes, Catherine Roche, Jonathan Sharp, and Marty Smits

**G**reen products are in vogue. Consumers are increasingly interested in products that use resources more efficiently. But outside certain niches, consumers have resisted paying the higher prices that these products usually require.

To profitably connect with environmental concerns, companies in the home improvement sector are beginning to reorient green products around the direct material benefits to consumers. They emphasize the other benefits that these products generate—not just their environmental credentials.

## A Challenging Opportunity

The housing bust of recent years further dampened what was already a mature home improvement market. With household formation and home construction slowed, companies in affluent countries are eager for any area of potential growth. On the face of it, sustainability offers a great deal of potential, but converting theory into commercial viability is difficult.

Like companies in many other industries, home improvement companies have worked on improving the sustainability of their products. They've developed new lines and features and explored emerging technologies. But the results of these efforts have so far proved largely disappointing.

Most companies have changed their business practices to boost sustainability, according to a recent survey of executives worldwide that BCG conducted jointly with *MIT Sloan Management Review*. Yet fewer than half the respondents from a variety of consumer goods businesses said that they have figured out how to boost sustainability *and* make a profit.

Similarly, surveys of consumers show that most are interested in buying green. But only a small minority do so systematically, and their numbers decline during economic downturns. Consumers in affluent countries cite high prices as the major constraint, whereas in emerging markets, high prices rank a close second to lack of availability. The vast majority of consumers just aren't willing to pay extra for sustainability for its own sake.

Adding to the challenge is consumers' confusion about what *sustainable* really means. A variety of terms get bandied about: low impact, energy efficient, renewable resource, local, and fair labor. Other feel-good concepts, such as healthfulness and "artisan made," get thrown into the conversation. The sustainability discussion can involve environmental, economic, and social resources. No wonder consumers are confused.

## Breaking Through

Yet some companies in the home improvement sector are working on ways to make green profitable. The key, they have found, is to clarify and reposition the category of green products and services. Instead of sustainability for its own sake, companies need to offer concrete, direct-to-the-consumer benefits. Sustainability, long an abstraction, needs to become direct and personally beneficial.

The first step is to pick one's battles. Sustainability can be compelling only in certain cost-benefit contexts. Basic consumer interest in sustainability can help tip the decision balance toward buying green, but it can't work by itself. Reducing carbon emissions, for example, is a worthy goal, but consumers are far more motivated to save on energy and water bills. Government regulations, subsidies, new technologies, and higher energy costs all work into the mix.

Just look at the success of the Energy Star program for household appliances in Europe and the United States. Governments have mandated that manufacturers report the energy efficiency of their appliances and estimate consumers' likely savings on utility bills. A model whose performance falls within a certain range earns an Energy Star. In certain categories, the government or local energy utility grants rebates to consumers who have bought those models. The program has encouraged manufacturers to give greater consideration to efficiency-boosting technologies such as reconfigured dishwasher drums that use less electricity at the cost of a longer cycle time. Energy Star appliances have also gained space in retail showrooms. Special markings on the appliances even promote "conspicuous conservation," appealing to people inclined to show off their virtue to visitors to their homes.

As a result, consumers who never before would have paid attention to energy efficiency can easily include this appliance attribute as a buying criterion. Those who live in areas with rising electricity rates have had the greatest incentive to buy these appliances. The overall energy efficiency of household appliances has risen dramatically under the program.

# Focusing Green Products on Consumers' Concerns

In areas for which the cost-benefit ratios are favorable, companies still need to make the financial benefits easily understood by and relevant to consumers. That means focusing the products on what consumers care about and can relate to.

In most European Union markets, many of the programs for reducing household carbon emissions include subsidies for low-carbon energy generation (such as solar energy), subsidies for home insulation, and regulations that require the measurement and certification of the carbon emission status of houses for sale. In today's regulatory environment, the carbon-reduction home improvement market is likely to grow significantly, generating many billions of dollars of new spending.

For retailers to go after this opportunity, they will need to develop their sales packages in a number of areas:

- *Customizable options.* Retailers need to develop a customer-friendly menu of options to match the variety of housing structures, energy costs and subsidies, and customer preferences. These options should allow homeowners to customize their purchases according to their available time, money, appetite for risk, and underlying interest in sustainability. This approach will also help retail sales teams understand and communicate product features and benefits.

- *Specific savings estimates.* Furthermore, retailers will have to demonstrate that these home improvement purchases would be rational investments with financial payback. For most households, even with subsidies, such investments are big purchases, amounting to thousands of euros. Retailers cannot guarantee actual savings in energy bills, but they can show how the improvements would raise a home's ratings in the certification program for home sales and explain the impact these changes would have on typical energy bills.
- *Convenient installation.* Price is not the only hurdle to conversion. Homeowners also weigh the inconveniences and risks of installation. Retailers need to establish a network of home surveyors and installers.
- *Long-term financing.* A final barrier to sales in this market is the insufficient availability of financing for homeowners. Because of the long time between purchase and payback, new consumer lending products are needed to fund these projects.

As these markets develop and well-prepared retailers increase their share in them, product costs can fall rapidly. In Germany, for example, a better organized and more efficient solar panel distribution chain led to prices falling 30 percent from 2004 through 2006, and another 30 percent from 2006 through 2009. The installed base of solar panel capacity more than quadrupled as consumers reacted to the lower prices.

## Timing the Market

Because these products and services are expensive and complex, manufacturers and distributors should proceed carefully. They should look carefully at the three key drivers in the marketplace: government requirements and incentives, local energy and water costs, and underlying consumer interest.

The importance of each driver varies a great deal by location. European countries, for example, are promising markets for energy, whereas Australia may be a leader in efforts to conserve water.

The drivers are evolving and their importance can change fast—moving in either direction. Concerns about sustainability have certainly increased in recent years. Yet the global recession has led many governments to pull back on sustainability initiatives.

A wait-and-see strategy, however, has risks as well. Aggressive, well-prepared first movers in this category can establish distribution networks, set standards for product packages, refine their selling and service models, and learn about household needs. Rivals would then have a harder time getting consumer acceptance for what they bring to the table. If a pioneering strategy seems too risky, companies should consider preparing now to jump in as fast followers.

Companies will also have to balance sustainability programs with other opportunities. Expanding into developing countries is on everyone's agenda, but expansion carries its own risks and complexities. In many sectors, the sustainability market represents one of the few organic domestic large-scale growth plays.

Whether because of executive conviction, public image, or stakeholder pressure, most companies have embraced sustainability as a concept and are searching for a hard business rationale. By orienting their products around solid and immediate consumer benefits—admittedly a less inspiring mission than saving the planet—companies can drive the strategic and organizational responses needed to make these efforts profitable. And that's the only way sustainability programs will themselves be sustainable.

# 17 Potential Impacts of the New Sustainability Champions

## David C. Michael, Kim Wagner, Knut Haanaes, Eugene Goh, Diederik Vismans, Jeremy Jurgens, and Lyuba Nazaruk

Sustainability is a hot topic in the West, but companies in rapidly developing economies (RDEs) are far more likely to face resource constraints. How can they meet the challenge?

BCG, in partnership with the World Economic Forum, conducted a study of sustainability practices in a variety of industries. We identified several sustainability champions in RDEs that combine a profitable, growing business with the efficient consumption of scarce assets. These champions have discovered innovative ways to drive sustainable growth, and they are reshaping the business landscape in developing economies. Collectively and individually, they are becoming inspirational models for their emerging-market peers. If other companies in the same industries were to emulate their approach, using existing practices and technology, RDEs would make enormous strides in sustainability—and the entire planet would benefit. In this chapter, we discuss two of these champions and their ongoing contributions to sustainability.

This chapter was written in collaboration with the World Economic Forum and is reprinted with permission.

## Innovations on the Ground

RDEs are often portrayed as the inevitable laggards in the drive toward sustainability. Just as affluent nations polluted far more as they industrialized than they do now, these fast-growing countries may be focused more on raising their populations out of poverty than on the impact they are having on the planet. Environmental improvements, says the conventional wisdom, are unaffordable luxuries.

That's often true on the governmental level, where regulatory bodies can be quite weak. But in several industries, companies are already threatened with shortages of key natural resources. Rather than wait until the crisis comes, some farsighted leaders have worked to change mind-sets and operating practices.

These innovations rarely follow the typical Western pattern of laboratory-based development. Our sustainability champions eschew expensive research in favor of adjusting what they already have to the needs of the market and the environment. Homegrown improvements drive most of the progress. And even when companies make use of technology from the developed world, they often tweak it to match their operating conditions. That's important, because employees and customers are far more likely to accept improvements adapted to the local context.

So far, these sustainability champions have stood out for their aggressive investments in efficiency and in resource-minded product development. What would happen if their rivals invested likewise? To get a ballpark sense of the opportunities, we have considered a few examples and extrapolated the savings that would likely result from the widespread imitation of their practices.

## Following the Leaders

Shree Cement is the biggest cement manufacturer in northern India and one of the biggest in the country as a whole. Its sustainability efforts arose from pressures that most developed countries never face. Frequent and unpredictable power outages required it to install monitoring equipment to protect its sensitive machinery. Company engineers found that they could easily modify the same equipment to give quick feedback on operational efficiency as well. Ongoing experimentation with the feedback enabled them to establish several ways to reduce electrical consumption substantially.

Their success inspired innovation in a variety of other areas, including the main kiln process for making clinker, a key ingredient in cement. They found a way to use fly ash and other waste—which meant less coal to be burned and less waste to be dumped. The company also dealt with limited local water supplies by switching to air cooling in some stages and by constructing an artificial lake.

The reduction in electricity usage alone was significant. Shree's improvements enabled it to use 9 percent less electricity than other Indian cement companies—and made it more efficient than almost every cement company in the West. If all Indian manufacturers reached Shree's level, they would reduce consumption of electricity by 18 terawatt-hours annually. Since the cement industry currently accounts for 3 percent of total Indian electricity consumption (that is, in 2012), these steps would eliminate 0.25 percent of the entire country's demand—helping lighten the burden on fuel supplies and improve air quality.

The sustainability of water supplies is another crucial issue. Farmers are by far the biggest consumers worldwide—and that's especially true in India, where farming currently accounts for nearly 90 percent of total water demand, much higher than the global average of 70 percent. Many small and medium-sized farms, which still account for half the total acreage, rely on flooding of the fields for irrigation. Larger farms moved over to drip irrigation years ago, but the equipment has been too expensive for smaller operations.

In stepped Jain Irrigation Systems, the leader in importing and adapting drip systems for small farms. The company innovated throughout the agricultural value chain to make its systems affordable. This included helping many illiterate farmers qualify for loans by promising to buy their produce at a set price. Although handling farm commodities has added to Jain's complexity and risk, the gains from increased sales have more than compensated.

Cotton farming provides a clear example of the necessity of drip systems. India is the world's second-largest producer of cotton, generating a fifth of total production, yet two-thirds of its farmers still rely on flood irrigation. If they all switched to drip systems, the annual use of water in cotton agriculture could fall by up to half, from 53 billion liters to 34 billion liters.

## Moving Forward

It's no easy matter for companies to make this kind of progress. Improvements in sustainability usually require not just new technologies or techniques but also shifts in habits and mind-sets. Otherwise, the gains are rarely permanent. What's most important is a culture that energizes people to solve practical problems. Every company—even within the same region—faces somewhat different production and market conditions. An approach that succeeds for one organization may need substantial modifications to work for another.

Still, as these leaders have shown, companies don't have to choose between sustainability and profitability. They've all prospered despite—and more often because of—their creative investments in resource efficiency. What's usually lacking is more the will than the means. The examples here can help inspire other companies to reorient around sustainability and to see constraints as opportunities. With enough effort, they could even leapfrog these current leaders into the future.

The extrapolation of the sustainability efforts shown here suggests the magnitude of opportunities available. RDEs face serious threats to their energy, water, and air resources. Yet they need not resign themselves to further degradation and shortages. They can grow rapidly while safeguarding their future.

# V Customer First

**G**reat brands find many ways to connect with their customers, aiming to create a deep emotional bond with them. At the very least, they transform their customers into repeat buyers and, in some cases, into true brand evangelists.

The real game changer occurs when companies manage to define the unique, authentic elements of a product or service experience that will stimulate that desired emotional connection. Pulling that off requires a multilayered understanding of the customer's hopes, dreams, and even dissatisfactions. In Chapter 18, "Breaking Compromises," we explore how companies can strike emotional gold by identifying the compromises that competitors are imposing on consumers. Breaking those compromises can unleash a tidal wave of emotional connection and loyalty.

Few companies excel at really understanding their customers' needs and translating that into action. Those that do it well never leave the thinking about customers and brands to the marketing department. Instead they are organized to deliver technical, functional, and emotional benefits to specific customer segments. Picking the right benefits and segments—the ones that will truly resonate—is both an art and a science. As we discuss in Chapter 19, "Brand-Centric Transformation: Balancing Art and Data," it requires a qualitative understanding of the customer predicated on active listening and a high degree of emotional sensitivity, as well as the ability to verify and size the market opportunity through advanced customer analytics. Do one without the other, and you'll miss the target.

True leadership happens when companies make it a priority—a mission, even—to *deliver* on the promises made to their customers. Doing that successfully requires aligning the entire company around the shared objectives of delivering on every single element, every moment of truth, in the customer's experience.

In our final two chapters we turn to two specific megatrends that are fundamentally changing where to look for new customers and how they make their decisions. As we describe in Chapter 20, "Unlocking Growth in the Middle: A View from India and China," unprecedented challenges and opportunities abound. The explosion of the middle class in rapidly developing economies, most notably India and China, will unlock new vectors of growth but will also demand new capabilities to understand, reach, and serve those markets.

Across all global markets, consumers have a growing desire to track down good deals—bargains—in some product and service categories. As we argue in Chapter 21, "Treasure Hunt," that pursuit not only is emotionally rewarding but also aligns with consumers' desire to "trade up"; in essence to use the money saved from successful treasure hunts to splurge in other areas more core to their personal identity or needs.

# 18 Breaking Compromises

## George Stalk, Jr., David K. Pecaut, and Benjamin Burnett

**M**any companies today are searching for growth. How and where should they look? One powerful way to grow is through innovations that break the fundamental "compromises" of a business. When a company successfully breaks a compromise, it releases enormous trapped value. Breakaway growth can be the result.

Compromises are concessions demanded of consumers by most of the companies in an industry. They occur when the industry imposes its own operating constraints on customers. Usually, customers accept these compromises as just the way the business works—inevitable trade-offs that have to be endured.

But a compromise is different from a trade-off. In choosing a hotel room, for instance, a customer can *trade off* luxury for economy by choosing between a Ritz-Carlton and a Best Western. Until recently, however, most hotels forced all customers to *compromise* by not permitting check-in before 4:00 PM. No law of nature or economics decrees that hotel rooms can't be ready before late afternoon.

## Uncompromising Opportunity

The idea of compromises can be a useful organizing principle to focus an entire company on growth. It provides a systematic way to search for

---

growth opportunities that are logical extensions of a company's existing business system.

Take the example of Circuit City, now bankrupt, and its foray in 1993 into the used car business through the creation of a network of used car superstores under the brand name CarMax, now an independent Fortune 500 public company. Few experiences are more fraught with compromises. Shopping for a used car is extremely time-consuming. And the buyer is at a fundamental disadvantage, ignorant about the actual condition of the product and subject to high-pressure sales tactics.

Circuit City concluded that many of the distinguishing capabilities of its consumer electronics business could be used to break the compromises imposed on used car buyers. Circuit City was known for the wide variety of its merchandise. CarMax took the same approach. The typical used car dealer has only 30 vehicles in stock; CarMax sites can have thousands. That makes it easy for customers to compare makes and styles.

CarMax didn't hesitate to deviate from the Circuit City model when the strategic logic required it. For instance, Circuit City paid percentage-of-sales commissions to its consumer electronics sales force, but CarMax opted not to follow that pattern in paying its sales force. Because a key compromise in used cars is pressure selling, the company created a compensation system that encourages no-haggle pricing and no-hassle guarantees. The result: an integrated business system that offers a fundamentally different experience to used car buyers and a business model that has allowed CarMax to capture a significant share in the markets where it is active.

# A Pathway to Growth

Compromises are inherent in any business. Even when a company breaks one compromise, it usually ends up creating another. By focusing on compromises, a company can continuously uncover fresh opportunities and thus sustain growth over time.

The financial services company Charles Schwab, for example, was founded on the breaking of a compromise. The company began as a discount brokerage in 1975, when the deregulation of U.S. security markets made it unnecessary for individual investors to pay high fees to full-service brokers.

But Schwab didn't stop there. Next, it broke the compromise set up by the discount brokerage houses themselves. Although these new firms offered low prices, most also provided unreliable service. By investing in computer technology that allowed almost immediate confirmation of orders over the telephone, Schwab was able to combine low prices with levels of responsiveness unusual for its industry. Subsequently, Schwab added to its value proposition such benefits as convenience, flexibility, and ease of transferring funds through the provision of 24-hours-a-day, seven-days-a-week service, the Schwab One cash management account, and automated phone and electronic trading.

Schwab used its compromise-breaking capabilities to enter the mutual fund business. Most people invest in several fund families to achieve diversification. But diversification often comes at the price of frustration. It means dealing with a confusing variety of statements, rules, and sales representatives. In 1992, Schwab introduced OneSource, a single point of purchase for more than 350 no-load mutual funds. Over the decades since its founding, Schwab has evolved from a simple discount broker to a comprehensive self-help financial supermarket.

# Creativity, Flexibility, and Nerve

For a company to grow by breaking compromises, it must have the creativity to translate customer dissatisfactions into new value propositions, the flexibility to engage in constant reorientation of its business system, and the nerve to challenge business as usual in its industry. There are three basic steps.

## Get Inside the Customer Experience

Start by asking your managers and employees to immerse themselves in the customer's experience. It is critical to develop a visceral feel for the compromises consumers encounter when they do business with you.

A compromise often becomes visible when customers have to modify their behavior to use a company's product or service. So, pay special attention to the compensatory behaviors customers engage in to get around the constraints that your product or service imposes on them. In the brokerage business, for instance, it was common knowledge that customers often called back a second or even a third time to confirm that their trade had gone through at the price requested. By paying careful attention to this behavior, Schwab realized that the ability to provide immediate confirmation when an order was taken would eliminate the extra calls, saving customers a lot of trouble and giving Schwab a significant advantage over its competitors.

## Travel Up the Hierarchy of Compromises

Once the organization is focused on the customer experience, learn to recognize three different types of compromises, each with increasing potential to create value.

Some of the most obvious can be found in your company's existing products or services. It was Chrysler's awareness of the compromises between station wagons (based on a car platform) and vans (based on a truck platform) that led to the minivan, a van based on a car platform. In the 10 years after Chrysler introduced the minivan in 1984, minivan sales grew eight times as fast as industry sales overall.

Other, more powerful compromises can be found at the level of an entire product category. Witness how Nike has transformed the athletic footwear category by combining continual innovation in shoe design with the proliferation of narrowly defined customer segments. Nike doesn't just make basketball shoes. It has made Air Jordans, Force, and Flight, each designed for a different playing style, with different design requirements, and a different image.

The most powerful compromises are often the hardest to identify: broad social dissatisfactions that may have little to do with your product or industry but a lot to do with how your customers live their lives. For example, long-term social and economic trends are causing more and more people to manage their own investments. And yet, lack of time and growing economic complexity can make this an immensely frustrating task. Schwab's ability to address that frustration is a big factor in its success.

## Reconstruct Your Value Chain

Defining new value propositions for the customer is necessary but not sufficient. You must also use the compromises you break to redefine the competitive dynamics of your industry to ensure that the economic value liberated by compromise breaking flows to you rather than your competitors.

So, think of compromises as an opportunity to reshape the value chain of your industry to your advantage. When Schwab entered the mutual fund business, its first thought was to create its own family of funds. Careful analysis of the industry value chain, however, revealed an even bigger opportunity: to become an intermediary between its own customer base and a large number of subscale mutual fund companies. Through OneSource, the firm serves the needs of the fund companies by providing them with economies of scale they could not achieve on their own. At the same time, Schwab interposes itself between the funds and the customer. Schwab's ownership of the direct customer relationship now provides a platform for growth in other financial services, such as insurance.

■ ■ ■

To break compromises, executives must first break with the conventional wisdom of their industry—about customers, about industry practices, and about the economics of the business. When they do, faster growth and improved profitability are the results.

# 19 Brand-Centric Transformation: Balancing Art and Data

Dylan Bolden, Antonella Mei-Pochtler, Rohan Sajdeh, Gaby Barrios, Erin George, Keith Melker, and Deran Taskiran

Google, Apple, Nike, Louis Vuitton...just a few of the names on any list of top global brands. These companies demonstrate without question that a *brand* can drive tangible financial impact and increase value for employees, customers, and shareholders. Of course, the inverse is also true: poorly crafted brand-building efforts can waste precious dollars from marketing budgets already stretched thin.

With so much at stake, brand building cannot be left to chance—or to creative advertising alone. The critical, strategic investment decisions required to shape and strengthen the brand must be tackled as such: debated by the most senior executives, grounded in data-driven insights, and embedded throughout the organization. Too often, however, brand transformation efforts falter because they lack the rigor and discipline that are applied to other business initiatives.

In developing their branding strategies, companies must move beyond qualitative research, such as consumer interviews and focus groups. These techniques can provide rich insight and emotional depth, but they are not conclusive. A more robust approach synthesizes a variety of insight sources—including internal financial information, competitive landscaping, and quantitative market research. Given the growing complexity of business, "going with your gut" can lead to bad decisions. As the hit movie *Moneyball* showed, the best moves are often counterintuitive—and revealed only by rigorous data analysis.

# Rules to Remember

Building a strong brand is not an end in itself but rather a way to drive customer loyalty, sales, profits, and shareholder returns. Executives looking for new avenues of growth or a turnaround in financial performance are often wise to consider a brand transformation as one component of their strategy.

To ensure that your brand transformation effort will succeed, we suggest keeping a few key rules in mind:

- *The brand can't live on emotions alone.* Although emotional resonance with the consumer is a prerequisite for brand value, it isn't the only critical element. Companies must firmly link the emotional connection to the underlying product or service attributes and to the customer experience.

- *The brand can't be everything to everyone.* Managers must make the tough trade-offs required to keep a brand on target and reject anything that isn't "on brand." For instance, an edgy energy drink company would do best to avoid adding a line of smoothies under the same brand.

- *The brand is not a separate entity.* The "brand" cannot be owned solely by marketing and its advertising partners. Brand-related decisions must be sold to the entire organization—including the sales force, field operations, and franchisees—through internal brand building.

- *The brand is a moving target.* Because technology, consumer needs, and business models evolve, any brand must continuously adapt its current positioning to remain relevant. Consider a food brand that helps mothers feel virtuous about feeding their children. The product attributes required to deliver on that emotional need might shift from "low fat" to "all natural" to "organic" as consumer trends evolve.

- *The brand balances art and data.* To make the right investment trade-offs, companies must draw on data from quantitative market research and economic analysis to answer key questions: How large and valuable are the different market spaces that the brand might occupy? How many consumers will respond to a particular cluster of emotional needs? What is the relative consumer preference for each product attribute or experience? What is the likely profit impact of various brand investment options?

# Understanding the Brand-Benefit Ladder

A data-driven approach to brand transformation requires that executives first understand what drives consumer choice in the product category and then translate that understanding into the core elements of the brand. To this end, we rely on the "brand-benefit ladder," a tool that describes how specific product benefits layer to support one another in delivering a brand experience to the consumer. A basic brand-benefit ladder includes the following elements:

- *Technical attributes:* the physical characteristics of a product or service, such as the ingredients, quality level, or aesthetics
- *Functional benefits:* differences in how consumers use or experience the product or service features
- *Emotional benefits:* the feelings that the product or service inspires
- *Social benefits:* the community connection and engagement a brand creates

Although technical attributes and functional benefits can vary between brands, they don't provide sustainable brand differentiation on their own. Emotional and social benefits are the key to creating customer loyalty, preference, and willingness to pay.

Every successful brand has a benefit ladder that is relevant, differentiated, and fully experienced by the consumer. For example, travelers on Southwest Airlines feel thrifty and savvy because of rock-bottom ticket prices and no-frills service delivered by high-energy employees. BMW owners feel proud to drive a superior-performance vehicle grounded in German engineering.

But simply using the brand ladder doesn't prevent suboptimal branding decisions. Many marketers stop at the emotional layer of the ladder instead of quantifying and fully understanding the links between the technical, functional, emotional, and social layers. And some companies are too focused on the technical and functional attributes alone, and do not build emotional and social connections to their target group. They may fail to use hard data to measure the value of potential brand investments and to prioritize trade-offs. Finally, they often struggle to implement the resulting brand-benefit ladder elements and hold the organization accountable.

Why is implementing a new brand strategy so difficult? Too often, one part of the organization owns the emotional and social benefits while other parts manage the functional benefits and technical attributes. These groups may have limited interaction, and their key performance indicators are typically misaligned.

Emotional and social benefits are typically owned by the marketing organization and external advertising agencies—passionate brand gurus who may envision brand building as more of an art than a science. They may focus mainly on developing catchy messaging and gloss over the fundamentals of the product and customer experience. What's more, they may fail to incorporate business metrics or opportunity sizing into their recommendations.

Meanwhile, technical attributes and functional benefits are often controlled by different company departments. Product development, pricing, merchandising, field operations, and real estate, for example, may each oversee different aspects of the product or service features. These departments often make day-to-day decisions and trade-offs independently, without considering the brand promise. Ultimately, coordination across these teams on any integrated brand transformation effort becomes a massive undertaking.

## A Four-Step Solution

The optimal approach to brand transformation ties together the brand-benefit ladder, the drivers of brand choice, and the company strategy and is grounded in deep consumer insight, including both qualitative and quantitative analysis. It conveys the product's technical, functional, emotional, and social benefits in a globally meaningful way. It ensures a consistently delivered experience using "brand drivers" across all the marketing Ps—such as placement, promotion, and people. It touches all parts of the organization to ensure buy-in and commitment. It is both creative and disciplined. It shapes what the company is (and is not) permitted to do and can be measured and tracked over time.

On the basis of our work with leading companies worldwide, we recommend a four-step methodology that quantitatively links the brand ladder to brand strategy and then enables the organization to translate strategy into reality.

## Step 1: Identify the Drivers of Brand Choice

How do consumers choose between different brands within a product category? Choice drivers are never entirely rational. The final purchase decision usually reflects the feelings that consumers have when experiencing the category. For example, a retail store might feel like a "relaxing escape" from the busy world outside or invoke a "sensible" feeling of having made good use of one's time and money.

Because the consumer sits at the heart of brand-centric transformation, so does exhaustive consumer research, which helps reveal the key drivers of choice. Combining this research with other data sources, such as a detailed assessment of the competitive landscape, can deliver a fuller perspective of the company's differentiated brand positioning—a primary input to inform hypotheses.

But the ultimate goal is to develop a very focused, large-scale quantitative survey of consumers to prove or disprove those hypotheses. This quantitative research should use multiple analytical techniques to identify emotional drivers overall and by market space.

The specific methodology should be adapted to a particular company's unique situation, but it will typically include analytical research techniques that make it possible to prioritize individual attributes, highlight key relationships among attributes and benefits, and cluster similar drivers of brand choice.

## Step 2: Select the Target Market Spaces

Which market spaces are best suited to the brand? The goal is to identify opportunities that are financially attractive and available—ideally, "white spaces" not already owned by an existing brand or adjacent to where the company's brand currently plays. Market sizing is critical in terms of the customer base but also in terms of dollars. Again, this step is heavily driven by analytics. Large-scale quantitative surveys can determine the size of each market space and identify which spaces enhance one another and which do not. It is also important to know where your brand has a competitive advantage.

## Step 3: Identify the Brand Benefits Needed to Win

Now it's time to build the brand-benefit ladder, using the market space and the key emotional and social benefits as a starting point. Link each benefit to the corresponding functional benefits or technical attributes that will make it real for the consumer. Research and analytics can help establish these links with quantitative precision rather than instinct and guesswork. Then companies can compare the prioritized list of technical attributes and functional benefits, along with key trade-offs, with their current product or service offering—and will likely find critical gaps. Be sure to factor in competitors' offerings and capabilities. Final brand investment decisions can be made on the basis of these findings.

## Step 4: Develop a Brand Execution Strategy and Playbook

The final step is to align the organization around the new brand. Senior executives must translate the brand positioning into something that can be communicated, understood, and acted on by all employees. Each relevant function needs an action plan for internal execution. At the same time, marketing must work with external advertising and public relations (PR) partners to develop communication plans that align messaging with the new emotional and social benefits and brand positioning. Together, these plans should create an integrated brand experience for the consumer. When a company has established effective "brand mirroring," each employee experiences and describes the brand in exactly the same way that the customer does.

A brand-centric transformation program can improve all aspects of *brand delivery*—from strategy, repositioning, and execution to organization and capabilities. Companies must also track *brand impact* by measuring brand equity, valuing the brand, and building brand reporting systems that can show how brand metrics tie directly to the financial performance of the company and its valuation.

■ ■ ■

In today's marketing landscape, the basics of brand management may seem obsolete compared with the latest digital tools and trends. But some things never go out of style. Company executives must reject complacency, rethink old ways of tackling brand issues, and apply a new, more disciplined approach. The result will be a brand-centric transformation that goes well beyond messaging and "the creative" to strengthen every aspect of the business.

# 20 Unlocking Growth in the Middle: A View from India and China

## Zhenya Lindgardt, Christoph Nettesheim, and Ted Chan

Over the next decade or two, one of the fiercest business battles will be for the billions of people joining the middle class in emerging markets—a group that will make up 30 percent of the global population by 2020. Emerging markets are forecast to grow at an annual average rate of 5.5 percent over the next 10 years to 2020, compared with just 2.6 percent for developed economies. In these countries, the big money increasingly clusters in the middle, where average income is growing at 8 percent per year and will reach an estimated $4 trillion by 2015.

Yet many multinational companies are not prepared to tap into this new stream of revenue growth, even if they're already active in emerging markets. Simply put, their business models were not designed to reach the new middle. Many have simply imported their existing high-end products and services through standard distribution channels to target the most affluent tier of customers in the largest cities, such as Delhi, Shanghai, Rio de Janeiro, and Moscow. This strategy has proved successful in the past, but the top-tier segment is becoming saturated.

If multinational companies are to reach the expanding middle classes in countries such as India and China, they will need to design and package their offerings differently, rethink their entire cost structure, and adapt their distribution systems. Many companies are familiar with the need to adapt a product to local tastes, usually through slight modifications to the offering. But fewer companies have acknowledged the need to substantially change their business model to gain a lasting advantage.

Multinational companies will also need to compete against a new threat: highly successful local companies that are already serving the middle market in their home countries—a group that BCG calls the global challengers—and now have ambitions to expand worldwide and dethrone the global leaders. Consider the market for wireless telecommunications equipment. In 2006, the top seven suppliers were all venerable companies based in the West. Today, four of those companies have been acquired or have merged, and two young Chinese companies, Huawei and ZTE, have broken into the top five. Any multinational company that starts pursuing the middle in emerging markets thus will also be learning to defend its markets at home.

# Four Steps to Business Model Innovation

To compete with global challengers and crack the middle market, multinationals will need to go through the same intense process of analysis and design they did to develop their current successful business models. In most cases, some degree of business model innovation will be essential, given the unique characteristics of emerging markets, such as lower consumer purchasing power, different competitive ecosystems, geographically dispersed customers, varying customer priorities and expectations, rapidly changing infrastructure, and political influence and regulation.

Business model innovation involves creating a new value proposition (Which customers do we choose to serve, with which offerings, and how are we compensated?), supported by a distinct operating model (How do we profitably deliver the new value proposition?), to address a new opportunity. This approach can be used to reinvent a dying core business, explore new avenues for growth, or create a durable competitive advantage.

Multinationals that have succeeded at business model innovation in emerging markets think systematically about the opportunities and threats. We have distilled their varied experiences into four steps that can guide executives as they launch their own endeavors.

## Uncover Opportunities through Customer Discovery

Business model innovation starts by developing a capability in each local market to understand customer needs, buying habits, and price points and to determine the potential size of the opportunity. Two avenues of discovery can be fruitful here: an analysis of megatrends that will encourage new types of demand and a deep examination of the unmet needs of the middle-market customer. Scoping out new customer segments within the middle should be done as precisely and quantitatively as possible.

Taking the first approach, Philips recognized that the rise of the middle class in emerging markets could greatly benefit several of its businesses. Increasingly affordable health care would spur demand for medical equipment, construction of new and better housing would raise demand for lighting, and greater wealth would spur demand for home health products and domestic appliances. That led Philips to develop a dedicated strategy and business model for emerging markets and an expanded portfolio of products relevant to local middle-class households.

The second type of consumer discovery—deep analysis—was undertaken by Indian conglomerate Godrej. When the company set out to design a new kind of refrigerator for middle-income consumers in India, it worked with many village women to modify its chotuKool prototype, then built the lightweight refrigerator using solid-state technology instead of a compressor and priced it between $65 and $75. Godrej also rejected the traditional channel of sales force plus distributors and dealers and instead enlisted nongovernmental organizations (NGOs) and microfinance institutions to distribute the refrigerators throughout India.

## Convert Opportunities into Viable Business Models

Once the customers' needs have been identified, a company must create a business model suitable to meet them, often entailing changes to the value proposition, value chain, organization, or cost structure to reach the middle in emerging markets.

KFC, for example, made substantial changes to its model to meet the demands of emerging markets. Developed world locations feature the dominant logic that made the company a global brand: a limited menu, low prices, and an emphasis on takeout. Under new management in the early 1990s, KFC stretched the brand so that it would better appeal to the demonstrated demands of middle-market consumers in China, with a wider variety of foods and traditional dishes than the standard fast-food outlet would offer. Managers enlarged the restaurants to about twice the size of those in the United States. They needed bigger kitchens to prepare Chinese food and more floor space so that customers could linger. KFC China thus positioned itself as a special occasion restaurant within reach of the middle class.

Configuring this new value proposition required operational changes as well. KFC had to reinvent its value chain and the manner in which it procured key resources for its restaurants. Because the network of distributors that KFC relies on in many countries does not exist in China, it built its own distribution arm—including warehouses, its own fleet of trucks, and a unit that monitors safety along the supply chain all the way back to animal feed companies.

## Test, Scale Up, and Iterate

Before committing valuable resources to new business projects in emerging markets, the corporate center should ensure that they are viable projects, by fostering experiments with different models. Such testing also includes a means to mitigate risks and to connect the dots among locally adapted business models. That means determining which platforms (in areas such as brand, manufacturing, and procurement) should be common across the enterprise and which will need to be modified for new markets. The center will need the right information, the ability to derive insights from that information, and the key execution capabilities—all of which can combine to produce smart trade-off decisions.

Business models can be tested cheaply to prove the main hypotheses and avoid ill-advised investments. For example, in developing its micro-entrepreneurship distribution mechanism, called Shakti, Unilever began with just a few micro-entrepreneurs. Only after finding that the concept was profitable did it continue with the new model.

After pilots have paid off, companies can take a variety of different approaches to quickly and efficiently scale up new models. KFC, for instance, shifted from franchises to primarily company-owned outlets, enabling the restaurants to more easily expand geographically, closely control operations, and centralize purchases. Philips, on the other hand, acquired a local producer, which offered a quick route to local expertise, cheaper manufacturing facilities, and closer relationships with hospitals and clinics outside the main cities. Finally, Tesco avoided the risks of going it alone or making a potentially risky acquisition by forming a joint venture with a local partner, RHB Banking Group, to launch cobranded credit/debit cards and in-store branches.

## Manage Emerging Markets Like a Business Model Portfolio

Once they reach middle-class customers in several emerging markets, companies will soon find it necessary to manage multiple business models and multiple brands. Just as executives aggregate individual products into a portfolio that can be managed, they should do this for their business models. Taking a portfolio approach allows them to assess and gain a view of the payback, risk level, and launch timing for the entire enterprise and to share lessons with other local units more readily.

As part of any restructuring, it is often advantageous to simplify decision making so that managers at the local level can take advantage of fast-moving opportunities. Serial business model innovator General Electric, for example, has found that having local units report to someone high up in the organization keeps emerging markets on the senior management agenda. This approach also enables reverse innovation and ensures that local units get the support they need from the corporate center.

More broadly, multinationals can use common platforms to support business model innovation in multiple markets so that local units don't have to start from scratch each time. Think "voice of the customer 101" or "distribution in a kit." Some of these platforms can be housed in regional centers or shared-services centers. Regional offices cluster markets that have common consumer characteristics, competitor sets, geographic proximity, or channel development and generate savings through best practices and automation.

Management of the portfolio should include hard targets and metrics with which to evaluate each of the business models, as well as the whole. Just as a business model in mature markets may not transfer to the developing world, so too may performance metrics need to be altered to reflect new realities. Forward-looking metrics such as market share may be more relevant than financial metrics when entering or expanding in a developing nation.

Organizational challenges in a portfolio of emerging-market businesses will be different from those in mature markets. Efforts to penetrate middle-tier markets through innovative business models often resemble a start-up operation, putting a premium on employees with an entrepreneurial mind-set. Local teams should think like business builders, considering the entire equation of business economics—thinking that goes beyond a narrow sales focus on exceeding the next quarter's quota. At the corporate center, meanwhile, leaders must be willing to consider alternatives to traditional business models, to free up resources accordingly, and to keep up a regular dialogue with multiple local teams.

# Early Questions for Executives

In the dynamic, even volatile environment of some emerging markets, business model innovation can be challenging for multinationals that have relied for years on exporting their standard models. To start the process and determine the fitness of the organization, we suggest checking the health of the current business model to identify areas of strength and areas that need improvement or radical change. As part of this diagnosis, the senior executive team, including representatives from emerging markets, should gather to address a set of key questions:

- Which countries and segments of the middle can we feasibly penetrate in the next five years? Which competitors exist there today—including global challengers—and what can we learn from them?
- What unmet needs are mid-market customers trying to fill, and what are their highest priorities?
- What new value propositions can we design to fill those needs? Does the organization excel at customization and flexibility in product design?
- How can we alter the operating model to best deliver a new value proposition to the middle at a lower cost? Will we require partnerships or acquisitions?
- Who are our business builders in emerging markets? Do managers at the local level have the capabilities to engage in customer discovery

and experimentation to test new models? Are they experienced in leading transformation?

- Does our organization tolerate diversity as well as standardization? Does the governance structure promote rapid decision making?
- Is our organization set up to promote experimentation and fast failure? Is it running enough experiments? Do we have a clear process to scale up promising, tested new opportunities?
- Is the organization ready to manage multiple business models to address different tiers of the market? Do we have the infrastructure to incubate new models, as well as modular global platforms to support business model innovation?

Depending on the answers to these questions, companies can start to reach countless businesses and the more than 1 billion consumers who make up the emerging middle and are eager for affordable products that solve their problems and fit in with their lives. That's an opportunity that could sustain at least another decade or two of profitable revenue growth.

# 21 Treasure Hunt

## Michael J. Silverstein

It was coming up to Christmas, and Alice Nelson wanted to make the holiday very special for her family. The Nelsons had not bought a new TV in 12 years. Alice's husband, Ben, was sick of the old television with its 27-inch screen and mediocre sound. Their three children looked with envy at the big flat screens of their friends and neighbors. Everybody in the family was tired of mediating who would get to watch what and when.

"We needed a new television," Ben says with conviction. "Especially me. I work a 75-hour week. Watching sports on television is one of my few luxuries. Alice and the children wanted a vacation as a Christmas gift. But I knew that if I could convince them to go with the TV as the family gift, we would get years of pleasure from it, rather than just a few days of vacation."

It was an unusual decision for an unusual family. Ben Nelson holds two jobs: one as an engineer; the other as a barber. Alice is a part-time nurse with health issues of her own to attend to. The Nelsons have three children—two girls and a boy—aged 18, 16, and 14. They live in a middle-class suburb. Alice drives a gas-guzzling Durango SUV and Ben tools around in an aging two-seater. He works hard, as much as 14 hours a day. His engineering work involves selling big-ticket durable accessories to purchasing agents in the railroad industry. His barbering is done in a

---

This chapter is based on Michael J. Silverstein and John Butman's 2006 book, *Treasure Hunt: Inside the Mind of the New Consumer*, published by Portfolio.

prestigious men's salon in Chicago, where cuts go for $40 or more. Ben loves his wife and children and hopes the children will achieve success that will far surpass his own. He is a kind man and devotes his life to providing for others. Even so, he really wanted a bigger-screen television far more than he wanted to go on a vacation that he felt would be little more than "a happy memory" within a few months.

So, one weekend in November, Alice and Ben went together to look at new TVs. They started at Best Buy, went on to Sears, and ended up at Circuit City. There, with the help of an unusually attentive salesperson, they studied dozens of sets and carefully compared features and prices. They decided they would have to spend at least $1,500 to get the big-screen television with the quality and features they really wanted. That was more money than they had thought about spending, and it would put a strain on their already-strained budget. The Nelsons' total household income—including engineering, barbering, and nursing—is about $100,000 a year.

The Nelsons did not think the television was overpriced. In fact, it seemed like a good value to them, considering its picture and audio quality, as well as its many controls and connection options. Plus, they could imagine the new TV in their lives and the benefits it would bring. Ben looked forward to watching football and baseball with the panoramic clarity of the new set. Alice pictured the whole family together on a weekend night, laughing at their favorite comedies on DVD.

But, as Ben and Alice discussed the purchase, they realized that it would probably make the "who watches what and when" problem even worse. As they talked, they continued to wander through the aisles, looking at different TV sets, which were arranged on the shelves according to size and price. At the very end, they noticed a 13-inch color television, a perfectly nice-looking little unit made by Daewoo. Ben checked the price and could not believe what he saw: $57. And, as an engineer, he was satisfied with the technical features and functional performance. The picture quality was good. The sound was fine. You could hook up cable or a DVD player. It came with a neat little remote.

A little nervous, but also quite excited, Alice and Ben debated a new idea. What if they were to buy not just one wide-screen TV, but *four* sets? A 32-inch LG wide-screen flat-panel TFT-LCD TV for $1,999 for the whole family and three 13-inch Daewoos, at $57, one for each of the children. The total purchase would come to more than $2,000, but it would bring tremendous pleasure to the family, reduce the number of squabbles, and make for a fabulous Christmas. They decided to go for it. On the way out of the store, Ben crowed, "It's gonna be a Daewoo Christmas!"

Christmas morning came, and the children were ecstatic. They could not believe that their parents, who were always looking for ways to save money, had sprung for four television sets. The kids would have been thrilled with one big-screen TV. Now they each had their own. It was nothing short of revolutionary. Ben and Alice loved seeing their son and daughters so happy. That evening, with the big screen set up in the family room, Ben surfed through the channels and the children dashed from bedroom to bedroom, and from set to set, squealing with delight.

A few days after Christmas, Alice called the family together. She said that they had spent a lot of money on the television sets, more than they had planned, but that it was definitely worth it. However, it would mean that they would have less money than usual for a little while. They would have to cut back on spending for things that weren't absolutely necessary. Alice said she would do all she could to save money on food and other household expenses. She expected the children to be frugal and not ask for frivolous things. Ben pledged that he would try to limit his spending on the little gifts he occasionally liked to spring on his family. No more $40 boxes of chocolates for Alice or $85 skirts for the girls or video games for the boy. And that's exactly what they did. For the first quarter of the family's "fiscal year," the Nelson family was like a company on an austerity budget. There was no additional capital spending. No unnecessary purchases. No dining out. Ben kept his splurging instinct in check. Alice cut out her weekly coffee date with her friends. She bought no new clothing. By April, the TV sets were paid for and the Nelsons breathed a little easier.

## The Dynamic Market Meets the Unpredictable Consumer

Whatever you think of the benefits of television, or the necessity of one family owning four of anything, the story of the Nelsons and their Daewoo Christmas is a good parable for what's going on in the consumer goods market today.

In the United States and around the world, the consumer markets are bifurcating into two fast-growing pools of spending. At the high end of the market, consumers are trading up, paying a premium for high-quality, emotionally rich, high-margin products and services. At the low end, consumers are relentlessly trading down, spending as little as possible to buy basic, low-cost goods that still deliver acceptable quality, reliability, and, increasingly, elements of fashion and current design.

In between the trading-up and trading-down pools lies a vast expanse of mediocre, often low-margin, goods that offer neither distinctive emotional appeal nor better value than cheaper competitors. Whenever they can, consumers steer clear of them. Many businesses that have long prospered by bringing mid-priced products to middle-market consumers suddenly find themselves facing "death in the middle."

Companies that succeed in this bifurcated market do so by understanding the attitudes, behaviors, and values of the middle-market consumers who are driving the transformation and by constantly adjusting and reinventing their product offering to satisfy the ever-changing "value calculus" of the consumer.

Consuming has become a treasure hunt—a constant search through the world's incredibly vast and ever-changing store of goods and services—with the goal of finding the perfect value every time. Consumers spend their money with great individuality, trading up in a few categories, trading down in most, avoiding some altogether, mixing upscale products with downscale ones, and creating customized lifestyles and standards of living that are uniquely their own.

# Why People Trade Down

Consumers trade down for four main reasons:

- *"I'm a smart shopper."* Buying and consuming have become skills as fundamental as driving a car or using a computer. As one consumer said to me, "I wake up every day and start a new battle. It's me versus the world. The world is trying to take money out of my wallet. It's my job to make sure it stays in there." These warrior-shoppers take advantage of every weapon and channel at their disposal: sales, coupons, promotions, everyday-low-price retailers, hard discounters, and the Web. Shopping is the work of the everyday trader-down. "I see it as my job to find bargains and get the lowest price," said a consumer in a conversation in a parking lot outside a Dollar General store. "I will shop in three different stores to save 50 cents."

- "*There's no material difference.*" Another reason that consumers trade down is that they often see no perceivable or material difference between goods at two price points. The quality of goods in many categories has risen such that the difference in price of a few pennies, even a few dollars, does not always translate into genuine technical, functional, or emotional differences. "I don't trade quality for price," one consumer told me. "Instead, I focus on finding the best value. These days you really can find high quality for a low price. You just have to be smart about how and where you shop."

- "*My mom taught me.*" Many trading-down consumers, especially women, were taught frugality at their mother's knee. They believe in being thrifty as a moral value. When they consider a purchase, they ask themselves, "Would Mom approve? Would she have bought this?" In fact, many middle-market consumers will seek their parents' advice and counsel, especially when it comes to a major purchase such as a car or kitchen appliance. The great word-of-mouth network, as well as the many online communities of shoppers and buyers, help people to consider and evaluate the features and benefits of every imaginable product, from pet food to food supplements.

- "*I can go without.*" Although Americans have gotten a bad rap for being careless spenders and wasteful consumers, particularly compared with other cultures around the world, most middle-class consumers do not believe in excessive consumption. They are willing to forgo buying an item to save some money. They prioritize their purchases and will buy certain items only when everything else has been paid for. As one shopper said to me, "Making ends meet is always something I'm worried about. We're very careful about where we spend our money. The kids' activities and needs are taken care of first, and we just find a way to make the rest of it work."

As a result of these trading-up and trading-down behaviors, middle-market consumers confound the traditional demographic and psychographic stereotypes. These people are unpredictable—completely, delightfully, exasperatingly unpredictable. Our definition of the middle class includes the $150,000-a-year professional who buys $19 jeans at Target, flies AirTran, splurges on shoes at Neiman Marcus, travels 50 miles to a Coach outlet store to buy a handbag, and pays $100 for her dog to have a "beauty treatment." It also embraces the $50,000-a-year plumber who leases a $27,000 BMW, never dines out, buys clothes at Kohl's, and is a connoisseur of cold-pressed virgin Italian olive oils. Both of them look for the best deals on TVs. Neither one really cares what brand of canned tomato sauce they buy or where they buy it. More and more, that's the market companies now face.

Trading down is hardly a solely American phenomenon. The same income and spending patterns that drive the trading-up and trading-down behaviors in North America are also causing market restlessness in Europe, China, India, and Japan. Throughout Europe, especially in Germany, the propensity to trade down in selected categories has led to the rise of hard discounting—medium-sized stores that offer little in the way of a shopping experience but a lot in the way of extremely low prices on a wide array of goods, especially groceries. In Japan, the consumer market is distorted by a single demographic group: young, single, working women with high salaries and few financial obligations. They trade up in fashion and dining out but are ruthless about trading down in many other categories.

There are differences from country to country, but the phenomenon is evident everywhere. You can see it in the streets of Shanghai and Seattle, Mexico City and Montreal, Tokyo and Topeka. Every city has its high street boutiques offering expensive goods with dramatic presentations—and with high operating costs. A few miles away are the discount retailers, such as Walmart, Carrefour, and Costco. Middle-class customers shop at both places on different occasions and with different motivations.

Worldwide, we expect to see continued growth at the bottom and top of the market and a further decline in the middle. New companies will emerge at both ends; well-known names will be humbled by their inability to escape the middle.

## Strategies for Winning

What does this pressure on the middle and transformation of the consumer goods market mean for businesses? Opportunity. And danger. There are three principal ways to succeed: trading down, trading up, and holding the middle.

### Trading Down

The trading-down market is massive, but it is extremely knockabout, with ferocious price competition and virtually no consumer loyalty. And you can't succeed at the low end simply by tapping into the global supply chain, taking cost out, and waging a price war with your competitors; consumers still expect value and performance from their low-cost products. More and more, they demand emotional qualities in their low-cost goods and a pleasurable experience while shopping for them.

For trading down, the mantra must be "basic, low-cost, and reliable" (BLCR). The mission is always to find ways to make a product or service cheaper and better. Not only cheaper, not just better—but both at once. As soon as you think your price is low enough and you stop trying to lower it further, a competitor will find a way to scrape a few pennies off the cost and offer the product at a lower retail price. As soon as you think your quality is good enough and stop trying to make it better, a competitor will incorporate a technical improvement or a functional feature that will grab the consumer's attention.

Trading down is a global game in which the global low-cost producer wins. Success requires the aggressive management of scale, raw materials purchasing, continuous experimentation in design to reduce costs, and a relentless drive to rethink the cost structure to establish advantage.

## Trading Up

There are still opportunities to succeed in trading up, but you must create distinctive products that offer technical, functional, and emotional differences for which consumers will pay a premium. This is not a onetime event. Competitors that rest on their laurels in trading-up categories will be matched and then trumped by newcomers.

For trading up, the mission is captured in the slogan coined by Ely Callaway of the Callaway Golf Company—"demonstrably superior and pleasingly different" (or DSPD). This is, essentially, a short way of saying that the product must deliver on the ladder of benefits—technical, functional, and emotional—in order to command a premium.

However, succeeding in trading up is not as easy as it might look, and there is plenty of congestion at the premium end of the market in many categories. I get a continual stream of e-mails from entrepreneurs who have developed yet another new and wonderful premium vodka, for example. My answer to them is this: maybe you should explore a less picked-over category. Vodka has traded up and is highly segmented. There are many other categories where the market is open to a trading-up offering, particularly financial services and health care.

## Holding the Middle

The middle of the market is still the biggest piece of the consumer goods pie. Companies that aim for the middle can still achieve share and profit growth. The point, however, is that the middle is steadily shrinking, which means that it just gets harder and harder for companies that have for years served the middle of the middle class to grow and strengthen their brands.

As the middle contracts, it's likely that a few competitors will remain there and new ones will emerge—companies that can strike a smart balance between low-cost functionality and premium emotion without resorting to bland, me-too conformity and empty marketing messages. What's particularly intriguing is that successful companies employ a nearly identical set of practices, no matter what strategy they have chosen to pursue in the bifurcating market:

- *Escape the middle.* If you are in the middle, begin moving up, down, or in both directions. Don't assume your customers will ever come back to the vast desert of mediocrity and don't get stuck there yourself. If you choose to play in the middle, be sure it's not your only playground.
- *Drive costs down and quality up.* Never stop searching for ways to provide ever lower prices and better quality, because consumers won't stop searching for more value. There is never a point where all the costs are out or all the quality is in.
- *Attack the category like an outsider.* Look at your offering from the perspective of a category outsider. What would it consider your weak spot to be?
- *Listen, listen, listen.* Understand all the detail and nuances about consumers' dissatisfactions. Track them down in your products and engineer them out.
- *Focus on your best customers.* Follow them up and down the aisles and tailor your offering to meet their needs. As Walmart teaches its associates, "The truth is in the stores."

# The Trend Will Continue with or without You

Wherever you now sit, no one will thank you, in the long run, for holding back, ignoring the data, or delaying action. No one will laud you for allowing your company to get caught in the middle. They will, however, be delighted to be with you when you have correctly understood the treasure hunt phenomenon and connected your company with the genuine needs of that most powerful market force in the world: the middle-class consumer.

# VI Fit to Win

Strategy is all about building sustainable competitive advantage. Having smart ideas isn't enough. Companies must also have the capability to execute on those ideas over the long term—what we call being fit to win.

In Chapter 22, "High-Performance Organizations," we describe our experience of what these companies do that others don't. We offer a framework of characteristics grouped into five broad dimensions: leadership, design, people, change management, and culture and engagement. We explore how leading companies take a strategic approach to cultivating and monitoring improvement in these key characteristics that drive performance and successful strategy execution.

Deploying capabilities with maximum effect requires a well-designed organization. Many companies have too many management layers, which diminish reaction times and impair decision making. In Chapter 23, "Shaping Up: The Delayered Look," we contend that by removing managerial layers, organizations can speed up information flows, lift morale, and improve decision making—without eliminating activities that create value.

Another way to dramatically improve performance is to apply lean principles throughout the organization, not just to manufacturing. But many companies struggle to achieve lasting results. Chapter 24, "Getting More from Lean: Seven Success Factors," focuses on the critical keys to success. By following the seven guidelines, companies can capitalize on the transformational power of a lean approach.

Finally we take a more detailed look at three specific areas of the organization that are often of strategic importance across the whole company: the supply chain, pricing, and IT.

Creating a supply chain that is fit to win has always been a challenge, especially given that needs often change. Even when forecasts are finely tuned, an unexpected shift in demand can wreak havoc on production schedules. Now, thanks to recent industry and technology changes, a truly demand-driven supply chain is finally possible. In Chapter 25, "The Demand-Driven Supply Chain," we explore the key factors needed to make this Holy Grail of operations managers a reality.

Pricing that is fit to win does so by persuading customers to pay a little more or buy a little more. Chapter 26, "Pricing Fluency," explores how companies can enhance their pricing models through better policies and improve the pricing platforms used to implement those policies throughout the organization. The payoff is a significant increase in earnings.

In our final chapter we look at how IT departments that are fit to win can drive business transformation. Chapter 27, "The IT Organization of the Future," identifies the key factors that characterize effective IT groups and explores how companies can put these insights into action.

As competition becomes demonstrably more intense and turbulence increases measurably, these timeless prerequisites for success are more important than ever.

# 22 High-Performance Organizations

## Vikram Bhalla, Jean-Michel Caye, Andrew Dyer, Lisa Dymond, Yves Morieux, and Paul Orlander

**W**hen you walk into a high-performance organization, you can feel the difference. Instead of just going through the motions, the people are energized. They are confident about their organization's strategy and the changes that are occurring, rather than confused or resigned. They know what they are supposed to be doing and how that relates to the tasks of their neighbors. Your casual observations can be confirmed quickly by checking performance measures such as sustained earnings and market share growth at corporations and, in the nonprofit world, social impact.

But how do organizations become high-performance organizations? We have compiled a list of 14 organizational and people characteristics that can be grouped into five broad dimensions and that lead to sustained performance.

- *Leadership*. An aligned leadership is effective deep within the organization.
- *Design*. A lean structure reflects the organization's strategic focus and has clear roles and accountabilities.
- *People*. The organization effectively translates business strategy into a powerful people strategy, attracting and retaining the most capable individuals.
- *Change management*. The organization has the ability to drive and sustain large-scale change and to anticipate and adapt to an increasingly volatile environment.

- *Culture and engagement.* The culture is shaped to achieve strategic goals, and its employees are motivated to go beyond the call of duty in pursuit of corporate objectives.

When organizations take a strategic approach to their pursuit of monitoring and improving these five broad capabilities—and the 14 characteristics that follow—they generate lasting performance gains and a competitive edge.

Tolstoy was right: each unhappy family is unhappy in its own way, but all happy families—or high-performance organizations—are alike. By understanding the common strands of organizational DNA, all companies can put themselves in a stronger position to achieve success.

# Leadership

Leadership is a scarce resource, both in developed markets suffering from an exodus of older executives and developing markets straining to keep up with rapid growth. Today's accelerated pace of change has weakened leadership conducted solely through command and control. Leadership starts but does not stop at the top of the pyramid. High-performance organizations create leaders at every level.

## High-Performance Teams of Leaders Drive Urgency and Direction

Leaders are comfortable with complexity, volatility, and change. In the face of ambiguity, they are able to mobilize the organization. Although leaders need to be visionary, they cannot be lone wolves or independent operators; the days of the heroic corporate leader are over. Today's leaders need to work cooperatively with their peers and recognize the collective strength generated through collaboration.

## The Pipeline Is Stocked with Future Leaders Whose Skills Are Matched to Future Needs

High-performance organizations have leaders in the wings who have been rotated through many types of positions and roles in many functions and regions and are groomed for success. These organizations identify potential leaders early in their careers—and cultivate in them the skills and competencies that will be required in the future.

## Middle Managers Embrace and Translate Strategy

Middle managers oversee the vast majority of employees, translating the strategy and vision endorsed by senior leaders into concrete plans for their teams. They also select and elevate the key issues from the front line that need senior management's attention. Despite the pivotal and difficult role middle managers play, they often get lost in the shuffle and receive insufficient development, support, and attention from senior leadership.

# Design

Organization design can help companies improve execution and achieve strategic goals. But for that to happen, the interplay among its key elements—structure, individual capabilities, and roles and collaboration—must be carefully coordinated and tightly linked with a company's strategy and sources of competitive advantage.

## Structure and Resource Allocation Reflect Strategic Trade-offs

Compromise is inherent in organization design. A well-designed structure should emphasize what matters most to an organization. In the real world, it is impossible to accommodate all dimensions equally. An organization's structure should also be dynamic, oriented around current and future—rather than legacy—priorities. When strategy, performance, or the competitive environment changes, an organization's structure may need adjustment.

## Few Layers Separate the CEO and the Front Line, and Spans of Control Are Wide

Lean structures allow organizations to focus on meaningful work, rather than coordination. Activities that don't deliver value are eliminated.

With fewer organizational layers, communication and decision making are faster, and senior leaders have a better view of day-to-day operations and customer interactions. With wider spans of control, managers become more ambitious in applying their leadership skills. They don't have time to micromanage but can grow comfortable in their ability to lead, coach, and inspire.

### Accountabilities, Decision Rights, and Collaboration Are Constructed with Thoughtful Consideration

High-performance organizations have clearly defined roles that are carefully assembled to form a highly efficient organization. People understand what is expected of them and which decisions are theirs to make. When accountability is shared, employees understand clearly when and with whom they need to collaborate. BCG helps companies achieve this clarity through *role charters*, but what they are called is less important than the need to have a path to achieve clear accountabilities, decision rights, and behavioral expectations.

### Individual Capabilities Are Matched to Role Requirements

Roles need to be staffed by the right people with the right skills. Depending on its needs, for example, a company might require a head of sales who is a great "closer" and can excite the sales force. Or it might need a solid manager who can implement a new sales management system. Unless the broader organizational needs are explicit, managers may hire and promote people on the basis of their perception of "fit."

## People

Although many companies boast particular strengths in recruiting, training, or performance management, high-performance organizations are effective at translating their business strategy into a compelling people strategy. At these organizations, the HR function acts as a strong advisor to business units on both operational and strategic people issues. It has short- and long-term plans for identifying, attracting, developing, and retaining the right people with the right capabilities.

## The Employer Brand Is a Core Asset

High-performance organizations have a well-defined employer brand. Employees and recruits alike know the broad range of benefits—beyond compensation—that employees enjoy, ranging from career advancement, job rotation, and prestige to flexibility and autonomy. This brand—or employee value proposition—contributes to an organization's strengths and competitive edge.

## Critical Roles and Key Talents Are Clearly Identified and Treated with Care

Talent management is a broader activity in practice than most organizations realize. It is not just reserved for those on the fast track. It also covers the people and roles critical to enterprise success. High-performance organizations identify these critical roles and individuals and focus retention strategies and contingency plans around them. This list of individuals and roles should be dynamic, changing with the firm's strategic priorities.

## HR Is a Strategic Partner and an Enabler of the Business

In leading organizations, people strategy is as prominent as business strategy. The human resources (HR) function has successfully translated business strategy into people objectives and enabled business priorities through people initiatives. The function operates with clear separation of strategic, functional, and transactional activities. It efficiently completes functional and transactional activities and effectively influences strategic topics.

# Change Management

In today's fast-paced world, the ability to change in two fundamental ways generates sustained competitive advantage. First, companies need to have a disciplined approach to drive shifts in focus, strategy, direction, structure, and culture. Second, they need to have the ability to adapt to rapidly changing developments in the market.

## Change Is a Disciplined Cascade

Despite the high rate of failure among change programs, a few organizations are beating the odds. They ensure that the leadership group is aligned on the goals and means of change, and they deliberately transfer that alignment to employees layer by layer throughout the organization. During a major change, senior executives receive feedback from deep within the organization, where the fate of change resides, in order to track progress and make adjustments. We call this process *cascading change*.

## The Organization Is Evolutionary

High-performance organizations are *adaptive*, continually detecting changes in the market and making strategic adjustments. This approach supplements rather than replaces the broad strokes of classic strategy. They empower the periphery of their organizations—far away from the classic strategy function—to spring into action in anticipation of market developments.

# Culture and Engagement

Culture is *the way things get done* in an organization and reflects employees' behaviors and attitudes toward work. It is the "secret sauce" of an organization, bringing a strategy to life or deadening it. Employee engagement, meanwhile, is the willingness of employees to go the extra mile for an organization, not merely out of obligation or for a paycheck but because work matters both personally and professionally to them.

## Culture Accelerates Strategic Objectives

Good corporate culture is not accidental. High-performance organizations set, manage, and monitor culture to achieve strategic objectives. A culture either works for a given enterprise—or it doesn't—*at a point of time*. As strategic priorities change, so should culture.

## Engagement Is Measured and Cultivated to Generate Discretionary Effort from Employees

At a high level, engagement is built through two equally important dimensions: personal motivators, such as recognition, and performance disciplines, such as performance management metrics. High-performance organizations keep a finger on the pulse of their people, regularly measuring engagement levels and actively managing engagement through difficult times, such as a reorganization or large-scale change effort.

# A New View on Organizational Success

Companies often make changes to their organization and people elements in knee-jerk response to external events. Others take a laissez-faire approach, with few deliberate initiatives. Neither of these approaches yields sustained performance records.

High-performance organizations just work differently. They understand the need to have all 14 characteristics present in their organization and take a coordinated approach to implementing them. They also decide which of the 14 are the most critical to sustained competitive advantage and actively work to improve weak spots by engaging in a disciplined set of interventions and activities. Furthermore, these organizations closely monitor and measure their adherence to these characteristics with the same intensity and skill they require of themselves for financial and operational performance.

The pursuit of the right organizational and people characteristics is no longer an undefined black box. Just as the development of magnetic resonance imaging (MRI) technology provided physicians with a previously unavailable visual image of organs and musculature, this framework gives companies a window into internal dynamics that have been only vaguely understood. Access to this knowledge can lead to sustained performance.

# 23 Shaping Up: The Delayered Look

## Ron Nicol

Even after all the job cuts of the past few years, many organizations are still out of shape—literally. They have too many layers, there are too many pay levels within those layers, and, not surprisingly, spans of control are too narrow. Companies are too lean in some places and too fat in others.

By *layers*, we mean the hierarchy of reporting relationships. *Levels* refer to pay grades. And *spans* refer to the number of direct reports. The costs to companies of being out of shape are enormous, particularly in terms of reaction time and decision making.

Why, then, are so many companies still out of shape? One reason is that belt-tightening (across-the-board layoffs and department closings), although fast and uncomplicated, is often a blunt and unfair instrument that does little to fix an organization's basic structure. At the other extreme, process redesign, which seeks to change the detail of organizational interactions, is a lengthy approach that often doesn't question whether something really should exist. "Value-based" cost reduction, which also focuses on process activities rather than the interaction of people, is another alternative, but it can miss the big opportunities and still doesn't improve decision making or responsiveness.

Focusing exclusively on delayering at the management level, on the other hand, speeds up both information flows and decision making. Moreover, with leaner managerial ranks and the focus on work rather than coordination, activities that don't deliver value get eliminated.

Jack Welch understood this when he took over at General Electric (GE). He inherited an organization that had at least 12 layers and an average span of control between 3 and 4. Imagine: on average, each manager had only 3 or 4 direct reports. Within a few years, there were only 6 layers at GE, and the average span of control was more than 10. It's clear now that Welch's "strategy" was focused on organization and human resources. Managers may be tired of hearing about the lessons they can learn from GE, but this is one they should remember.

Nonetheless, they would rather forget it. Delayering is certainly not a new idea, but it has been shelved for more complicated schemes because it is hard to let people go when you work directly with them or they are your friends' friends. It is much easier, or at least less personal, to order the elimination of frontline employees. Taking out layers of management, particularly middle management, requires discipline, a willingness to confront sacred cows, and a clear sense of where you want your company, division, or unit to go. Outsiders hesitate to offer help because flattening a steep organizational pyramid is an emotionally bruising process for everyone involved. If it is conducted mechanically or in a way that seems unfair or inconsistent, the delayering process can damage relationships across an organization.

## Mapping the Problem

So, how do you do this right? First, find out if you really have a problem. Conduct a detailed analysis of the layers, levels, and spans in your organization. The data exist in your company to help you assemble—within a few weeks—a "before" and "after" picture. You may be surprised by what you see.

One hypothetical large company, before delayering, had no fewer than 18 officers who were separated from the CEO by 4 reporting layers. Almost 40 percent of the company's managers were 8 or more layers deep, and more than 800 people were in reporting chains of 11 or 12 layers. (Imagine how fast decisions got made in this company.) What's more, middle management had the narrowest spans of control, not the top or bottom layers. This is typical. In most cases, the CEO is well aware of the top few layers, so the spans are usually good. And the bottom of the organization is lean as a result of traditional cost cutting. But the middle ranks of management seem to remain immune to shape-up efforts.

Assembling a picture like this allows you to see both the kind of organizational challenge you face and the value of reshaping the pyramid. In the company mentioned here, management decreased the layers from 12 to 8 and achieved savings of roughly 30 percent. If flattening the organization will produce savings of 10 percent or less, you don't have a big problem—at least not one worth solving with delayering. Just assign your managers to reduce costs in the course of their budget execution. But if your excess structure represents more than 10 percent of excess costs, then you need to consider a more formal process that will maintain morale and retain the right people.

Keep this reality in mind: any process that aims to restructure an organization by taking out significant numbers of people can't be executed without an iron will. That means CEO ownership of and commitment to a fact-based and transparent approach. There is no such thing as a covert reorganization. Treat your employees like adults and be clear about the what, the why, and the how of the delayering process.

Debate the issue with your top team and then establish some principles such as the following to guide the process:

- We are not a democracy—all decisions are subject to senior management's approval.
- Our commitments, once we agree on them, are set in stone.
- We will deal in an open and direct fashion on all issues.
- We will restructure to create competitive advantage.
- We will complete all organizational changes by a certain date.
- We will count cost reductions only when the costs are off the books.
- We will put together the best team (the lowest performers will have to leave).
- We will execute quickly without taking shortcuts that undermine success.
- We will use the same process and timing throughout the company.
- If we violate any of our principles, we will be required to change them.

# A Cascading Process

Organizations are geometric structures and therefore require a geometrically scalable process to redesign them. Senior executives who think they can redesign a major corporation over a weekend are fooling themselves, considering that everything two layers below them recedes into a fog. The best way to delayer an organization is for managers to participate in a cascading process. The people who are closest to the problems are best able to solve them, and when senior management sets the right example, others will follow. All this means that you start the delayering process at the top, not at the bottom.

One objection we hear to this approach is that it will take too long and reduce productivity because it increases uncertainty. On the contrary, well-communicated processes result in less disruption and better execution than blitzkrieg reorganizations, which rarely work.

Delayering is an honest, effective, and empowering way of reducing costs while speeding up decision making. The goal is to put the right people in place and let them make decisions about what is important. Delayering looks to the future, not just at the present. After getting the structure right, there are fewer "jump balls," less confusion over who follows up, increased responsiveness to customers, and, in general, cleaner ways of doing business.

Delayering's success rests on a couple of hypotheses. The first is that increased spans of control force managers to do their jobs differently. If you have just three or four direct reports, you will be tempted to meddle and micromanage. But if you have 15 reports, you have time to do only two things: communicate your goals and manage exceptions. Effective management requires trust in your reports and an ability to focus on the trouble spots. The second hypothesis is that breaking down hierarchy sets the stage for the formation of networks that cut across processes and functions and that these networks, properly engaged and motivated, are the key to superior performance.

Flattening the pyramid is just the first step, but arguably the toughest one, toward leaving a legacy of organizational readiness and agility—a legacy far more important than any particular strategy or market position.

# 24

# Getting More from Lean: Seven Success Factors

## Pascal Cotte, Adam Farber, Amyn Merchant, Petros Paranikas, Harold L. Sirkin, and Michael Zinser

**W**hen Toyota created its lean production system in the late 1950s—drawing on the thinking of Henry Ford and W. Edwards Deming—the Japanese company revolutionized auto manufacturing. Since then, lean techniques have moved far beyond the shop floor. Still, the principles of lean production remain the same: an integrated, end-to-end process viewpoint that combines the concepts of waste elimination, just-in-time inventory management, built-in quality, and worker engagement— supported by a cultural focus on problem solving and the use of tools such as *kaizen* (continuous improvement), *kanban* (ongoing replenishment), *poka-yoke* (error proofing), 5S (workplace organization), and value-stream mapping.

Despite the ongoing popularity of lean tools and techniques, however, we've seen a variety of outcomes in our work with major companies around the world. Toyota's success with lean is, of course, legendary. But what types of results are other companies getting from their lean initiatives? And what are companies with the best outcomes doing differently than their less successful peers? To find the answers, BCG conducted interviews with executives at a wide range of companies with varying degrees of lean experience. We then combined those insights with our own observations, gleaned from helping clients succeed in their lean initiatives.

# Different Definitions and Evolving Goals

The executives we spoke with defined *lean* in various ways: as continuous improvement, as a way to drive out waste or increase process efficiency, and as a means to better understand client needs. Underscoring this lack of consistency, one interviewee summed up the issue as follows: "The organization doesn't define lean because it doesn't understand lean."

In many cases, cost was the primary catalyst of lean efforts. But other drivers included the desire to increase productivity or efficiency, stimulate cultural change, achieve greater agility or flexibility, improve quality, and shorten cycle times.

Goals tended to be narrower. Many pointed to cultural change as the key outcome. One executive explained that "[lean] has to become part of our DNA, part of our daily activity." Others defined goals in terms of efficiency. Another executive noted, "Success is defined not by the amount of waste taken out of the system but by whether it's enabled researchers to do their jobs better." Few defined success in terms of cost savings alone.

Goals for lean initiatives have evolved, however. Today the primary focus is continuous improvement of processes and corporate capabilities, which leads to improved competitiveness and business results.

# It's Tough to Do Well

Most of the executives we spoke with said that lean programs are difficult or very difficult to implement. The reasons they gave varied. Some executives cited cultural resistance, lack of skills, or leadership issues. Others noted that their companies' processes aren't well understood or that their employees have trouble absorbing new strategies and methods. "People forget that their job is to serve the customer," observed one executive.

But despite initial difficulties, once a lean program has been successfully executed in one facility, rollouts to other facilities are generally successful as well, especially if word of mouth has been positive—success in one area can generate interest in other areas. Having a well-documented methodology and a process for sharing knowledge also helps pave the way for subsequent lean projects.

That said, our experience indicates that lean hasn't reached critical mass at many companies. This inability to truly embed lean and its principles may arise partly from the fact that few companies are making the necessary organizational changes—in roles and responsibilities, management structure, and teams.

# Seven Key Success Factors

Although some companies met their lean targets, others reported mixed results. So what does it take to achieve the greatest success? Our research revealed seven critical keys to success:

## Choose Strategic, Customer-centered Projects

Start by focusing on the customer, clearly defining goals that add value or address specific customer needs. Vague productivity or cost-cutting targets don't energize the hearts and minds of employees. But initiatives that are aligned with overall corporate strategy and focused on important issues related to customers can mobilize line management and cross-functional lean teams to work together more effectively. Moreover, there is a critical need to clarify and align the links among corporate strategy, annual operating objectives and incentives, and lean projects. Improved production efficiency or other incentive targets, for example, should not promote overproduction that leads to inventory pileups. Rather, incentives should reinforce the notion that production will take place only when parts are demanded by the next process (and, ultimately, by a customer).

## Think Big, but Start Small

Lean programs must be ambitious and far-reaching to drive real change. Think about the total value that the initiative can unlock. For instance, aim to transform your entire production system rather than settling for spot improvements. But start with small test projects that focus on the highest-priority areas. Use these pilots to refine new ways of working before rolling them out to the organization at large. To be clear, small simply means manageable in scope—not limited in terms of strategic importance or potential solutions. Besides being more feasible and manageable, smaller efforts are more focused, have clearer start and finish points, and allow teams to own a problem and optimize its solution. Success at smaller projects also builds momentum and positive word of mouth. After early wins, teams can roll out successful lean initiatives enterprise wide.

## Involve Everyone—from Top Managers to Line Workers

Managing change by involving people at all levels of the organization is critical to the success of any lean initiative. The direct involvement of everyone, from line management to supervisors to shop floor workers, makes available a great deal of knowledge and insight, creates company-wide enthusiasm and buy-in, and embeds lean principles and capabilities throughout the ranks. Although some lean initiatives are seen as too driven from the top, the reverse can also be true: lean is perceived as just a shop floor initiative with limited relevance for the rest of the organization and no buy-in from senior management. However, delivering value and results in one part of an organization can attract interest in lean initiatives and encourage their adoption elsewhere.

## Tailor Your Approach to Your Culture

Different cultures present different challenges, so companies should customize their approach accordingly. For instance, people in an entrepreneurial culture that rewards individual initiative may not welcome enterprise-wide programs and generic communications. A better approach is to use a "cascading" process in which managers tailor lean messaging and metrics to their groups. This increases buy-in and better addresses the specific objectives at different levels of the organization.

Similarly, a culture that prizes skilled individual contributors may not welcome team-based structures, yet teams are a basic tenet of the lean philosophy. This type of culture demands an employee-led, bottom-up approach that doesn't dampen creativity; a top-down mandate would likely backfire. Then there are companies with a strongly hierarchical culture and independent fiefdoms, and little standardization or sharing of knowledge. Here, lean programs must focus on breaking down silos and empowering employees. The first step is to promote cross-functional and cross-organizational understanding so that people begin to think more broadly. The key is for companies to strike a balance among employee empowerment, top-down mandates, and centralized execution and tracking—and the right balance depends on your culture.

## Assign Dedicated, Experienced Resources

By assigning dedicated, full-time people with deep knowledge of—and expertise in—lean principles, tools, and techniques, company leaders send a clear message throughout the organization that lean is a priority. That commitment greatly increases the odds of success. With these resources, lean programs gain traction more quickly and show results sooner, which helps build momentum and enthusiasm. These experienced people can take on the important role of teacher and coach during the ramp-up period and thereafter.

Although a centralized cadre of dedicated resources should kick-start a lean initiative, the ultimate goal must be to build lean capabilities in the workforce so that continuous improvement can happen without an outside catalyst. Over time, companies should migrate to line ownership of lean efforts. This will typically mean changing job descriptions and incentive systems.

## Use Metrics to Drive Progress

As a starting point, make sure that all metrics are tied to the overall strategic goals of the organization. The right set of metrics will help your lean teams focus on the right things and measure their progress. Unfortunately, too many companies either don't measure the results of their lean efforts or use the wrong set of metrics. For instance, a European industrial goods company used the 5S tool to create a cleaner, safer, more orderly production facility following the principles of sort, simplify, shine, standardize, and sustain. The improved work space should have led to productivity improvements, but whether it did or not may never be known for sure. The company failed to link its 5S activities to specific bottom-line targets. Absent the expectation of higher production rates, the operators may simply be taking longer coffee breaks now that their tasks take less time to complete.

BCG's research shows that time, financial impact, and behavior are the three factors that drive successful implementation. The best set of metrics tracks all three. Cost metrics are most commonly used, but on-time delivery, process speed, quality, safety, and morale can also be measured. Consider tracking behaviors as well—especially those that support new ways of working. The wrong behaviors, or falling back into old ways of doing things, can sabotage results.

## Communicate, Communicate, Communicate

A strong and ongoing communication plan speeds the adoption of lean principles, techniques, and tools. It's also important for top management to maintain its visibility and create a continuous feedback loop. Be sure to tailor, monitor, assess, and adjust communications as needed. Face-to-face gatherings—such as town hall, breakfast, and lunchtime meetings—are especially effective. Performance scorecards are another good way to emphasize lean goals and demonstrate progress. Written communications such as newsletters and e-mails are also good channels for sharing information and updates. And be sure to celebrate and reward success.

■ ■ ■

Despite the enduring popularity of lean principles, tools, and techniques, few organizations have come close to achieving the success of Toyota and its lean production system. For most companies, the ideal of an unwaveringly customer-focused and engaged workforce aligned around common principles and practices is just that—an ideal, and an elusive one at that. But by following these seven guidelines while building and sharing knowledge over time, companies can capitalize on the truly transformational power of lean.

# 25

# The Demand-Driven Supply Chain

## John Budd, Claudio Knizek, and Bob Tevelson

A true demand-driven supply chain (DDSC) has always been the Holy Grail of operations managers around the world. Even when forecasts are finely tuned, an unexpected spike or drop in demand can wreak havoc on production schedules, leading to problems such as stock-outs and lost sales; inventory pileups, markdowns, and write-offs; poor capacity utilization; and declining service levels. Today, these margin-sappers are increasingly avoidable thanks to recent advances in technology that finally can make the DDSC a reality.

The advantages are substantial. According to research in 2012 by BCG, some companies with advanced DDSCs carry 33 percent less inventory, improve their delivery performance by 20 percent, and reduce supply chain costs dramatically. DDSCs are becoming even more critical as supply chains become more global and complex and as new challenges emerge.

But few companies wholly understand the profound changes they must make to their organizations to reap the full benefits of a supply chain that is truly driven by demand.

## What Is a DDSC?

A DDSC offers real-time information on current demand and inventory levels to all supply chain participants so that they can react quickly and effectively—by revising forecasts given to their own suppliers, for instance, or by altering production or distribution plans—when unexpected changes arise. This allows companies to optimize planning, procurement, production, inventory replenishment, and order delivery for better service, higher sales, and lower costs overall.

Supply and demand are easily matched if demand is steady over time with no change in volume or mix. As soon as demand changes, however, a company must adjust the supply levels accordingly at each step of the supply chain. But given the lag time before changes in demand are detected at various points along the chain, their effects are often amplified when they hit, leading to inventory shortages or pileups. Product promotions—which are becoming increasingly important to retailers—further exacerbate the problem by altering demand. Companies then tend to overcompensate by slowing down or speeding up production lines, which can cause inventory levels to fluctuate wildly. This whipsaw effect is costly and inefficient for all participants.

The goal of a DDSC is to tightly align and coordinate all players across the supply chain. With a true DDSC, companies can become more responsive to changing market conditions, minimize stock-outs and lost sales, maintain lower inventory levels, sharply reduce the costs of expediting orders, and make far better use of their operating assets.

## Evolving Capabilities

The concept of a DDSC is not new, of course. Toyota's demand-driven *kanban* system is a key part of its just-in-time (JIT) production system. But recent industry and technology changes are driving the DDSC evolution forward. In the past, retailers were reluctant to share real-time point-of-sale (POS) data with their suppliers. Now, many companies (including Walmart) provide that information, because they recognize that partnering with suppliers can reduce stock-outs, improve service levels, and boost overall sales and customer satisfaction. Moreover, dramatic improvements in processing speed and computing power can support the rapid, data-intensive processes underlying a DDSC. External storage capabilities—once unavailable or cost-prohibitive—are now virtually unlimited through external platforms and cloud-based systems. Taken together, these developments are making the DDSC a reality.

Real-time visibility into demand and supply levels allows for unprecedented supply chain performance. Inventory can be reduced throughout the system without hurting service levels. In fact, by lowering costs and improving forecasting accuracy, DDSCs benefit all supply chain participants: suppliers, manufacturers, retailers, and consumers.

# Six Success Factors

Despite the advances in technology and the growing willingness among supply chain players to share information, creating a DDSC is far from a plug-and-play exercise. Old processes, structures, and behaviors can hinder true change and sharply limit results. Getting all supply chain participants committed and involved is another challenge. Unfortunately, partial adoption leads to only partial benefits. By evaluating the experiences of leading companies that have implemented true DDSCs—and achieved major benefits—we've identified six critical success factors.

## Set Up the Right Technology Infrastructure

Information is integral to DDSCs. This is why a fast data-exchange platform that can share inventory data in real time among all participants is the backbone of any implementation. A DDSC also requires strong processing capabilities to manage the high volume of data, a secure and trusted source of data storage, a simple user interface, and a scalable architecture that is flexible and robust enough to incorporate needed changes as they arise. Finally, the system must support operations; close coordination is needed between the IT and supply chain functions to select and roll out the best tools.

## Revisit Data Collection and Analysis

Most companies trying to implement a DDSC will need to collect and share data on inventory levels more frequently and increase the degree of data granularity they analyze. Effective DDSCs typically require detailed information on inventory levels at plants, as well as SKU-level detail on items in stores, on warehouse shelves, and in distribution centers. Because the exact volume of on-shelf SKUs is hard to measure in a non-DDSC environment, it may need to be deduced on the basis of shipments to a store minus customer sales. It also may be necessary to remap customer information to make it more usable.

## Rethink Operations

The classic elements of flexible manufacturing—such as short changeover times, access to temporary labor and external capacity, and the ability to produce small batches cost-effectively—make it easier to respond quickly to spikes and dips in demand, a key aspect of DDSC success. Companies should analyze their production capabilities and remove any obstacles that hinder agility. Otherwise, excess inventory will be needed as a cushion. Flexible logistics are also critical. Companies need to rethink delivery planning and scheduling so that logistics are optimized overall. The key is to analyze your specific situation and delivery targets and capitalize on the greater visibility you have into inventory levels throughout the supply chain.

Finally, procurement must change how it operates by finding flexible, highly responsive suppliers to work with and by recalculating inventory "safety cushions" and ordering habits.

## Align Metrics and Incentives

The ultimate goal of a DDSC is to ensure the best service at the lowest cost. To this end, the performance targets and incentives of all supply chain players must be aligned so that everyone is marching in the same direction. Only with transparency and common incentives can end-to-end economics be optimized. With the proper metrics, a company can constantly benchmark its supply chain performance and identify gaps and inefficiencies that can be addressed in partnership with suppliers. The most common measurements of DDSC success are reductions in inventory levels, working capital, and stock-outs; faster and more accurate order fulfillment; and higher rates of customer satisfaction. Supplier contracts must be modified to guarantee that decisions made to improve the performance of the supply chain as a whole don't hurt individual parties.

## Manage the Cost and Service Trade-offs

Before getting too lean, be clear on the trade-offs of maintaining lower inventory levels. Segmenting products according to specific characteristics can reveal where the benefits of a DDSC would offset the added costs. These categories typically include high-margin products, high-tech or other products with a high cost of obsolescence, food or other perishables for which freshness is critical, products with highly variable demand, and products with rapid inventory turnover. Segmenting customer accounts on the basis of purchase volume and profitability can also reveal where higher service levels could pay off.

The key is being able to quantify the end-to-end costs and benefits of supply chain decisions. Because companies often lack the ability to perform these complex analytics, many default to pure cost reductions without considering the potentially negative impact on revenue or service. A DDSC promotes greater visibility into the bottom-line impact of higher service levels, greater manufacturing flexibility, and lower inventory levels across the supply chain.

### Change the Organization and Employees' Behavior

Encouraging a supplier's employees to take a more proactive role—such as suggesting a larger or smaller order if consumption data show the need—is one challenge. Another is persuading workers to move from a manual order fulfillment process to an automated one. A DDSC also requires cross-functional coordination, because silo-based decision making rarely considers the end-to-end impact of various actions. But perhaps the greatest behavioral challenge for all DDSC participants is learning to trust one another. For instance, retailers must be willing to share their data and trust that suppliers will deliver the right merchandise at the right time. Consumer goods manufacturers must trust that retail buyers will reward their performance—and that closer alignment will lead to greater benefits for all.

## Benefits of a DDSC

Only companies that truly understand the profound changes they must make to their organizations will reap the full benefits of a DDSC—and achieve a sustainable advantage in today's fiercely competitive global economy.

# 26 Pricing Fluency

## Sylvain Duranton, Jean-Manuel Izaret, and Rich Hutchinson

Pricing is the language of business. Through pricing, companies tell customers which products have the greatest value or when costs have gone up. Through pricing, companies can "ask" customers to change their behavior. As with all languages, fluency matters in pricing. Organizations fluent in pricing can persuade their customers to pay a little more or to buy a little more. Consequently, they routinely earn 1 to 3 percent more in revenue than their competitors do—an advantage that falls straight to their bottom line.

Fluency in the language of pricing—as in any other language—requires discipline. Yet it is not managed as a discipline in most organizations. Many people *touch* pricing, but no one *owns* it. Pricing decisions, expertise, and information are fragmented across a company's regions, business units, and functions.

Some organizations recognize this language barrier in pricing and try to address it. But too often they resort to narrowly focused initiatives—one-off pricing projects that provide only superficial results. To switch metaphors momentarily, that's like relying on a crash diet for a quick—and short-lived—fix when a lifelong regimen of exercise and discipline is needed to achieve sustainable goals.

One of BCG's clients learned this the hard way. Convinced that the sales force was giving away too much in price negotiations in order to capture volume, this company undertook a pricing project in which it analyzed accounts, identified opportunities to raise prices, and provided a new set of pricing guidelines. The resulting profit boost was quick and significant. Unfortunately, a short while later, the company found itself back in its original position and in need of another pricing remedy. The problem resurfaced because the leaders of the sales force continued to drive a culture that emphasized volume, rather than profitability. Without changing its incentives, processes, and people, the company could not achieve sustainable impact from pricing improvements.

Pricing is multifaceted and requires significant change management to hardwire new approaches. The effort will take most organizations more than 12 to 18 months and require a comprehensive program, rather than a single project. Yet changing pricing strategy can be done in stages that yield significant value along the way. Following is a brief description of the program we have found that organizations fluent in pricing use to become competitively advantaged.

# A Master Program for Pricing

A comprehensive pricing program for an entire organization focuses on two clear goals: improving the pricing model through better policies on how prices are set and improving the pricing platform used to implement those policies throughout the organization.

## Improving the Pricing Model

Companies have three types of lever for pricing improvement:

- *Tactical levers.* These offer quick, no-risk fixes for pricing policies and anomalies. Solutions might include tightening the terms of payment, setting strict guardrails such as minimum profitability levels, increasing prices on products or product features that have low visibility, and monetizing giveaways (such as freight and service). Tactical levers can be decided upon quickly and rolled out for immediate impact.
- *Strategic changes in price levels.* These involve moving prices on key items up or down—as much as 5 percent or more—by changing list prices or redefining the terms of trade promotion. Such actions are

not to be taken lightly. To predict how customers or consumers will react, companies considering strategic price-level changes must make extensive use of analytic tools, such as conjoint analysis, price elasticity measures, profit parabolas, and in-depth customer interviews. These changes also require companies to use game theory and industry structure analysis to predict how competitors will respond. The investigation phase takes some time, but once a decision is made, implementation is fast—and so are results.

- *Fundamental reshaping of pricing schemes.* This is a step change that requires a company to creatively rethink its overall pricing structure. It could lead to overhauling the product lineup or completely rebuilding the discount structure. It might also involve pricing-model innovations such as pricing for performance, subscription pricing, or dynamic pricing, which is pegged to an external variable, such as time of day. (In some vending machines, for example, the price of the products varies from the morning to the afternoon.) These types of changes require managers to carefully segment their customers and opportunities. Piloting and testing are crucial before pricing schemes are rolled out; therefore, implementation takes longer than for other, less complex moves.

## Improving the Pricing Platform

In this cyclical effort, the company reviews its progress and redesigns its processes when necessary. It encompasses the following dimensions:

- *Roles and responsibilities of stakeholders.* Actions in pricing will depend on a company's market and how the company is structured to serve it. Companies with fragmented customer bases, for example, should enable their field representatives to make informed pricing decisions by supplying them with effective tools. By contrast, business-to-business companies that focus on a few megadeals might appoint a "pricing czar" to manage price negotiations. Most companies lack sufficient pricing resources and would benefit from creating a central pricing support team to raise the visibility of pricing positions at the business unit level and to ensure that all key functions have input into pricing policy and final decisions.

- *Market intelligence.* Too often, managers are forced to make decisions on the basis of incomplete or inaccurate information, anecdotes, or even gut instinct. Establishing a clear process for collecting, analyzing, and interpreting market data is critical. Heavy industry players, for example, have created significant value by improving their ability to forecast market cycles and adjusting their price levels accordingly.

- *Business processes.* Surprising as it may seem, very few companies have hardwired pricing into their key business processes. Without adequate lines of reporting and fine-tuned key performance indicators (KPIs), companies can't use information to drive better forecasting and decisions.

- *Human resources.* Learning any language requires training by experts, and pricing is no different. Companies should be open to recruiting new expertise in pricing from outside the organization. For example, to prepare for auctions organized by large original equipment manufacturers (OEMs), an electronics manufacturer invested in a training program that taught the sales force game theory and had them role-play auction bidding. The training generated pricing rewards that totaled 10 times the program's cost.

- *Information technology.* We've found that the best-performing companies out-invest their competitors in tools and technology to support stakeholders in pricing. For example, an industrial goods company purchased a tool that helped it set the best prices by determining how much each product reduced labor costs for individual customers. The tool resulted in an immediate hike in profits and a big boost to the sales team's morale.

- *Incentives and compensation.* General managers and sales teams are more likely to be given incentives for increasing volume and earnings before interest, taxes, depreciation, and amortization (EBITDA) than they are for meeting explicit price realization targets. Yet promoting price realization can be a powerful lever. A North American company, for example, introduced price realization targets and publicized individual sales reps' performance on a monthly basis. It didn't take long to see the company's overall price performance increase by more than one percentage point, thanks to increased awareness and healthy peer pressure.

# Implementing the Master Plan for Long-term Success

So far so good. The goals are clear, as are plans for tactics, levers, and tools. But how do those who are fluent at pricing get a program started and then keep it going? All worthwhile transformations take time and effort: it's a several-stage process—albeit with rewards along the way.

We have found that effective programs consist of five phases, which can be piloted in selected business units that have high potential for success and then rolled out in waves to other units. The program begins by sizing the prize and developing a road map for pricing improvements. The next two phases, conducted in parallel, involve optimizing price levels to eliminate price leaks and adjust high-stakes price points, as well as redesigning processes and the organization to fill key positions and implement decision-making bodies, KPIs, and incentives, among other steps. In the final two phases, we return to the pricing model to simultaneously align the pricing structure with value (creating a new product lineup or pricing scheme, for example) and hardwire the new pricing platform using best practices and tools.

# Support for the Journey

Building a foundation for pricing fluency throughout the organization is a transformational effort that requires careful change management. Sales teams and business unit management teams will need to revise the very "grammar" that guides their business practices—and it will take experience and hard work to get it right. The following principles have, in our experience, proved useful for creating the desired momentum, accelerating implementation, and keeping the effort running smoothly:

- *Invest heavily in early pilots to demonstrate success.* For instance, a country manager for an animal health products company enrolled in the corporate pricing program and then took it upon himself to organize field tests with vets and conduct workshops to train sales reps. As a result, implementation of the pricing program went faster and more smoothly in his country than it had in any other market.

- *Plan for implementation from the first day and recognize that time is money.* To avoid missing important opportunities, the company should synchronize the new program's road map with the schedule of price negotiations with customers. To make sure everyone is prepared, the company should appoint pricing responsibilities within the first week of starting. And to build a results-driven momentum, it should aim to announce quick hits within three months.

- *Mobilize a central expert team.* High-stakes pricing decisions often require pricing expertise beyond the capabilities of the business units. The risk of failure should therefore be mitigated through the use of sophisticated tools, such as elasticity assessment and game theory. The central team should provide this support, as well as help monitor progress, track impact, develop tools, and communicate with other functions.

- *Actively manage the human resources agenda.* Companies often move too slowly and tentatively to renegotiate sales force incentives and make key appointments effectively. Sometimes it's best to rip the bandage off quickly—communicate the difficult news and get on with the program.

- *Involve the legal department early in the process.* Too often, the legal department is brought in only at the end of a pricing program to green-light final proposals. To prioritize opportunities for legally complex pricing issues, it is best for companies to seek help from legal experts early on.

■ ■ ■

Establishing an organization's fluency in pricing doesn't end with the initial effort. Once well-run pricing processes are in place, best-practice companies adopt an agenda of continuous improvement. They actively manage the new pricing ideas in their "innovation pipelines," focus on defensible competitive advantage, and sustain a price premium of 2 to 3 percent over competitors. And because mastery of the grammar, vocabulary, and syntax of pricing is a capability difficult to imitate, achieving fluency in pricing can provide sustainable competitive advantage long into the future.

# 27

# The IT Organization of the Future

## Jeanne W. Ross, Stephanie L. Woerner, Stuart Scantlebury, and Cynthia M. Beath

A s companies build digitized process platforms to replace large port-folios of isolated, and often redundant, systems and processes, they are fundamentally transforming the business.[1] But business transformation demands leadership. Where does that leadership come from?

This question featured prominently in a survey of chief information officers (CIOs) conducted by the MIT Sloan School of Management's Center for Information Systems Research (MIT CISR) and BCG. One of the survey's key findings was that CIOs believe that business leaders are *not* positioned to lead IT-enabled business transformations.

If business leaders are not able to drive the digitization of business processes, the need for IT to do so becomes acute. And the rewards for IT organizations that fill this role, as well as the benefits to their companies, are sizable. Indeed, CIOs of companies that are building and leveraging digitized process platforms are much more likely to describe the IT unit's

---

BCG is a patron of the MIT Center for Information Systems Research, which published the results of this research in a CISR Research Briefing by the same title in 2010.
[1]We define a digitized process platform as a coherent set of business processes, along with supporting technology, applications, and data.

role as "business change driver" rather than "order taker."[2] What characterizes these IT organizations—the ones that are not just supporting transformation but driving it? And what benefits have they realized?

## Why Should the IT Unit Drive Business Change?

The benefits to companies in which the IT unit acts as a change driver—rather than as an order taker—are substantial. According to our survey, such companies spend a smaller percentage of their IT budget running—as opposed to building—systems. The spending ratio is important because we found that companies that apportion more of their IT spending to new initiatives, rather than to sustaining initiatives, had a significantly higher overall return on assets and higher net margins relative to their competitors.

In addition, IT units that act as change drivers enjoy faster realization of the business benefits from new systems. On average, business change drivers reported an interval of nine months between the project's start date and the delivery of business value. This is 33 percent faster than in companies where IT's role is that of an order taker.

Finally, scores on IT employee satisfaction surveys are higher in business change–driving IT units. The enhanced satisfaction translates into recruitment advantages.

## Adopting the Mind-Set of a Business Change Driver

As part of a company's transition to greater digitization, IT staff must shed an order-taking mentality and work to identify ways in which they can contribute to business success. One CIO we interviewed is pushing this shift by reminding both the business and IT people that they wear the same company badge and thus have shared goals.

---

[2]We relied on respondents' descriptions of their architecture maturity to assess whether IT was building a digitized platform. For more information, see Jeanne W. Ross, "Maturity Matters: How Firms Generate Value from Enterprise Architecture," *MIT Sloan CISR Research Briefing*, IV, no. 2B (July 2004, revised February 2006). MIT Sloan CISR working papers and research briefings are available for download at http://cisr.mit.edu.

Chris Perretta, CIO of State Street, told us, "I think the real challenge is whether the job I'm doing is relevant to the things that the CEO really cares about. For instance, I know that our CEO wants to extend lean, which is business process design, throughout the whole organization. If I incorporate business process design into the IT function, then I position the IT organization in a leadership role. If I retreat, then I am simply a service provider, and we waste a lot of knowledge capital."

Frank Luijckx, the Dow Chemical Company's director of business services and environment, health, and safety for India, the Middle East, and Africa, told us that the CIOs in his company have been very active in "shaping the company's future." He noted, "The CIOs have been very close to the transformation of the company—they have enabled it, probably because they have the most structured approach to it. I think leadership in information systems is *increasingly* important. The technology is *decreasingly* important." He also said that the company does not do IT projects anymore; rather, it does projects for the company. In a supply chain project, for example, the people who are skilled at doing the IT part and the people who do major product and facilities engineering all work together in one big project organization. According to Luijckx, "Our project support center is no longer called the IT Project Support Center. It's broader, and we continue to pull more and more functions into it."

Luijckx believes that the business leaders may have forgotten what it takes to run a business, because so much is automated in the background. He told us, "We increasingly find that we need to reeducate the business leaders about the engine on which they rely on a daily basis."

A CIO for a manufacturing company told us, "I think the boundaries of IT are expanding. What we have done well up till now, which is all of the basic plumbing—operations, security, controls, disaster recovery, continuity, and so forth—doesn't stop being important. As a matter of fact, as you do those things better, you can move up the value pyramid in IT. We started with standardizing and delivering infrastructure and operations services. Then we moved to shared applications, and we helped the business get the most value from them. Now it's really about expanding into process leadership. We went from being a service provider and a process *participant* to being a process *leader*, mainly because business processes are increasingly built into the applications. Everything is integrated, so IT has a greater impact on the defining and transforming of processes through the use of technology."

Recently, this CIO said that his IT organization established the role of chief business process officer, responsible for optimizing business processes—both general processes, such as an internally developed proprietary process that is similar to Lean Six Sigma, and specific end-to-end processes, such as hire to retire, bench to plan, order to cash, make to ship, and account to report. The people in his area now have a much higher level of business acumen than was previously typical in the company's IT unit.

## Developing the Capabilities Necessary to Drive Business Change

Securing the right talent to realize the IT organization's ambitions is a critical challenge. In particular, many CIOs struggle to hire or develop strong IT architects, business process engineers, and business relationship managers. However, a number of CIOs noted that domain knowledge and existing relationships with the business areas that IT serves were extremely valuable attributes for such roles. As a result, these CIOs believe that it makes far more sense to develop talent internally than to scour the marketplace.

But developing such talent isn't easy. A number of CIOs said that they had tried to transform good developers into IT architects, only to find that the talents intrinsic to good developers do not necessarily make for good architects. One CIO said that she could identify developers who would make good architects by the consistency with which they asked questions about how their projects linked to other projects.

One popular development technique is to recruit people into the IT organization from the business functions—especially people with project or program management or technology management expertise. Said Luijckx of Dow Chemical, "I think IT professionals are going to have to be more rounded individuals. They probably will come out of the business and go back to the business, and come out of the [IT] function and go back to the [IT] function." Almost 78 percent of the CIOs who described their IT organizations as business change drivers said that their organization used this approach.

The CIO of a manufacturing company, for example, told us, "Our head of sales systems for North America is someone who had been an outstanding technical program manager and happened to be part of the sales force. We recruited him into the IT organization, and he brought his business experience and acumen, along with his technical project leadership. We've done the same thing in some of our supply chain areas, where we've taken folks out of the supply chain who were strong project and program managers and made them heads of these application areas in the IT organization."

Business change–driving IT organizations also rely on formalized talent management. Most have defined multiple career paths—such as general management, technology expertise, and project management—and have some type of multiyear IT workforce development plan. Furthermore, almost all of these organizations use resource pools, centers of excellence, and competency centers to some extent. Several CIOs said that their organizations have instituted carefully developed job families and career ladders, specifying the skills and learning required for each employee to advance along a path that appeals to the individual and that addresses the company's emerging IT staff needs.

# Engaging Business Leaders

A litany of failed enterprise resource planning (ERP), customer relationship management (CRM), and other technology-inspired initiatives bear witness to the limitations of IT leadership. If business leaders do not share ownership of both the implementation process and the outcomes associated with digitization efforts, the IT unit cannot bring about a transformation.

Given that they cannot "go it alone," IT leaders are working to engage business leaders in the types of visioning exercises, governance processes, and business change efforts needed for effective digitization. CIOs are encouraging engagement by delivering IT services efficiently and effectively. These efforts build credibility and trust. IT organizations that are not providing excellent traditional IT services (such as infrastructure, applications, and help desk services) are rarely asked to expand their service offerings into business process design, product design, business transformation program leadership, business strategy, and other activities that business change–driving IT organizations often take on.

Beyond building credibility, CIOs in companies where IT drives change spend a great deal of time talking with their colleagues on the business side about business opportunities that *might* involve IT. These discussions afford CIOs some insight into how IT can make a difference.

If a CIO cannot generate widespread agreement among business executives on the desirability of a vision and the IT-enabled business changes it requires, any efforts to increase business process digitization will constitute a lonely, and ultimately disastrous, journey. But CIOs who create demand for increased business process digitization are likely to create critical leadership roles for themselves—and potentially a powerful competitive advantage for their companies.

# VII

# Value-Driven

Certain principles of management and leadership are timeless and enduring. One principle in particular is as old as commerce itself: the mandate to create value. Organizations that don't deliver value cannot last. Value is both an objective measure and the engine of future growth. It is what attracts shareholders and rewards them. And it is the currency for attracting and retaining the best people. It is not the only objective function and is not always particularly inspiring. But without it, nothing else is viable in the long term.

The quest to create value for our clients is at the very center of what has driven BCG since its founding. In this section, we open with a chapter on where it all started for us: with founder Bruce Henderson's assessment of the experience curve he pioneered, "The Experience Curve Reviewed." He wrote his original *Perspective* on the topic in 1966, and it's no exaggeration to say it changed the business world. It was the first systematic approach to business strategy and literally spawned a new management discipline. It was also the genesis of strategy consulting as an industry.

For Henderson, the experience curve was emblematic of his fundamental desire to search out the underlying truth, based on a unique blend of empirical facts, experience, and insight. With the experience curve, he observed something that now is widely understood as a general principle yet had never before been articulated: that every doubling of experience (cumulative production volume) results in a predictable decrease in unit costs. Built on the economic principle of the learning curve, Henderson's insight unleashed a focus on market share and market leadership. There were massive implications for everything from pricing to mergers and acquisitions.

In 1976, Henderson published the first version of the next chapter in this section, "The Rule of Three and Four: A BCG Classic Revisited," which extended his thinking on experience curve analysis. His argument was seemingly simple but as profound as the experience curve itself: that in a stable, competitive environment there would be three generalist players, with the market leader having roughly four times the relative share of the third player. Relative profitability would also accrue to the leader. The quest for industry leadership was unleashed with a fury. In 2012, we set out to test the durability of this concept. The results were revealing. The rule has stood the test of time quite well across many stable industries. In industries with greater volatility, however, the more adaptive approaches defined earlier in this book are more appropriate.

Fifty years after Henderson founded BCG and began his prolific thinking and writing, the quest for value continues. In our next two chapters, we fast-forward to a more modern perspective. In Chapter 30, "The CEO as Investor," we make the case for taking a long-term ownership approach to the business and contend that aligning the strategic and investment agendas of a company is absolutely essential for long-term value creation. We build on these ideas in Chapter 31, "Focusing Corporate Strategy on Value Creation." Here we explain the ways in which real-world corporate strategy is often not in fact sufficiently focused on value creation and describe what to do about it.

Next we consider postmerger integration (PMI), an activity that can create—but often destroys—significant value. In Chapter 32, "Powering Up for Postmerger Integration," we describe how best-practice design and execution of an integration, tailored according to the strategic intent of the merger, can beat the odds and create significant value.

Finally, we look at value creation in family businesses. Large, successful family-run firms, it turns out, are typically managed differently than are nonfamily companies. They tend to focus on *resilience* rather than short-term performance—a tack that has helped them weather volatile times and generate superior long-term financial results. Chapter 33, "Resilience: Lessons from Family Businesses," describes this orientation and highlights defining elements, including how these companies approach capital expenditures, debt levels, acquisitions, international diversification, and talent retention.

# 28

# The Experience Curve Reviewed

## Bruce Henderson

*As the 1960s unfolded, fattish, complacent American companies found themselves confronted with competition from unexpected quarters—foreign manufacturers, smaller upstart enterprises in their own backyard. What was going on? What to do about it? The Boston Consulting Group had the answer to both questions in the form of the experience curve. The experience curve was, simply, the single most important concept in launching the strategy revolution...*

*While its basic truths are so ingrained today that we take them as eternal and unchanging laws of nature—"everyone knows that"—when first proclaimed, they were electrifying: businesses should expect their costs to decline systematically, at a rate that can be accurately predicted.*

—Walter Kiechel III, in *The Lords of Strategy:*
*The Secret Intellectual History*
*of the New Corporate World*[1]

**E**xperience curve is the name applied in 1966 to overall cost behavior by BCG. The name was selected to distinguish this phenomenon from the well-known and well-documented learning curve effect. The two are related but quite different. In this article, originally published in 1973, BCG's Bruce Henderson reviews the experience curve concept and describes its enduring impact on corporate strategy.

■ ■ ■

---

[1]Walter Kiechel, *The Lords of Strategy: The Secret Intellectual History of the New Corporate World* (Boston: Harvard Business Press, 2010).

It has been known for many years that labor hours per unit decline on repetitive tasks. This effect was particularly easy to observe in such things as aircraft production in wartime. The rate of labor decrease was characteristically approximately 10 to 15 percent per doubling of experience. This expectation has long been a part of military contracting.

The so-called learning curve effect apparently had somewhat limited application, however. It applied only to direct labor. Unless the job changed, this meant *the time required* to obtain a given cost decline tended to double each cycle of experience. This masked the far-reaching implication of the possibilities of job element management with volume changes.

BCG's first effort to formulate the experience curve concept was an attempt to explain cost behavior over time in a process industry. Long-continued successful cost reduction by the client had resulted only in its survival as a marginal competitor. The correlation between competitive profitability and market share was strikingly apparent. The pattern of the learning curve was an attractive initial hypothesis to explain this. The client was chasing its larger competitors down the cost curve.

Later, a study of the cost of television components showed striking differences in the rate of cost improvement between monochrome parts and color parts. This was difficult to explain given that the same factory, the same labor, and the same processes were involved at the same time. Again the idea of progress down a cost curve provided a plausible hypothesis.

Semiconductors provided the evidence on which to build the experience curve concept itself. The wide variety of semiconductors offered a chance to compare differing growth rates and price decline rates in a similar environment. Price data supplied by the Electronic Industries Association were compared with accumulated industry volume. Two distinct patterns emerged.

In one pattern, prices, in current dollars, remained constant for long periods and then began a relatively steep and long continued decline in constant dollars. In the other pattern, prices, in constant dollars, declined steadily at a constant rate of about 25 percent each time accumulated experience doubled. That was the experience curve. That was 1966.

Work with clients since 1966 has proved the universality of the experience curve relationships. A real understanding, however, required many, many client assignments.

Application of the experience curve to problem solving and policy determination discloses many technical questions:

- What is an appropriate unit of experience where the product itself changes too? The transport airplane is an example.
- What is the relationship between experience effects on similar but different products such as semiconductors?
- How are technological changes integrated into experience effects?
- What effect does capital investment intensity have?
- Does the same effect appear in overhead and marketing functions?

Accounting data are frequently misleading for cost analysis. The choice of treatment as expense versus capital can distort apparent cost change.

Over time, the experience curve has become recognized as essentially a pattern of cash flow. The average cost is by definition the total expenditure divided by the total output. The unit cost is the rate of change in that ratio. Projection of this relationship is frequently both simpler and more accurate for cost forecasting than even the most elaborate conventional accounting analysis.

Understanding of the underlying causes of the experience curve is still imperfect. The effect itself is beyond question. It is so universal that its absence is almost a warning of mismanagement or misunderstanding. Yet the basic mechanism that produces the experience curve effect is still to be adequately explained. (The same thing is true of gravitation.)

It can be observed that if high return-on-investment thresholds are used to limit capital investment, then costs do not decline as expected.

It can also be observed that extensive substitution of cost elements and exchange of labor for capital is characteristic of progress down a cost experience curve.

The experience curve is a contradiction of some of the most basic assumptions of classic economic theory. All economics assumes that there is a finite minimum cost that is a function of scale. This is usually stated in terms of all cost-volume curves being either L- or U-shaped. It is not true except for a moment in time.

The whole concept of a free enterprise competitive equilibrium assumes that all competitors can achieve comparable costs at volumes much less than pro rata shares of market. That is not true either.

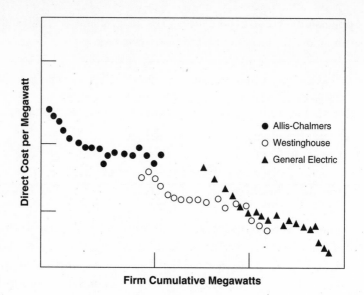

**Firm Cumulative Megawatts**

Note: Each dot represents a year. The horizontal scale is the total cumulative output of the specific firm involved to that year.

**FIGURE 28.1** Direct Costs per Megawatt Steam Turbine Generators, 1946–1963
Source: Confidential information from Allis-Chalmers, Westinghouse, and General Electric made available in public records as the result of antitrust litigation.

Our entire concept of competition, antitrust, and non-monopolistic free enterprise is based on a fallacy if the experience curve effect is true.

The experience curve effect can be observed and measured in any business, any industry, any cost element, anywhere. Figure 28.1 shows the effect in steam turbine generators.

Most of the history of insight into the experience curve effect and its significance is still to be written.

# The Rule of Three and Four: A BCG Classic Revisited

## Martin Reeves, Michael Deimler, George Stalk, Jr., and Filippo L. Scognamiglio Pasini

In "The Rule of Three and Four," written in 1976, Bruce Henderson put forth an intriguing hypothesis about the evolution of industry structure and leadership. He posited that a "stable, competitive" industry will never have more than three significant competitors. Moreover, that industry structure will find equilibrium when the market shares of the three companies reach a ratio of approximately 4:2:1.

Henderson noted that his observation had yet to be validated by rigorous analysis. But it did seem to map closely with the then-current structures of a wide range of industries, from automobiles to soft drinks. He believed that even if the hypothesis were only approximately true, it would have significant implications for businesses.

Fast-forward to 2012. Has the rule of three and four held? If so, to what degree? Does it merit the attention of today's decision makers? Our analysis yielded compelling findings.

The authors thank Can Uslay, Assistant Professor of Supply Chain Management & Marketing Sciences, Rutgers Business School; Ekaterina Karniouchina, Assistant Professor of Marketing, Chapman University; and Ayça Altintig, Assistant Professor of Finance, Claremont Graduate University, for their collaboration.

# Testing the Rule of Three and Four

To test Henderson's theory, the BCG Strategy Institute, working in collaboration with academics from Chapman, Claremont, and Rutgers Universities, studied industry data from more than 10,000 companies dating back to 1975. Our analysis allows us to confirm that Henderson's hypothesis was indeed valid when he conceived it: it accurately described the market share structures current at the time and trends in a wide range of industries. We can also confirm that the rule of three and four has remained a predictor of the evolution of industry structures in "stable, competitive" industries over the decades, with the caveat that many industries have experienced a departure from such stable conditions.

To facilitate our analysis, we divided companies into two categories: those with market shares of more than 10 percent (generalists) and those with shares of 10 percent or less. The prevalence of industries with no more than three generalists (the "three" part of Henderson's rule) was striking. From 1976 through 2009, industries with one, two, or three generalists ranged from 72 percent to 85 percent and averaged 78 percent. The most common industry structure throughout the period was the three-generalist configuration, which prevailed in 13 of those 34 years and was the second-most common in 20 out of 34 years.

Industries with three-generalist structures have also proved the most profitable for industry participants, with an average return on assets a full 2.5 percentage points higher than in industries with four, five, or six generalists. In addition, three- and two-generalist configurations appear to have the greatest stability and to act as the strongest "basins of attraction"— that is, more companies gravitate toward these structures every year than toward any other (Figure 29.1).

Our study also confirmed the "four" part of Henderson's rule—the 4:2:1 market-share ratio that tends to characterize equilibrium in these industries. We found that, over the period studied, the top players in nearly 60 percent of industries with three-generalist structures had relative market shares of $1.5\times$ to $2.5\times$, reasonably close to Henderson's prediction of $2.0\times$. And we confirmed that today, the 4:2:1 relationship remains the most prevalent among industries led by three generalists.

Current examples of the rule of three and four are easy to find. The U.S. rental car industry is one. In 2006, four competitors—Avis, Enterprise Holdings, Hertz, and Vanguard Car Rental—had market shares exceeding

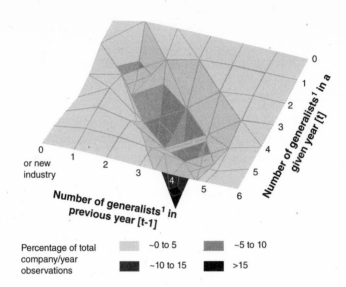

Note: N=121,859 company/year observations, >10,000 companies, and approximately 450 industries from 1975 to 2009. Industries were aggregated based on four-digit SIC codes.

[1]A company or segment of a company with a revenue market share equal to or greater than 10 percent of overall industry revenues for any given year.

**FIGURE 29.1** Three- and Two-Generalist Configurations Are the Most Stable and Act as the Strongest Basins of Attraction
Sources: Compustat; BCG analysis.

10 percent. The March 2007 acquisition of Vanguard by Enterprise, however, gave the latter nearly half the market—and it set in motion competitive dynamics implicit in the rule of three and four. In fact, the market has closely followed Henderson's script. In 2011, the three market leaders—Enterprise, Hertz, and Avis—had market shares of 48 percent, 22 percent, and 14 percent, respectively, close to the 4:2:1 ratio Henderson predicted. Hertz's 2012 acquisition of Dollar Thrifty, which held a 3 percent market share at the time, made the numbers align even more closely with the rule.

All told, the rule of three and four appears to be very much alive and well in 2012. But its applicability, as Henderson proposed, remains confined to "stable, competitive" industries characterized by low turbulence and limited regulator intervention. Other examples, beyond the U.S. rental car industry, of industries where the rule applies today include machinery manufacturing (companies such as John Deere, Agco, and CNH), household appliances

(Whirlpool, Electrolux, and General Electric), and credit-rating agencies (Experian, Transunion, and Equifax).

The rule of three and four does *not* seem to apply to the growing number of more dynamic, unstable industries, such as consumer electronics, investment banking, life insurance, and IT software and services. Nor does it apply to industries where regulation hinders genuine competition or industry consolidation, such as telecommunications in the United States (witness, for example, the government's antitrust action against the merger of AT&T and T-Mobile). The difference in applicability is stark. For companies in low-volatility industries led by three generalists, we measured a return on assets 6.1 percentage points higher than that of companies in low-volatility industries led by a larger number of generalists. Yet we found no such trend in high-volatility industries—the three-generalist configuration had no advantage over others. A possible explanation for this is that experience curve effects, which Henderson supposed underpinned the rule, are less applicable in industries where technological innovation and other factors shift the basis of advantage before the benefits of a lower cost position can be realized.

Rising turbulence in many industries has also reduced the rule's impact over time. The higher return on assets associated with three-generalist structures, for example, has decreased over the decades, falling from an average of approximately 3 percentage points in the 1970s to roughly 1 percentage point today. The same holds for the prevalence of the 4:2:1 market-share ratio among industries led by three generalists—that ratio is still the most common in such industries, but it is less common than it was at its peak.

## Implications for Decision Makers

For corporate decision makers, the rule of three and four has important implications. First, an understanding of the industry environment is critical. Is the industry one in which classical "rules" of strategy, such as the rule of three and four, apply, or does it demand an alternative—for example, an adaptive—approach? Next, decision makers must determine whether their companies have a long-term viable position in their industries. Where the rule applies, this is largely determined by market share. Being the industry's largest player is the most desirable position; the number two and three spots are also sustainable. Any other position is likely to be unsustainable.

Once they understand their company's position, decision makers must shape their strategies accordingly. If the company is a top-three player, it should aggressively defend its share. If it is outside the top three, it should attempt to improve its position through consolidation or by shifting the basis of competition—or it should exit the industry. (As Henderson wrote, "cash out as soon as practical. Take your writeoff. Take your tax loss. Take your cash value. Reinvest in products and markets where you can be a successful leader.") If the company operates in an environment where the rule does not apply, it should employ adaptive or shaping strategies, which we describe in more detail in Chapter 1.

The rule has implications for other stakeholders as well. Investors, for example, should factor an industry's dynamics and likely trajectory into their investment strategies. And policy makers should consider the rule and its ramifications as they weigh antitrust issues.

As we have seen, the rule of three and four remains relevant more than three decades after its conception—in a business environment that is, in many respects, profoundly different—and its implications continue to provide guidance for decision makers working in environments where classical business strategies hold. For companies in increasingly unstable environments, a new set of rules applies, calling for more adaptive approaches to strategy.

# 30 The CEO as Investor

## Gerry Hansell
## and Dieter Heuskel

O f the many roles played by the modern CEO, one of the most important is among the most neglected: the role of the CEO as investor.

A company's investment choices constitute a critical and underestimated part of the CEO's agenda. These choices have extremely high stakes: typically, a company allocates investment cash flows equal to half or more of its market capitalization over a three- to five-year period. These choices are extensive in scope, encompassing not only decisions about reinvestment to drive the business (capital expenditures, acquisitions, and brand and technology investments) but also decisions about the company's deployment of its cash flow other than for operations (for example, for dividends, share buybacks, and capital structure adjustments). At first glance, some of these may not seem to involve much choice—just being in a business requires some reinvestment. But taking a passive attitude toward portfolio exposures and managing reinvestment "democratically" is, in itself, a choice—and in many cases, a poor one.

Many CEOs and senior teams struggle in the investor role. Strikingly few companies have a coherent process for managing their investment choices and linking these choices to the company's value over time. Investment failures are surprisingly common. More than one-third of the $8 trillion of invested capital in the S&P 1500 does not earn the cost of capital. Over a five-year period, half the companies experience a significant write-off, divest a major business, or see a decline of 50 percent or more in company value.

Many CEOs assume that "financial discipline"—especially in the form of a tough chief financial officer (CFO) who approves or rejects spending requests using tools such as discounted cash flow and earnings per share (EPS)—will protect them from investment failure. Unfortunately, the lesson of experience is that such financial tools are like a racecar's speedometer: they sometimes provide useful guidance, but they neither prevent accidents nor deliver power to drive the car forward.

There is a better way. By developing an explicit corporate investment thesis, much as professional investors do, a CEO and his or her team can allocate capital to support more attractive value creation with less risk.

## What an Investment Thesis Is—and Is Not

An investment thesis is not an equity story that describes how a company's leaders wish outsiders would see the company's opportunities. Rather, it's a clear and focused summary—grounded in the granular realities of the company's competitive situation, opportunities, and risks—of how the company will create value over time.

In contrast to the typical strategic plan's lengthy list of actions and ambitions, a good investment thesis highlights three to six critical actions that are required to achieve attractive performance over a specific time period (usually three to five years). A company's opportunity to create value at any point in time is driven by just a few factors, and a good thesis focuses managerial energy.

A good thesis explicitly considers enterprise risks and embraces contrarian viewpoints. After all, from an owner's standpoint, you shouldn't invest in a company unless you can first describe why the consensus view driving today's valuation is too conservative and you can also see where the short seller's logic is misguided.

## A Tale of Two CEOs

To understand the difference a clear investment thesis can make, consider the experience of two consecutive CEOs of a large, highly diversified consumer products company. The first CEO was a disciplined operator whose agenda was that each of the company's businesses should "be the best growth company" in its respective sector. He challenged each business unit to become the biggest competitor in its served market, raise operating margins, and beat its budget each quarter. And he measured business unit performance using a comprehensive list of more than a dozen measures—from revenue growth and inventory turns to operating profit margins.

Operationally, these priorities generated good results. Working capital efficiency improved; selling, general, and administrative expenses (SG&A) were reduced; and a number of acquisitions drove top-line growth. What's more, the company was able to exploit attractive borrowing rates to fund share buybacks with debt, which contributed to raising the company's EPS nearly 50 percent over a four-year period.

And yet, the company's competitive position was steadily eroding. Whatever progress the company had made in growing its profits was more than offset by a series of poor investment choices. Under pressure to deliver quarterly earnings, some unit managers cut back on long-horizon technology investments. The aggressive search for growth resulted in sizable acquisitions in segments with fundamentally weak returns, diluting earnings quality. In the context of declining gross margins, investors interpreted the cuts in SG&A as bad news—a sign that the company was on a commoditizing trajectory (however much EPS was growing at the moment). As investors fled the stock, the company's valuation multiple compressed more than its earnings increased, putting the company's total shareholder return into the bottom quartile of its peer group. This poor value-creation performance cost the CEO his job.

His replacement developed a more integrated strategic and investment agenda. The new CEO continued the push for operational excellence, but he also engaged openly with the company's long-term owners, seeking to understand their views. The new CEO developed an explicit thesis that was backed by a financial model linking operational performance to the company's market value over time. That thesis came to be known as "8 + 6 = 14": driving sustained operating profit growth of 8 percent while throwing off a 6 percent cash flow yield would generate annual shareholder returns in the neighborhood of 14 percent.

Deceptively simple, this way of articulating the company's financial goals focused attention on the key trade-offs. The company's operational agenda remained important, but the new model clarified the critical role of investment discipline. To create value, the executive team had to focus not only on revenue growth and margins but also on the capital strategy. The executives had to manage the trade-off between *reinvested cash* to drive profitable growth and *distributed cash* (including dividends, share count reductions, and debt paydowns), which provides cash flow yield.

The new investment thesis also pushed the senior team to focus on three key changes that unlocked significant value. First, instead of aiming to grow all the company's many business units opportunistically, the team developed an explicit portfolio strategy that was grounded in a view of competitive advantage and its drivers. The team clearly differentiated priorities for the various businesses in the portfolio, detailing how each should contribute in its own way to creating value. A few platforms merited disciplined investment in growth, other businesses required a turnaround, and still others were structurally worth more to different companies and were candidates for divestment.

Second, they developed a more rigorous and disciplined approach to acquisitions to ensure that each dollar of cash flow reinvested to drive growth would deliver well above a dollar of value to owners. Meaningful acquisition investment would continue to be a key part of the agenda, but—from target screening and deal board approvals to integration management and postmortem reviews—the company developed new tools and resources to manage the M&A process more effectively.

Finally, the senior team adjusted the control system so that the new investment thesis was reinforced meaningfully and tangibly at the operating units. Metrics, performance assessment, and unit-level incentives were simplified and aligned with sustained value creation over a three-year period. The team also worked intensively to communicate the logic of the corporate-level thesis, empowering the units to bring forward bolder investment ideas that reflected a more differentiated range of growth-to-yield trade-offs in the various businesses.

These moves transformed the company's performance. Business unit heads no longer perceived capital as free and growth as the only way to create value. Rather, each dollar of cash flow was allocated toward the best alternative for driving sustainable returns. Investors regained confidence when they saw strategically disciplined, high-return acquisitions and expanding gross margins that were the result of focused increases in innovation spending. The valuation multiple expanded, and the company's value-creation three- and five-year track records were the best of its peer group.

# Identifying the Right Value Pattern ——

One of the greatest challenges management faces when developing an investment thesis is to identify the right shortlist of focus areas that fit well with the company's starting position. Every company wants to grow profits and value over time, but the path and relevant priorities of a Google, a Gazprom, a Gilead Sciences, or a General Dynamics will be radically different. Sometimes the best long-term path requires short-term pain—shrinking a troubled business or reducing risk from the balance sheet for greater liquidity. Other times, shifts in the competitive landscape require a bold rethink of the business model or of where and how to compete. Many companies find themselves with limited growth prospects in their core business but unclear linkages to the many potential adjacent businesses. How does the senior team develop an investment thesis that truly fits the company's starting position and its opportunity set?

Although starting positions are multidimensional and vary widely across companies and industries, analysis by BCG suggests that there is a limited set of common archetypes, each with a distinct set of preferred pathways for creating value. Each of the archetypes—*healthy high-growth, high-value brand, utility-like,* and *distressed,* to name a few—has its distinct profile and priorities. BCG refers to these starting positions as *value patterns.*[1] Knowing the value pattern of a company can help management define the boundaries of its investment thesis and identify the most promising value-creating initiatives on which to focus.

---

[1] For more details on *value patterns,* see bcgperspectives.com.

# 31 Focusing Corporate Strategy on Value Creation

## Jeffrey Kotzen, Eric Olsen, Frank Plaschke, Daniel Stelter, and Hady Farag

In theory, corporate strategy should define how a company will use its organizational capabilities, financial resources, and competitive advantages to create superior value for its investors. But in practice, what passes for corporate strategy at most companies does not achieve this goal because it does not include a detailed consideration of how the company actually creates value. Senior executives need a more comprehensive and more integrated approach, one that emphasizes delivering sustainable total shareholder return (TSR) over the medium to long term.

## The Logic—and Limits—of Traditional Corporate Strategy

Every business needs its own individual business strategy—that is, a plan to create and exploit sustainable competitive advantage. The role of corporate strategy, however, is to define pathways for a company to generate value in excess of what its business units would create on their own and to make sure the company's portfolio sustains that superior shareholder value over time.

Ideally, a company's corporate strategy defines the fundamental portfolio logic that explains why a particular set of businesses are together in the first place. For example, it should identify the parenting advantages or financial and operational synergies that make the company the best owner of its particular set of businesses. And it should define the precise role of each business unit in the company's overall value creation strategy—for example, a growth engine that delivers above-average profitable growth, a cash machine that funds the growth of other units, or a distressed unit that creates value through a turnaround.

Corporate strategy also defines how a company's portfolio of businesses evolves over time. As businesses inevitably mature, the ways they create value will change. And some may no longer be able to create value at a level that matches the company's aspirations. A company needs to continually reposition the value creation strategies of its business units. It also needs to weed out those that are no longer creating enough value under its ownership and develop or acquire new businesses with greater value creation potential because they offer operational, financial, or parenting advantages that can be captured.

Finally, corporate strategy is the process by which senior management aligns its financial and investor strategies with its business strategy to optimize value creation. How much of the company's cash flow will be reinvested in the businesses, and how much will be returned to investors in the form of dividends or share repurchases? How will reinvested capital be allocated among the various business units? And how will the company ensure that the capital markets value its portfolio of businesses appropriately? What is the ideal capital structure and credit rating for the company?

That's the theory. Unfortunately, corporate strategy as it is actually practiced at most companies rarely performs all these tasks effectively. In our experience, the corporate strategy process at most companies typically suffers from the following four shortcomings:

- *Too much incrementalism.* A company's current business model—including its existing portfolio of businesses and financial policies—both frames and constrains the entire corporate strategy process. Legacy assumptions remain unexamined. And although the process typically incorporates forecasts of trends in the company's current markets at the individual business unit level, it rarely examines potential discontinuities in the external environment that could affect the company as a whole.

- *Sequential planning.* Planning and decision making tend to flow in only one direction. Once the strategies of the various business units are defined and specific financial targets and plans are set, those choices then determine the parameters of a company's financial policies and the communications necessary to "sell" the strategy to investors.

- *"Siloed" decision making.* Because planning and decision making are sequential, they also end up being highly fragmented across different operational and functional silos. Corporate strategists work with business unit management to set business strategies. Corporate finance determines the financial policies. Investor relations crafts investor messaging. But each does its work in relative isolation. The final result is often the product of negotiation and legacy thinking rather than that of an objective fact-based analysis of what it will take to create value.

- *Weak connection to value creation.* The result of all these limitations is a pervasive disconnect between corporate strategy and value creation. Few companies have an explicit goal for shareholder value (for instance, top quartile TSR over the next five years). And those that do rarely incorporate that goal explicitly in their planning processes or quantify the potential TSR contribution of their business plans. As a result, value creation may be a desired outcome, but it is not an actual driver of, or perspective considered in, strategy development.

Companies need a better approach. First, they need to make value creation an integral part of the corporate strategy process. Second, they need to extend the scope of corporate strategy to give equal consideration to the company's business strategy, its financial policies, and the priorities and goals of its investors. Finally, business strategy, financial strategy, and investor strategy need to be examined in parallel (not sequentially) by the entire senior executive team (not isolated functional experts) in order to identify and reach agreement on critical trade-offs and achieve alignment and consistency across the three strategies. (Figure 31.1 contrasts the traditional approach to corporate strategy with this new approach.)

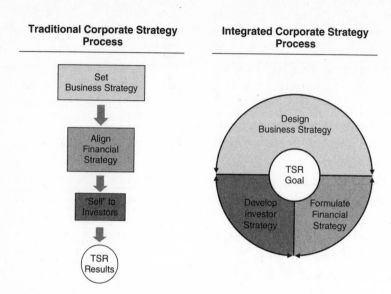

**FIGURE 31.1** An Integrated Approach to Corporate Strategy Focuses on Value Creation
Source: BCG analysis.

# An Integrated Model of Value Creation

Most senior executive teams believe that they are already committed to increasing TSR. After all, they talk about it all the time. Some may even have set a target for relative TSR performance or improvement in TSR. But in most cases, they are not really focused on value creation, because their corporate strategy process does not consider the full range of factors affecting TSR.

BCG recommends using an integrated model of value creation incorporating three critical dimensions. The first is profit growth represented by the combination of top-line growth in sales and margin improvement. The second is improvements in a company's valuation multiple, driven by investor expectations that shape how capital markets value a company's future performance at any given moment in time. Taken together, these two dimensions determine a company's capital gain. The third is free cash flow contribution through direct payments to shareholders in the form of dividends and share repurchases.

The key point about this model is that these three dimensions exist in dynamic interaction. For example, a company may create value through profitable growth. But precisely *how* a company goes about achieving that growth can have either a positive or a negative impact on its valuation multiple and, therefore, on its TSR. Alternatively, the level of a company's multiple, compared with those of its peers, can enable certain business strategies and make others impossible. For instance, an especially strong multiple can make a company's stock a powerful currency for acquisition; conversely, a weak multiple can make a company vulnerable to takeover. Finally, cash payouts not only can contribute directly to TSR but also can have a positive impact on a company's multiple by strengthening the investment thesis and thus increasing the loyalty of existing investors and attracting new investors.

Unless a company has a corporate strategy process that takes these interactions and linkages into account and allows executives to manage the trade-offs among them, it is not really focused on value creation. Its senior executives are unlikely to take full advantage of the company's value creation potential, are more likely to make decisions that inadvertently destroy value (for example, driving growth while maintaining a value-focused investor base), and may even find themselves vulnerable to pressure from activist investors. The way to avoid these negative outcomes is to make a company's financial strategy and investor strategy an integral part of the corporate strategy process.

# Business Strategy, Financial Strategy, and Investor Strategy

A key aspect of our approach is to see business strategy, financial strategy, and investor strategy as three integrated parts of a company's corporate strategy and to treat them in parallel rather than sequentially. This integrated perspective is critical because both a company's financial policies and the goals and priorities of its dominant investors can have important implications for the company's corporate and business unit strategies (and vice versa). They also can have a direct—and, sometimes, quite substantial—impact on TSR in their own right.

Financial strategy is the result of many different decisions about issues such as a company's capital structure, preferred credit rating, dividend policy, share repurchase plan, tax strategy, and hurdle rates for investment projects or mergers and acquisitions (M&A). Often, these seem like discrete issues. But it takes a holistic approach to optimize a company's overall financial strategy.

For example, consider the impact of a business unit's proposed growth initiative. Business unit managers will naturally be focused on the initiative's return on investment—that is, whether it has a positive net present value (NPV). But even when a proposed growth initiative delivers returns above the cost of capital, a company may have been able to get even greater returns by, for instance, returning the cash to investors. Companies that are overleveraged, that are undervalued compared with their future plans, or that suffer from a low valuation multiple relative to peers can often realize major improvements in their valuation multiples and TSR by paying out more cash to investors or by using that cash to reduce debt. Put simply, every investment option needs to be considered against alternative uses of capital. Unless senior executives integrate considerations of financial policy with considerations of business strategy, managing such trade-offs is extremely difficult.

The same is true for a company's investor strategy. It's essential that a company's corporate strategy be aligned with the priorities and expectations of its investors. Those expectations will drive the company's valuation multiple relative to its peers, which is the key source of short-term TSR and a critical influence on the company's long-term value creation.

One typical source of misalignment is the difference in how executives and investors assess business opportunities. Most managers evaluate the potential of a business initiative incrementally—that is, whether it adds to EPS today or has a positive NPV, given reasonable assumptions about future cash flows and likely risks. But investors tend to focus not just on EPS or on stand-alone NPV but also on how a company's initiatives fit in with their view of its overall TSR profile.

Another potential source of misalignment is that different types of investors have different expectations for company performance. For example, value investors tend to reward increasing the payout of free cash flow over growth. Growth at reasonable price (GARP) investors, by contrast, favor stable, low-risk EPS growth. And growth investors target organic revenue growth greater than 10 percent. Unless a company's corporate strategy corresponds to the priorities of the specific groups that dominate its investor mix, it will not realize the value from its strategy that executives expect.

Taking investors' priorities and goals into account doesn't necessarily mean doing whatever current investors say they want. In some cases, the correct response to misalignment may be to migrate to new categories of investors who are more in sync with the company's strategy. In others, the solution may be to educate existing investors to convince them that the current strategy will meet their goals. And in still others, a company may decide to "take a hit" to its near-term valuation to pursue a sound strategy that will pay off in the future. But whatever the situation, executives need to anticipate the likely results of their decisions and plan for them in advance.

When senior executives address business strategy, financial strategy, and investor strategy simultaneously, as part of an integrated management process, they forge a powerful link between corporate strategy and value creation. That link helps companies avoid corporate strategies that are incremental responses when larger opportunities are within reach or bolder moves are required. It also results in far greater commitment on the part of the organization to whatever path the senior team chooses and makes these goals quantifiable, thus ensuring more effective implementation and a stronger and more sustainable TSR over the medium to long term.

# 32

# Powering Up for Postmerger Integration

Jean-Michel Caye, Jeanie Daniel Duck, Daniel Friedman, Dan Jansen, Joe Manget, Alexander Roos, and Peter Strüven

Roughly half of all mergers and acquisitions (M&As) fail to create shareholder value, and about one-quarter actually destroy it. One of the biggest pitfalls is that companies tend to treat post-merger integration (PMI) as a mechanical process that occurs after the deal is done. But it is the strategic and tactical choices that are made before the deal is legally closed—and often before the bid has even been made—that ultimately determine whether the integration will succeed or fail.

## Finding the Strategic Pulse of a PMI

It is an ostensibly simple yet critical question that is sometimes overlooked: What is the strategic logic of the deal? Is it to consolidate and generate cost synergies? Is it to grow more rapidly by acquiring new technologies and capabilities or entering new geographies? Most often it is a combination of many things. The answer will determine virtually every aspect of the integration.

As a general rule of thumb in a consolidation merger, if the lion's share of the cost synergies is not delivered 12 to 24 months after a deal is signed,

The authors would like to thank their colleague Patrick Campbell for his contribution to this chapter.

the merger is unlikely to be successful. Consolidation acquirers need to approach the merger in the spirit of a takeover—with a directive, top-down leadership structure.

Growth mergers require a more collaborative approach, engaging the target more as an equal. The top priorities are to "do no harm," to retain and nurture the critical ideas, people, and customers of the acquired business, and to understand the cultures of the two companies deeply in order to define both their common aspiration and the degree to which alignment is needed.

In reality, most mergers are a hybrid. Accordingly, the PMI should be segmented by function, business unit, product line, and geographic region, with different approaches depending on the types and scale of synergies offered and the nature of the products and services.

## An Opportunity to Challenge the Status Quo

Most mergers enable companies to do what they have always done, but a bit more efficiently and expansively than before. However, mergers also provide an unrivaled—and underused—opportunity to question and transform the entire business model and unlock new sources of value.

Take the example of a merger that combined two midsize companies into the new number one player in the industry. The combined company created a consolidated back-office service center that allowed it to support a broader range of product lines more cheaply than any of its competitors. It then used its newfound cost advantage to seize price leadership in its industry and to invest in value-added services and offer customers a significantly more attractive value proposition.

## Optimizing Synergies as Rapidly as Possible

One of the biggest challenges acquirers face is setting realistic, yet stretch, targets. Set the bar too high, and the markets will punish you if you fail to reach it. Set the bar too low, and value will be squandered. Since Michelangelo's wisdom is still valid today—people fail not because they miss targets that are too high, but because they meet those that are too low. Therefore, different targets for the market and the internal merger team can be very useful.

Compounding this pressure, acquirers rarely have full access to the target's financial and commercial data until the deal is legally closed. Using benchmarks instead can be dangerously misleading. For example, in our experience average cost savings in purchasing are approximately 9 percent, but they can be as high as 32 percent and sometimes close to zero.

These difficulties can be overcome by creating a clean team, a dedicated PMI team chartered to validate targets through an iterative top-down, bottom-up approach. Using real data can give an acquirer a head start of several months.

## Creating a Clean Team

A clean team operates in strict legal isolation, in a room that is physically or electronically separate (or both) from the acquirer and the target. It is given privileged access to both parties' data, including competitively sensitive information, before the deal is closed. This enables the team to find and quantify potential synergies, to set provisional targets, to identify potential risks, and to prepare a preliminary implementation plan.

If the merger is not approved, the managers who have been exposed to a competitor's data may not be able to return to their previous positions and may even need to leave the company. The best solution to this is usually to rely on capable outsiders to staff the team. Retired company executives, such as the former heads of manufacturing or procurement, are good candidates, because they combine deep industry knowledge and good business judgment. So are third parties with deep integration expertise. They should be supported by strong analytical and financial modelers.

## Establishing a Dedicated PMI Team

Most companies delegate responsibility for the integration too far down the organizational hierarchy and try to fold the managerial tasks associated with a PMI into the existing management practices and processes of the company. Successfully executing an integration requires best-practice management in time compression. This demands top-flight senior leadership and a dedicated PMI team.

Particular attention should be paid to selecting the PMI team leader: more than anyone, he or she will determine the fate of the integration.

Ideally, he or she should be a widely respected executive and confidant of the CEO, a strong independent thinker, tolerant of ambiguity, and capable of making fast decisions on limited information.

At the head of the PMI team is the steering committee. It sets the top-line targets on the basis of data provided by the clean team and monitors progress against these goals. Line teams are responsible for executing the integration in the line organizations. Platform teams provide specialist support to core functions, such as finance and HR. An HR platform team will typically be responsible for consolidating the HR organization itself while also for providing information such as staff counts, evaluations, and legal requirements. Special issue teams resolve specific short-term issues—for instance, disposing of excess real estate. They need to develop options quickly and then move on.

Finally, the project management office (PMO) is the beating heart of any large integration. Headed by the PMI team leader, it is responsible for chartering teams and tracking their progress, for orchestrating the entire PMI effort, for coordinating culture integration efforts, and for overseeing communications and change management.

The PMO orchestrates the target-setting process. First it translates the original top-level targets provided by the steering committee into concrete metrics that line managers can act on. Next, each line team has to put forward bottom-up targets that it thinks it can achieve, supported by specific actions, with clear milestones and responsibilities for delivery.

Finally, the PMO and the line teams compare, contrast, and discuss the top-down and bottom-up targets. Where there are gaps—inevitably there is a tendency for line managers to aim below the ceiling—the office has to challenge and question. Line managers' compensation should be linked directly to synergy targets in order to provide them with focus and incentives.

The PMO also tracks the line teams' progress in hitting their goals. In the early days of a PMI, when it is too soon for integration efforts to show up on the bottom line, this means monitoring actions carefully. Later, it may be perfectly acceptable to decide not to do what a team initially said it would do. But it is unacceptable not to know if a line team is meeting its goals or not.

## Thinking Hard about the Soft Side

One of the common mistakes in a PMI is to assume that logic and facts will win the day: communicate the strategic rationale of the merger and most employees will see the light and throw their weight behind it. Actually, people will be asking themselves: "Do top executives know what they're doing? Can they pull it off? Is this company where I want to risk my future?"

Cultural differences between the two companies invariably add to the emotional cauldron. In a merger between a European and a U.S. company, for example, when a European executive proposed using a detailed system for tracking the merger's progress, his U.S. counterpart snapped back, "Cowboys don't fill out forms"—signaling the start of a long and rocky journey. Understanding the cultural differences between the two companies—how their beliefs, behaviors, and expectations differ—is an essential first step in developing an effective, targeted communications strategy. Cultural differences between two companies can create more challenges in a merger than those between countries.

Regularly monitoring morale and confidence helps in deciding which individuals or groups need targeted support. Although frequent, formal surveys are an option, another excellent approach is through informal, grass-roots feedback from a group of networkers—individuals who are plugged into the corporate grapevine.

## Recognizing That Silence Can Be Deadly

As soon as a company loses "radio contact" with its employees, others fill the silence—and rumors spread. In one hostile takeover, the prospective acquirer announced its desire to buy the target and then fell silent, allowing the target to set up a 24/7 hotline to explain its side of the story. Members of the acquirer's staff naturally called the number and were so influenced by the target's story that they became hostile toward their own management. Communication is the one task within a PMI that is more often than not undervalued: you can never communicate too much but always too little.

Everything that is said and done must be consistent with the merger's goals. For example, don't describe the merger as "all about top-line growth" if the primary goals are cost synergies and job cuts. Don't emphasize "collaboration" and then appoint a command-and-control executive to head the new business. Actions speak much louder than words, and incongruence leaches credibility.

## Promoting Dialogue, not Feel-Good Dictates

Formal communications never match the power and effectiveness of informal, face-to-face dialogue during which employees can test their leaders' sincerity up close. At one company, each member of the newly formed executive committee held a series of breakfasts with groups of 10 to 15 managers. This allowed the committee to connect directly and much more deeply with thousands of managers across the organization and to turn skeptics into missionaries.

## Understanding That Management Appointments Send Messages

The top appointments can send powerful signals about the future roles and responsibilities of individuals further down the chain. Therefore, it is vital to clarify the timetable and selection criteria for the next three to four layers as soon as possible—to remove uncertainty and prevent employees from guessing, often wrongly, who will stay and who will go.

People must perceive the appointment process as fair. At a minimum, the top executive team should systematically interview all potential candidates for senior management positions. One frequent global acquirer regularly assesses the top 80 to 100 people in the companies it acquires as part of its standard PMI process.

## Retaining Key People

As soon as the deal is announced, headhunters will be circling, so it is essential to reach out to top talent quickly, systematically, and (ideally) personally. A clear, legally vetted plan should detail who should talk to whom and what they can promise. An acquirer should not hand out unconditional retention bonuses—that is, bonuses that are free of concrete performance targets. At BCG, we have seen many companies waste millions trying to retain top people this way—only to see them leave soon after receiving the bonuses. A better solution is to link retention payments to performance, including hitting synergy targets.

## Our Lesson

Before a company initiates a PMI, it needs to lay effective strategic and tactical foundations. By making the right strategic choices in powering up for PMI, executives will enable their companies to accelerate in the right direction, retain the key people, and create value as rapidly as possible.

# 33

# Resilience: Lessons from Family Businesses

## Nicolas Kachaner, George Stalk, Jr., and Alain Bloch

To many, the phrase *family business* connotes a small or midsize company with a local focus and a familiar set of problems, such as squabbles over succession. Although plenty of mom-and-pop firms certainly fit that description, it doesn't reflect the powerful role that family-controlled enterprises play in the world economy. Not only do they include sprawling corporations such as Walmart, Samsung, Tata Group, and Porsche, but they account for more than 30 percent of all companies with sales in excess of $1 billion at the time of writing (2012).

Conventional wisdom holds that the unique ownership structure of family businesses gives them a long-term orientation that traditional public firms often lack. But beyond that, little is known about exactly what makes family businesses different. Some studies suggest that, on average, they outperform other businesses over the long term—but other studies prove the opposite.

To settle that question, we and Sophie Mignon, an associate researcher at the Center for Management and Economic Research at École Polytechnique, compiled a list of 149 publicly traded, family-controlled businesses with revenues of more than $1 billion. They were based in the United States, Canada, France, Spain, Portugal, Italy, and Mexico. In each business a family owned a significant percentage, although not necessarily a majority, of the stock, and family members were actively involved both on the board and in management. We then created a comparison group of companies from the same countries and sectors, which were similar in size but not family controlled. (We didn't look at Asian companies because so many of them are family controlled that it's difficult to find a suitable comparison group.) Then we did a rigorous analysis of the ways in which those two sets of companies were managed differently and how that affected performance.

Our results show that during good economic times, family-run companies don't earn as much money as companies with a more dispersed ownership structure. But when the economy slumps, family firms far outshine their peers. And when we looked across business cycles from 1997 through 2009, we found that the average long-term financial performance was higher for family businesses than for nonfamily businesses in every country we examined.

The simple conclusion we reached is that family businesses focus on resilience more than performance. They forgo the excess returns available during good times to increase their odds of survival during bad times. A CEO of a family-controlled firm may have financial incentives similar to those of chief executives of nonfamily firms, but the familial obligation he or she feels will lead to very different strategic choices. Executives of family businesses often invest with a 10- or 20-year horizon, concentrating on what they can do now to benefit the next generation. They also tend to manage their downside more than their upside, in contrast with most CEOs, who try to make their mark through outperformance.

At a time when executives of every company are encouraged to manage for the long term, we believe that well-run family businesses can serve as role models. In fact, in our research we were able to identify several companies with dispersed ownership whose strategies mimicked those of family firms. Those companies also exhibited a similar performance pattern: below their peers during upturns but leading the pack in times of crisis. (See the feature "It Operates Like a Family Business—But It's Not," later in this chapter.)

So how do family-run firms manage for resiliency? We've identified seven differences in their approach:

1. *They're frugal in good times and bad.* After years of studying family businesses, we believe it's possible to identify one just by walking

into the lobby of its headquarters. Unlike many multinationals, most of these firms don't have luxurious offices. As the CEO at one global family-controlled commodity group told us, "The easiest money to earn is the money we haven't spent." While countless corporations use stock grants and options to turn managers into shareholders and minimize the classic principal-agent conflict, family firms seem imbued with the sense that the company's money is the family's money, and as a result, they simply do a better job of keeping their expenses under control. If you examine company finances over the last economic cycle, you'll see that family-run enterprises entered the 2008 recession with leaner cost structures, and consequently they were less likely to have to do major layoffs.

2. *They keep the bar high for capital expenditures.* Family-controlled firms are especially judicious when it comes to capital expenditures. "We have a simple rule," one owner-CEO at a family firm told us. "We do not spend more than we earn." This sounds like simple good sense, but the reality is, you never hear those words uttered by corporate executives who are not owners. The owner-CEO added: "We make roughly €450 million of free cash flow every year, so we try to spend no more than €400 million per year, and we keep the balance for rainy days."

   At most family firms, capital expenditure investments have a double hurdle to clear: first a project must provide a good return on its own merits; then it's judged against other potential projects to keep spending under the company's self-imposed limit. Because they're more stringent, family businesses tend to invest only in very strong projects. So they miss some opportunities (hence their underperformance) during periods of expansion, but in times of crisis their exposure will be limited because they've avoided borderline projects that may turn into cash black holes.

3. *They carry little debt.* In modern corporate finance, a judicious amount of debt is considered a good thing because financial leverage maximizes value creation. Family-controlled firms, however, associate debt with fragility and risk. Debt means having less room to maneuver if a setback occurs—and it means being beholden to a nonfamily investor. The firms we studied were much less leveraged than the comparison group; from 2001 through 2009, debt accounted for 37 percent of their capital, on average, but for 47 percent of the

nonfamily firms' capital. As a result, the family-run companies didn't need to make big sacrifices to meet financing demands during the recession. "People think we are rich and courageous," one executive from a family firm told us, "but in fact we are cowardly—we leave most of the cash in the company to avoid giving away too much power to our banks."

4. *They acquire fewer (and smaller) companies.* Of all the plays a manager can make, a sparkly transformational acquisition may be the hardest to resist. It carries high risks but can pay large rewards. Many family businesses we studied eschewed these deals. They favored smaller acquisitions close to the core of their existing business or deals that involved simple geographic expansion. There were significant exceptions to this rule—when the family was convinced that its traditional sector faced structural change or disruption or when managers felt that not participating in industry consolidation might endanger the firm's long-term survival. But, generally, family companies aren't energetic deal makers. On average, we found, they made acquisitions worth just 2 percent of revenues each year, whereas nonfamily businesses made acquisitions worth 3.7 percent—nearly twice as much. Family businesses prefer organic growth and will often pursue partnerships or joint ventures instead of acquisitions. As the HR director of a leading family-owned luxury goods company described it: "We don't like big acquisitions—they represent too much integration risk, you may get the timing wrong and invest just before a downturn, and more importantly, you may alter the culture and fabric of the corporation."

5. *Many show a surprising level of diversification.* Plenty of family-controlled companies—such as Michelin and Walmart—remain focused on a core business. But despite a generation's worth of financial wisdom that diversification is better done by individual investors than at a corporate level, we found a large number of family business—Cargill, Koch Industries, Tata, and LG—that were far more diversified than the average corporation. In our study, 46 percent of family businesses were highly diversified, but only 20 percent of the comparison group was. Some family firms had expanded into new lines of business organically; others had acquired small entities in new fields and built on them. The CEOs we spoke with say that as recessions have become deeper and more frequent, diversification

has become a key way to protect the family wealth. If one sector suffers a downturn, businesses in other sectors can generate funds that allow a company to invest for the future while its competitors are pulling back.

6. *They are more international.* Family-controlled companies have been ambitious about their overseas expansion. They generate more sales abroad than other businesses do; on average, 49 percent of their revenues come from outside their home region, versus 45 percent of revenues at nonfamily businesses. But family businesses usually achieve foreign growth organically or through small local acquisitions—without big cash outlays. And they are very patient once they enter a new market. "We accepted that we'd lose money in the U.S. for 20 years, but without this persistence we would not be the global leader today," says one executive from a family-run global consumer products company.

7. *They retain talent better than their competitors do.* Retention at the family-run businesses we studied was better, on average, than at the comparison companies; only 9 percent of the workforce (versus 11 percent at nonfamily firms) turned over annually.

The leaders of family companies extol the benefits of longer employee tenures: higher trust, familiarity with coworkers' behaviors and decision making, and a stronger culture. These businesses have a lot in common with what the academics Karlene Roberts and Karl Weick call high-reliability organizations, in which long-serving teams of specialists develop efficient team dynamics and a collective mindset that helps them achieve goals. Says the CEO of one $10 billion diversified group: "We don't have the smartest guys out there, but they know their job like nobody else, and when a problem hits they can act immediately as a team—one that has been there before."

Interestingly, family businesses generally don't rely on financial incentives to increase retention. Instead, they focus on creating a culture of commitment and purpose, avoiding layoffs during downturns, promoting from within, and investing in people. In our study we found that they spent far more on training: €885 a year per employee on average, versus an average of €336 at nonfamily firms.

Examine these seven principles, and it becomes clear how coherent and synergistic they are: adhering to one of them often makes it easier to follow the next. Frugality and low debt help reduce the need for layoffs, thus improving retention. International expansion provides a natural diversification of risks. Fewer acquisitions mean less debt. Money saved through frugality is invested wisely if the company keeps a high bar on capital expenditures. Instead of working in isolation, these principles reinforce one another nicely.

When we talk with executives at family-controlled firms, they speak derisively about competitors who "bet the farm" or "swing for the fences." They talk about what keeps them up at night. Although they realize they are missing opportunities by being overly prudent, they hope to generate superior returns over time as business cycles turn from good to bad.

It's evident that those cycles are speeding up. If that trend continues, the resilience-focused strategy of family-owned companies may become more attractive to all companies. In a global economy that seems to shift from crisis to crisis with alarming frequency, accepting a lower return in good times to ensure survival in bad times may be a trade-off that managers are thrilled to make.

## IT OPERATES LIKE A FAMILY BUSINESS— BUT IT'S NOT

It makes sense that family-controlled companies would focus on resilience instead of performance, but why can't other companies mimic that strategy?

In fact, some do. Consider Nestlé. It slightly underperformed its three major competitors during the economic expansions of 1997–1999 and 2003–2007—but consistently outperformed them in periods of financial stress and crisis. Its leverage is lower: debt accounted for 35 percent of its capitalization, versus an average of 47 percent among its competitors. Nestlé relies less on acquisitions: as of 2012, newly acquired businesses accounted for an average of 3.9 percent of its annual revenues, versus an average of 7.8 percent for its competitors. Nestlé is also the most diversified of the world's four food giants, in terms of both geography (67 percent of its sales came from outside its home region, compared with 56 percent for its competitors) and product lines.

Essilor, the world leader in optical lenses, is another nonfamily firm that mimics these behaviors. It has a culture of cost consciousness, maintains a very low level of debt, and has little staff turnover. Essilor is highly international—and has made many small acquisitions close to the core. Like Nestlé, it has weathered downturns exceptionally well. In the United States, Johnson & Johnson isn't a family-owned business, but it acts like one, with a low debt-to-equity ratio, a diversified product line, and skepticism toward the large transformational mergers that other pharma players routinely attempt.

For years managers have been advised to "think like an owner." The rules of family business show how to translate that thinking into actual strategies. What Nestlé and other nonfamily companies prove is that it's possible to benefit from these rules regardless of ownership structure.

# VIII Trusted

We've covered many of the attributes that companies need to win in their respective markets. Long-term success isn't possible without trust, however. A company that isn't trusted will never build strong customer relationships or a positive reputation in the global community. Trust is the glue that binds together coworkers in high-performing organizations, turns supply chain participants into true business partners, and allows dispersed networks of individuals to collaborate on many of today's greatest innovations.

Trust isn't shown on a balance sheet, but it is, nevertheless, a company's most valuable asset—the hardest to build and the easiest to lose. How can companies nurture trust and better leverage the power of trust to gain strategic advantage?

The impact of business on the world's natural and social environments has grown. Today's corporation must maintain a social license to operate. Citizens and nongovernmental organizations (NGOs) alike are better informed and able to mobilize if they believe companies have negatively affected the local quality of life. Investors, meanwhile, increasingly consider social performance and purpose when assessing companies rather than just financial metrics.

In Chapter 34, "Social Advantage," we provide a framework for aligning a company's business model with a broader social and ecological context. We suggest that companies can operate profitably and deliver value in nontraditional ways, such as by meeting unmet social and environmental needs, finding ways to replenish scarce resources, and creating new markets for marginalized consumers.

The digital world offers unprecedented opportunities to accelerate and expand the process of reputation building. In Chapter 35, "From Reciprocity to Reputation," we discuss how companies can achieve global legitimacy in just a few short years by capitalizing on the proliferation of relatively inexpensive online channels. The blogs, social media, and websites that offer reviews and recommendations have arguably become more powerful shapers of reputation than TV advertising and telemarketing.

The changing relationship between the public and private sectors elevates the value of social trust. The march of trade liberalization and deregulation that marked the seeming triumph of global capitalism is giving way to a reassertion of government influence, not only in nations such as China and India but also in the West. In Chapter 36, "The Return of the Politician," we explore the implications for businesses as they move to accommodate the greater role of the state—often bearing more of the social costs as they globalize while losing some of the benefits of low-cost labor and favorable regulatory policies.

Trust also fosters rich, flexible collaboration. The Toyota Production System and the open-source software community that brought us Linux seem very different on the surface. Yet both are self-organizing networks that remain highly productive and inventive. In Chapter 37, "Collaboration Rules," we contend that at the core of the Toyota and Linux communities are similar rules about how individuals and small groups work together, how they communicate, and how leaders guide them toward a common goal. The chapter offers proven principles for building vibrant human networks.

When organizations win and maintain the trust of their people, of other organizations, and of society, they have acquired an invaluable source of strategic advantage.

# 34 Social Advantage

## Martin Reeves, Dieter Heuskel, and Thomas Lewis

**M**ost companies now understand the necessity of maintaining a social license to operate. But the increasing interdependence between business and society magnifies strategic risks and opportunities alike—and calls for new approaches.

The impact of business on the natural and social environment has grown and become more visible. Citizens and nongovernmental organizations have higher expectations for the social role of business and are better informed, engaged, and able to mobilize when they believe that business has overstepped its social contract. Investors are beginning to augment financial metrics such as total shareholder return with measures of social performance and risk when assessing long-term investment potential. In the wake of the global financial crisis, there has been a shift of legitimacy and influence away from business and toward national governments, arguably ushering in a period of greater activism directed at business. The need for clear thinking on business and social strategy has never been greater.

We define *social advantage* as a company's ability to generate value and achieve competitive advantage by sustainably aligning its business model with its broader social and ecological context. This chapter offers an integrated framework for realizing such alignment.

# Obstacles to Integration

Many companies have struggled with the ambiguities of corporate social responsibility, corporate responsibility, and sustainability and have failed to achieve the advantage that is possible by integrating the business and social aspects of strategy.

Some common traps that companies fall into include the following:

- *Financial focus.* Some companies assume that if their financial metrics are healthy, they have captured their business's net benefit to society. But such a narrow approach fails to explicitly address social risks and opportunities, thus undermining the sustainability of the business model.
- *Marketing and lobbying focus.* Other companies attend to social issues mainly through public messaging or by lobbying governments to prevent unfavorable action or legislation. These activities can temporarily mitigate threats, but they fail to address underlying tensions and contradictions. Marketing campaigns promoting lofty social values unaccompanied by action can precipitate mistrust and consumer or governmental sanctions, such as boycotts or new regulations.
- *Separation from the core business.* Another common approach is to make well-intentioned and visible contributions to social causes that are unconnected with the core business. Even when such contributions are in business-relevant domains, they are often driven through a separate staff function and are based on policies that are unrelated to the fundamental business strategy. Such efforts rarely address critical social issues or generate advantage.
- *Misaligned incentives.* Finally, as we have seen recently in the widespread public disapproval of the investment-banking sector, misaligned incentives can, over time, pervert good intentions and undermine the sustainability of a company's business model.

# Aligning Social and Business Dimensions

Companies can avoid the traps described here and create social advantage by better aligning their business and social strategies. The first step is to acknowledge and understand the broader context in which the business is embedded. A company conducts its affairs within a social setting, which is regulated by a political and institutional system—all, in turn, rooted in a natural environment. Mapping and understanding the various stakeholder groups and their aspirations and interests in each of these interdependent layers is an important prerequisite to developing strategies for managing social and business value.

The second step is to determine how value flows between the company and each of these layers. Positive flows such as providing useful products and services, replenishing scarce resources, and building trust and inclusiveness—as well as negative flows such as depletion, spoilage, and marginalization—must be identified, calibrated, and projected. This enables the identification of both tacit risks and untapped opportunities.

In the third step, the company can identify integrated strategies that align and maximize the flow of value between the business and its social context. There are three broad ways to achieve this:

- *Replenish scarce resources or goodwill.* Every company's business model depends on specific depletable resources. These can be physical or intangible resources. Trust, for example, is critical to a business's sustainability. Although it is often treated as a mere sentiment, it has economic value and can be systematically developed and enhanced through transparency, repeated interaction, contracts, appropriate incentives, and verification mechanisms. To avoid depletion of shared physical resources, it may be necessary to develop strategies at an industry level. By promoting smart regulation and collective restraint, businesses can avoid the "tragedy of the commons" and thereby uphold the sustainability of their business models.
- *Get paid to do the right things.* By identifying the social and ecological values of customers, treating these values as unmet needs, and building business models to respond to them, companies can effectively be rewarded for doing the right thing. The resulting incremental increase in price or market share can be thought of as an "ethical premium."
- *Create new markets.* Creating new markets for marginalized consumers through innovative products and services provides companies with access to new income streams, in addition to generating social value. Similarly, creating new markets and business models around

alternative and renewable resources is another way of aligning business and social interests.

Finally, to ensure long-term success in these efforts, a company must constantly monitor the changing environment and identify new opportunities for action.

## Creating Social Advantage

Some companies have succeeded in building social advantage by combining, in different ways, the three mechanisms described in this chapter. For example, the refuse disposal industry has often been censured for degrading the environment. Waste Management, however, a market leader in waste collection and recycling in the United States, has built businesses that not only promote environmental values but also generate attractive returns. Its Wheelabrator business turns refuse into electricity and addresses public concerns about both energy conservation and waste disposal. Wheelabrator generated 12.5 percent of the company's 2009 income from operations, despite bringing in only 7 percent of revenues. Thus, Waste Management is blending all three mechanisms to create social advantage: conserving resources, being paid to meet the ecological aspirations of its customers, and establishing profitable new markets in the process.

The video game industry has also come under increasing fire for fostering sedentary and asocial lifestyles among youth. In response, Nintendo, the video game company, created the Wii Fit, which addresses public skepticism about the social value of video games by promoting exercise and personal fitness. The Wii Fit combines aspects of game play with a fitness routine designed to help users get into shape. The product has expanded the company's reach well beyond its traditional youth market into segments that previously had little experience with gaming. Today, it is among the best-selling video games ever and is used in physiotherapy facilities worldwide. Thus, Nintendo combined the second and third mechanisms for achieving social advantage: getting paid for satisfying an unmet social need and in so doing creating a new market for video-assisted exercise.

Finally, Cemex—one of the world's largest cement producers—created a business model to profitably address socially marginalized consumers. Nearly 40 percent of Cemex's home market in Mexico consists of low-income do-it-yourself homebuilders, who frequently struggle to meet their housing needs. In 2000, Cemex launched Patrimonio Hoy, a program that addresses problems of affordability, limited distribution, and safe building standards. The program allows low-income families to pay a small weekly amount in exchange for materials, warehousing services, and technical support. By 2010 Patrimonio Hoy had reached more than 250,000 families and contributed to better living conditions, increased net worth for program participants, and improved savings habits. Furthermore, Patrimonio Hoy is a profitable and growing business for Cemex. The social and business value that Cemex has generated with this program in Mexico is only the tip of the iceberg—at the time of this writing in 2010 the company was expanding Patrimonio Hoy internationally.

## Starting the Journey

For many companies, achieving social advantage will require fundamentally rethinking their social and business strategy. Executives who want to lead their organizations into this unfamiliar territory might begin by posing the following questions to their management teams:

- What are the social and ecological costs generated by our current business model?
- Who bears these costs, and what are the likely consequences? How sustainable is our current business model?
- How structurally robust is the level of trust that we inspire in our employees, customers, suppliers, and regulators?
- To what degree are our company's social contributions integrated into our core business mission and purpose?
- Where are the opportunities to renew critical resources or goodwill, to profitably meet the social expectations of our customers, and to address new social markets?
- What obstacles are impeding these opportunities, and what traps could we fall into?
- Where can our company shape the industry ecosystem and gain social—and business—advantage?

As the economy begins to recover, companies might be tempted to think that they can return to business as usual. If they do, they may overlook the need to respond to rising expectations for social legitimacy and fail to align their social and business purposes. Equally important, they may miss out on opportunities for long-term value creation and advantage. Structurally aligning a business with its social contributions results not only in more sustainable business models, but also in a seat at the table in shaping the political and social context. Social advantage, once attained, becomes self-reinforcing.

# From Reciprocity to Reputation

## Philip Evans

*This chapter was first published in 2006. Although the Internet has continued to evolve rapidly since then, the principles set out here are as true today as the day it was written.*

**T**rust bypasses the rigidities of hierarchy and greases the wheels of markets. But it can take different forms. Technology is driving the substitution of one form of trust for another: *reputation* for *reciprocity*. This has consequences for strategy and for organization.

## Reciprocity

We used to live in a world where information channels were expensive: they required proximity, trips, introductions, advertising, and so on. In such a "thin" network, the parties (whether corporations or people) are mutually vulnerable, depending on each other to convey true information and fulfill obligations. Apart from market contract or hierarchical control, we address this vulnerability through trust. The form of trust that we employ is reciprocity: we respond positively to cumulative, collaborative signals from the other party.

But the time and effort required to build trust through reciprocity are themselves a cost, further raising the cost of making those connections productive. When this feedback loop is strong enough, we economize on connections to the point where we operate within the thinnest possible trust network: the hierarchical org chart, the linear supply chain, or the loyal customer relationship. In these networks, the need and capacity for reciprocity are maximized while the number of channels is minimized. Such networks, thin and brittle, are all-or-nothing: we break a connection infrequently, but when we do, the break is sudden and complete and comes at a high cost.

Thin networks both require and enable thick relationships. Reciprocal trust can be transitive—A trusts B, and B trusts C, so A is willing to trust C. Such chains, however, quickly peter out. As a result reciprocity does not scale. In general, reciprocal trusting relationships have to be built one at a time. Large swaths of organizational practice, marketing wisdom, and industry structure are based, unconsciously, on this logic.

Reciprocal trust of this kind is an asset, unrecognized by accounting conventions, and companies very often underinvest in it. The comparative innovativeness of Toyota's supply chain, for example, is in substantial measure explained by Toyota's reliance on (and willingness to invest in) reciprocal trust with its suppliers.

# Reputation

But in a context where information channels are cheap, another kind of trust can flourish: trust based on reputation. A, with whom I do *not* have a trusting relationship, tells me about B. But the abundance of channels means that I can access lots of As. I may not trust any one of them (each one is a "noisy signal"), but I trust the aggregate. So when there are *lots* of pieces of information, diffused over *lots* of routes, the noise (as information theorists tell us) simply cancels out. Moreover, B's behavior is affected by the knowledge that people are talking about her: she now has a *reputational asset* that she will rationally protect. As long as the gain from taking advantage of me is less than the consequent penalty to her reputation, I can be reasonably assured that she will not behave opportunistically. That, then, gives me a further reason to trust her.

Reputation requires multiple and redundant information channels: ideally, everyone would communicate with everyone else. If this is ensured, then reputation scales powerfully. In the language of information theory, double the size of a network and you multiply the signal-to-noise ratio of any one message sent to you by about the square root of two (this is Metcalfe's law of reputation). In the language of common sense, the bigger the group, the more robust the signal becomes. That, in turn, increases the value (positive or negative) of your reputation within the network, making it more likely to influence your behavior.

And whereas reciprocity creates an asset that is specific to the reciprocating pair, reputation facilitates near-costless re-pairings among any of a network's members. The reason: it is based not on *my* knowledge of you but on the *network's* knowledge of you (and my understanding of your dependence on the network's knowledge). The trust asset belongs not to the pair but to the reputed individual or, in a different sense, to the network itself.

The catch, of course, is that, in general, there is no incentive, contractual or reciprocal, for the many As to give me information about B. Some positive incentive can be created with norms and by making one's own reputation a function of one's contributions to the reputations of others. But if communication imposes significant costs on the As, they will not proffer anything. The acuity and influence of reputation are limited by the size and communication costs of the network within which it is embedded.

# Technology

But technology changes all that—and therein lies the revolution. Technology enables cheap and redundant connections across which reputation can emerge. It enables parallel information channels ("trust technologies") for aggregating reputation: people (deliberately or implicitly) contribute information, and the technology summarizes the data, publishing the results at negligible cost.

eBay's technology for aggregating ratings of buyers and sellers, Amazon's for creating reputations for books and for Amazon Marketplace vendors, and Google's for aggregating hyperlinks into votes on content all work in similar ways. One crucial element of this movement is that reputation requires persistence of identity. I cannot build my reputation from anonymous transactions. And transactions under a pseudonym will build a reputation for that pseudonym—but not for me.

The more people do this, and the more interconnected the human networks within which their reputations are embedded, the more valuable those reputations become. That enhanced value reflects not only the information content (signal-to-noise) but also, more important, the fact that those reputations serve as an earnest sign of their owners' moral reliability. Moreover, whatever the size of the population *not* participating in the reputational network, there is a self-sustaining process of positive selection: it will always pay for the "upper half" of nonparticipants to reveal their reputations, to achieve advantage over the "lower half," with whom they are otherwise being averaged. The bigger the reputation-sharing network, the greater the pressure to join: the classic increasing returns pattern of network economics.

## Implications

The implications of these developments are manifold. But consider just one. What if a company implemented these trust technologies internally? What if we all had reputations, aggregated from weak signals, that we could selectively reveal? What would that do to collaboration patterns? To the standard thin network/thick relationship paradigm of reciprocity? To the cost of wiring and (more important) *re*wiring the network? To the need for internal markets and hierarchy? To the need for the apparatus of human resources management? To the meaning of *leadership?* To behavior? To why people care?

And why stop there? Why not open the reputation network to people who are recruits and customers and suppliers? What would *that* do to behavior? And to brand? Would the company lose because the mixed signals are no longer "on message" as the recruiters and marketers and purchasing agents would define it? Or would the company—like Amazon with its book reviews—gain more from authenticity than it loses from honesty? When it first emerged, the World Wide Web seemed a vast and alien toy, irrelevant to serious business. Soon, however, it became a daily tool. Now reputation-based networks have emerged: another vast but alien toy. Is the cycle about to repeat?

# 36

# The Return of the Politician

## Dieter Heuskel and Martin Reeves

Today, Vilfredo Pareto, the Italian economist and philosopher, is best known for his principle that 20 percent of a group is responsible for 80 percent of its results. In the early part of the twentieth century, however, Pareto was equally well known for his theory about the rise and fall of power in society. In Pareto's view, power rotates among different groups of elites. Overlooked in recent years, Pareto's "circulation of elites" theory may be about to make a comeback.

For the past 30 years, business leaders have essentially called the shots, proclaiming markets, deregulation, and globalization as their mantras. Global capitalism has triumphed at the expense of national governments. The world of business has attracted the brightest talent and offered the most attractive careers and compensation.

The next few years will likely witness the return of the politician and the advent of a larger role for the state in the economy. When this article first went to press in 2010, Barack Obama, Angela Merkel, and Nicolas Sarkozy had shoved business titans off the front page. Politicians are now the ones in the driver's seat.

Evidence for the swing in power from corporations to governments is all around us: new trade barriers, the 2009 U.S. takeover of General Motors, the nationalization of banks, greater regulation of financial markets, and the reshaping of economic activity in the interest of climate control. Business leaders need to be prepared for the return of the politician into the affairs of business and adapt to that new reality.

## Taking Back the Power

Politicians—or, more broadly, government officials—have always played a role in the economy, but that role has been significantly downplayed in recent years. If free markets, free trade, and technological innovation have largely defined the modern era, we tend to forget that they owed some of their initial success and development to governments. In the early 1980s, President Ronald Reagan in the United States and Prime Minister Margaret Thatcher in the United Kingdom triggered the worldwide trend toward liberalization, deregulation, and privatization. Meanwhile, the rapid expansion of China, India, and other developing nations over the past decade was facilitated by government officials and state-influenced economic policies as much as it was by the activities of entrepreneurs. In addition, in the United States, federal funding starting in the 1960s provided the spark that ignited the Internet and the subsequent explosion of creativity and wealth.

The influence of government can be expected to increase in the future. As China has shown, the integration of politics and economics, under the right circumstances, can provide a tremendous advantage in speed and coherence. China has accelerated out of the global recession faster than most other nations by virtue of a broad array of innovative industrial policies and market interventions, not just traditional Keynesian government spending.

The return of the politician is not merely a temporary outcome of the financial collapse, which required government intervention to repair. It is a consequence of business elites defining their roles and responsibilities both too narrowly and too extremely. As Indra K. Nooyi, chairman and CEO of PepsiCo, said in a 2009 speech, "Somewhere along the line, the advocates of the joint stock company began to believe they were running a sovereign entity. They forgot that a company operates under license and therefore has to give something back." Now, the true sovereigns—or, at least, the representatives of the people—are taking back the power.

Many of today's leading economic, environmental, and social challenges will require forceful and concerted action by politicians. Take, for example, the emergence of the so-called next billion in China, India, and other developing nations. This emerging class of new consumers is straining global demand for natural resources—which are often located in regions where nationalization is a risk or even a reality. If the next billion are to fully join the middle class, businesses and governments will need to work together to provide natural resources, infrastructure, and social services. Climate change is another issue that will require a strong role for government.

# Responding to the New Realities

The consequences of a shift in power from business executives to politicians are profound. Four, in particular, stand out.

## The Reallocation of Social Costs

Companies have long avoided bearing the full costs of doing business. Climate change and financial risk taking are two examples of businesses passing along costs to society. National and international efforts to reduce carbon dioxide emissions and government action in the United States, United Kingdom, and France to curb pay (and consequently risk) suggest that this reallocation is under way. Businesses need to broaden their strategic perspective to embrace social and ecological dimensions, not just as risks but also as sources of potential advantage.

## A Less Global, More National Footprint

The globalization genie cannot—and should not—be put back in the bottle. But it will be increasingly constrained. The power of political institutions is bounded by national—or, in the case of the European Union, regional—borders. Politicians will be more sensitive to local needs and—as the financial crisis shows—more willing to nationalize banks and other companies essential to the domestic economy. Companies will need to rediscover the importance of national interests, local markets, and interactions with politicians. So, in developing growth strategies, multinational companies will have to consider a larger array of constraints, such as higher regulation, taxes, tariffs, and foreign subsidies that are essentially local in nature. And business leaders must keep in mind that a crisis in one part of the world can have significant impacts in other nations. Case in point: the nuclear moratorium imposed by Germany's chancellor, Angela Merkel, following the Fukushima disaster in Japan.

## Lower Profitability, Tougher Regulation, and Reduced Growth

Tighter regulation and the restructuring of financial markets will limit long-term risk taking. The capital markets will eventually recover. But for the foreseeable future, the leverage and speculative excesses that powered the rise in asset prices will be held in check. Outside of financial markets, politicians will likely limit the ability of companies to take advantage of lower labor and production costs—and lower standards in safety and environmental protection—in developing markets. In the United States, the Buy American campaign created as part of the American Recovery and Reinvestment Act of 2009 is just one example of the impulse of politicians to prop up local industry. And the regulation of carbon dioxide emissions by the state of California underscores the fact that tougher environmental regulation is likely to become the norm.

## The Reorientation of Talent

The most talented people in society gravitate toward elite positions in order to achieve personal growth and career aspirations. The new elites will increasingly be attracted to government positions as the public sector regains credibility, visibility, and even admiration. Executives will need to rethink their recruiting strategies in order to compete with the public sector. Businesses will no longer be able to simply lavish recruits with more money when government jobs offer prestige, status, and real power. They will need to better define their social purpose and contribution in order to create meaningful careers.

Business leaders can no longer draw comfort from Milton Friedman's belief that "the business of business is business." Fortunately, one of the enduring features of capitalism is its ability to evolve, and it will need to demonstrate this strength in accommodating the return of the politician and the increasing influence of the state on the economy. Executives will need to share power with a new class of elites, become more astute politically, and recognize a legitimate role for government in their affairs. If Pareto were alive, he might tell them that the business of politics is now business too.

# 37

# Collaboration Rules

## Philip Evans and Bob Wolf

Corporate leaders seeking growth, learning, and innovation may find the answer in a surprising place: the open-source software community. Unknowingly, perhaps, the folks who brought you Linux are virtuoso practitioners of new work principles that produce energized teams and lower costs.

By any measure, Linux is a competitive product. Its advantages extend beyond cost and quality to the speed with which it is enhanced and improved. The product's success is inseparable from its distinctive mode of production. Specifically, Linux is the creation of an essentially voluntary, self-organizing community of thousands of programmers and companies.

But Linux is software, and software is kind of weird. Toyota, however, is a company like any other—any other consistently ranked among the world's best, that is. The automaker has long been a leader in quality and lean production. We have found that Toyota's managerial methods resemble, in a number of their fundamentals, the workings of the Linux community; the Toyota Production System (TPS) owes some of its vaunted responsiveness to open-source traits.

An analysis of the characteristics shared by Linux and Toyota suggests how high-performance organizations remain productive and inventive even under grueling conditions. We believe those lessons can significantly improve the way work in most organizations gets done.[1]

## Tuesday, December 2, 2003

Near midnight, Andrea Barisani, system administrator in the physics department of the University of Trieste, discovered that an attacker had struck his institution's Gentoo Linux server. He traced the breach to a vulnerable spot in the Linux kernel and another in rsync, a file transfer mechanism that replicates data among computers. This was a serious attack: any penetration of rsync could compromise files in thousands of servers worldwide.

Barisani woke some colleagues who put him in touch with Mike Warfield, a senior researcher at Internet Security Systems in Atlanta, and with Andrew "Tridge" Tridgell, a well-known Linux programmer in Australia. They directed Barisani's message to another Australian, Martin Pool, who had been a leader in rsync's development.

By morning Trieste time, Pool and Barisani had found the precise location of the breach. Pool contacted the rsync development group, while Barisani connected with the loose affiliation of amateurs and professionals that package Gentoo Linux. Pool and Paul "Rusty" Russell (a fellow Canberran who works for IBM) then labored through the night to write a patch, and within five hours, Gentoo user-developers started testing the first version. Meanwhile, Tridge crafted a description of the vulnerability and its fix, being sure (at Pool's urging) to credit Barisani and Warfield for their behind-the-scenes efforts. On Thursday afternoon Canberra time, the announcement and the patch were distributed to Linux users worldwide.

No one authorized or directed this effort, and no one was paid for participating or would have been sanctioned for not doing so. Nonetheless, a group of some 20 people, scarcely any of whom had ever met, employed by a dozen different companies and living in as many time zones, accomplished in about 29 hours what might have taken colleagues in adjacent cubicles weeks or months.

---

[1]We use the term "Linux" as shorthand for the free/open-source software community that developed and continues to refine the operating system and other open-source programs. We use "Toyota" as shorthand for the Toyota Production System, which comprises Toyota and its direct, or tier 1, suppliers in Japan and the United States.

It's tempting to dismiss this as an example of hacker weirdness—admirable, yes, but nothing to do with real business. Consider, however, another story.

# Saturday, February 1, 1997

At 4:18 AM, a fire broke out in the Kariya Number 1 plant of Aisin Seiki, a major Japanese automotive parts supplier. Within minutes, the building and virtually all the machinery inside were destroyed. Kariya Number 1 produces 99 percent of the brake fluid–proportioning valves, or P-valves, for Toyota's Japanese operations—parts required by every vehicle Toyota builds. And Toyota, true to its just-in-time principles, had less than a day's inventory. The Japanese TPS faced the possibility of a shutdown lasting months.

Within hours, Aisin engineers met with their counterparts at Toyota and Toyota's other tier one suppliers. The group agreed to improvise as much production as possible. As news spread through the supplier network, some tier twos volunteered to play leadership roles. Aisin sent blueprints for the valves to any supplier that requested them. Aisin and Toyota engineers helped jury-rig production lines in 62 locations: unused machine shops, Toyota's own prototyping shop, and even a sewing machine facility owned by Brother.

Everyone was surprised when a small tier two supplier of welding electrodes, Kyoritsu Sangyo, was first to deliver production-quality valves—1,000 of them—just 85 hours after the fire. Others followed rapidly, and Toyota started reopening assembly lines on Wednesday. Roughly two weeks after the halt, the entire supply chain was back to full production.

No one individual or organization planned this effort, and no one at the time was paid for contributing. Months later, Aisin compensated the other companies for the direct costs of the valves they had delivered. Toyota gave each tier one supplier an honorarium based on current sales to the automaker, encouraging—but not requiring—them to do likewise for their own tier twos.

Few communities appear more different than the anarchistic world of hackers and the disciplined world of Japanese auto engineering. But the parallels between these stories are striking. In both of them, individuals stepped into roles without a plan or a command-and-control structure. A human network organized itself in hours and swarmed against a threat. And despite the lack of any authoritarian stick or financial carrot, those people worked like hell to solve the problem.

Now, obviously, these were emergency responses. But a look at the day-to-day operations of the Linux community and TPS reveals that those responses were merely intensifications of the way people were already working.

# Obsession, Interaction, and a Light Touch

At the core of the Linux and Toyota communities are rules about three things: how individuals and small groups work together; how, and how widely, they communicate; and how leaders guide them toward a common goal.

Taken together, these three principles seed a continuously adapting system. Over and over, ideas are formulated in tight, testable packets; they are communicated through direct, person-to-person connections; and where links are absent, widely connected leader-practitioners create them as needed.

## A Common Work Discipline

Both communities are composed of engineers who are extraordinarily disciplined and rigorous. They pay attention to small details, eliminate problems at the source, and trim anything resembling excess. Linux members, for example, share an obsession with writing minimal code. TPS engineers are relentless in applying short cycles of trial and error and focusing on one thing at a time.

## Widespread, Granular Communication

In both the Linux and Toyota communities, information about problems and solutions is shared widely, frequently, and in small increments. Most Linux hacker communication is not between individuals but by posting to open, searchable LISTSERVs. The Toyota philosophy of continuous improvement likewise comprises a thousand small collaborations.

### Leaders as Connectors

Linux and TPS leaders play three critical roles. They instruct community members in the disciplines we've just described. They articulate clear and simple goals for each project. And they connect people, by merit of being very well connected themselves.

# What They Know and How They Know It

At the heart of Linux and TPS is a new form of collaboration that relies on two infrastructure components: a shared pool of knowledge and universally available tools for moving knowledge around.

### Common Intellectual Property

The General Public License under which Linux is published requires that all distributors make their source code freely available so that others can emend it. Similarly, Toyota's supply chain is predicated on the principle that although product knowledge (such as a blueprint) is someone's intellectual property, process knowledge is shared. Toyota's suppliers regularly share process improvement lessons both vertically and laterally, even with their competitors.

### Simple, Pervasive Technology

Linux developers produce state-of-the-art software using communication technology no more sophisticated than e-mail and LISTSERVs. Toyota also prefers simple and pervasive internal technology. An empty *kanban* bin signals the need for parts replenishment; a length of duct tape on the assembly line floor allots the completion times of tasks on a moving vehicle; quality control problems on the assembly line are announced via pagers and TV monitors.

# The Power of Trust and Applause

Such open, flexible collaborations have positive psychological consequences for participants and powerful competitive ones for their organizations.

## Rich Semantic Knowledge

A rigorous work discipline, common intellectual property, and constant sharing combine to distribute knowledge widely and relatively evenly across human networks. That knowledge includes not just the formal, syntactic information found in databases but also the semantically rich knowledge about content and process that is the currency of creative collaboration.

## Modular Teaming

Modularity is a design principle by which a complex process or product is divided into simple parts connected by standard rules. In modular arrangements of teams, each team focuses on simple tasks that together make up a larger whole. Modularity allows an organization to run multiple, parallel experiments, making many small bets instead of a few large ones.

## Intrinsic Motivation

Monetary carrots and accountability sticks, psychologists have found, motivate people to perform narrow, specified tasks but generally discourage people from going beyond them. Admiration and applause are far more effective stimulants of above-and-beyond behavior. Psychologists also emphasize the motivational importance of autonomy. Linux programmers decide for themselves how and where to contribute. Compared with their counterparts in the rest of the auto industry, TPS workers enjoy fewer controls, greater encouragement of individual initiative, and louder peer applause.

## High Levels of Trust

Workers know their reputations are at risk, and that serves as a guarantor of good behavior—the equivalent of contracts in a market or audits in a hierarchy. Hence the obsession in the Linux community with acknowledging code contributions and including personal e-mail addresses in the comment fields of LISTSERVs. Hence the collective celebration of Kyoritsu Sangyo's heroic efforts.

# Cheap Transactions and Plenty of Them

The classical sources of transaction costs are mutual vulnerability in the face of uncertainty, conflicting interests, and unequal access to information. We spend cash on negotiation, supervision, and restitution to reduce those imperfections.

In the Linux and Toyota communities, agreements are enforced not by the sanction of a legal contract, nor by the authority of a boss, but by mutual trust—lowering transaction costs dramatically. Moreover, holding property in common—as certain kinds of intellectual property are held within these communities—lowers the monetary stakes among the joint owners. Transaction costs fall because there is simply less to negotiate over.

When the Aisin Seiki plant was destroyed, Toyota and its suppliers simply got on with the job, trusting that fair restitution would eventually be made. Jeffrey Dyer, a professor of strategy at Brigham Young University, has estimated that transaction costs between Toyota and its tier one suppliers are just one-eighth those at General Motors, a disparity he attributes to different levels of trust.

# A Model for Many

Bring together all these elements, and you have a virtuous circle. A self-organizing network creates the conditions for large-scale trust. Large-scale trust drives down transaction costs. Low transaction costs, in turn, enable lots of small transactions, which create a cumulatively deepening, self-organized network.

The Linux community and TPS are strikingly different. The fact that they achieve so much in such similar ways points to some principles others can follow.

The discipline of science is surprisingly adaptable to the organization of corporate—and even intercorporate—work.

Under some circumstances, trust is a viable substitute for market contracts and hierarchical authority, not just in small teams but also in very large communities.

Across supply chains, organizations that are able to substitute trust for contracts gain more from the collaboration than they lose in bargaining power.

Low transaction costs buy more innovation than do high monetary incentives.

Perhaps the effectiveness of these collaborations suggests the ultimate emergence of something altogether new. Not markets, which can be self-organizing but rely on the use of cash or contracts at critical junctures. Not hierarchies, which enjoy low transaction costs but impose predefined roles and responsibilities on their members. But a powerful combination of both—and a signature of the networked society.

# IX  Bold

In today's volatile world, industry leadership is far more fleeting than it used to be—and businesses must adapt to stay relevant. Forward-looking companies that can continually reinvent their business models through ongoing experimentation and innovation are far less likely to be blindsided by changing markets and maverick competitors. Although rethinking the tried-and-true is not without risk, the opportunities that can emerge as a result may drive future growth—and ultimately save your business. The industry landscape is littered with companies that didn't evolve with the times.

Experimenting with new business models requires bold leadership. It encourages innovation that seeks entirely new models for going to market, adding value, or operating a business. In Chapter 38, "Thinking in New Boxes," we argue that the breakthrough ideas needed for this innovation rarely appear at random. They require a disciplined process that guides exploration and increases the odds of discovering truly game-changing opportunities.

Bold leadership requires a willingness to take the proverbial leap of faith. Part of that process is thinking boldly. In Chapter 39, "Rethinking Scenarios: What a Difference a Day Makes," we offer a new approach to scenario planning that can help companies operate in a turbulent environment and react more quickly to change.

Sometimes more radical measures are needed to stay one step ahead. Business model innovation (BMI) goes far beyond just making changes to product or service offerings. It may include rethinking your company's underlying operating or commercial model—or even the entire ecosystem or network in which your business operates. We explore this game-changing approach in Chapter 40, "Business Model Innovation: When the Game Gets Tough, Change the Game."

The mandate for bold leadership with regard to business models has never been clearer. Business model life cycles are shrinking rapidly—from 15 years on average in the 1980s to as little as 5 years today in some rapidly changing sectors. The pace of change is not entirely surprising. As value chains in nearly every sector deconstruct, companies are facing competitors that are increasingly specialized and focused. And with the globalization of business, a new breed of potent challengers has emerged—many from low-cost countries. We examine the implications of this evolution in Chapter 41, "The Deconstruction of Value Chains."

Business models come in many flavors, from low-cost and asset-light to time-based operating models focused on breaking the compromises between quality, customer uptake, and speed to market. In Chapter 42, "Time-Based Management," we reprint a classic article that showed that by looking through the lens of "time," companies could sharply improve their operations—and reinvigorate themselves. Many companies went on to do just that.

Next, in Chapter 43, "The New 'Low Cost,'" we examine a new wave of companies with low-cost business models that are taking market share from established companies in many industries and locations.

Strategy in all of its forms requires resolve and, at times, a boldness of action that applies not only to BMI but more broadly to finding the best way to compete and win. There are times when boldness of action may not require changing the game per se, but playing the current game better. In a provocative chapter—Chapter 44, "The Hardball Manifesto"—we explore a range of tough-minded or hardball strategies that can increase your odds of winning.

Whether changing the game or playing the current game better, transformation of an organization is often required. It's hard—change is rarely popular, often actively resisted, and very rarely will a CEO have the luxury of time. In our final chapter in this section, Chapter 45, "Leading Transformation," we hand the microphone to nine very different CEOs who have successfully transformed their organizations. They describe how they did it, and we find clear parallels between their approaches.

# 38 Thinking in New Boxes

## Luc de Brabandere and Alan Iny

The ability to survive in a world of accelerating change and challenge calls for ever greater creativity in our thinking. But to become more creative, we need to understand how our minds work. Once we do, we will recognize that we must do more than simply think outside the box, as the traditional business manuals suggest. We need to think in *new* boxes. In this way, business leaders can marshal their companies' creativity and give them a real competitive advantage.

## We Cannot Think without Models

We constantly simplify things in order to make sense of the world around us. Take three examples:

- How many colors are there in a rainbow? You will probably say seven. But why seven, when there are actually thousands? The fact is that *thousands* is not a manageable figure—so we are forced to simplify, and seven is what we have been taught.

---

"Thinking in New Boxes" has become a book on creativity in business, to be published by Random House in 2013.

- How many columns are at the front of the Parthenon? You are probably hesitating and might say anywhere from 5 to 10. Actually, there are 8. But to have an image of the Parthenon in your mind's eye requires only that you have a general grasp of the details.
- How many grains of sand does it take to make a pile? More than a few, obviously. But there is no exact answer because a *pile* is, by definition, an approximation: we do not need to know the precise number.

In the business world, we also simplify. Take three more examples: *market segments* are conceptual categories and do not add up to the same thing as the market itself; *balance sheets* are models based on rules relating to currency and accounting and do not represent financial reality; and Maslow's hierarchy of needs, devised by the behavioral scientist Abraham Maslow, is an abstract rendering of human nature rather than a precise profile of your customer.

These six examples demonstrate that the human mind needs to invent models and concepts and frameworks as stepping-stones on the road to interpreting reality. They are not precise representations of reality—they are working hypotheses. They allow us to think and then work. They help us to "freeze" part of reality in order to make things manageable.

# The Art of Thinking in New Boxes (Because Thinking outside the Box Is Not Enough)

Models and concepts and frameworks are—to use another phrase—mental boxes within which we comprehend the real world. And ever since the 1960s, we have been taught to be creative by thinking outside the box.

Although the precise provenance is obscure, the phrase *thinking outside the box* was associated with a popular nine-dot puzzle whose challenge is to connect nine dots on a square grid by drawing four straight lines through them without lifting the pen from the paper. The solution is to extend one of the lines beyond the boundaries of the grid—and so, outside the box.

The trouble is this: once you have mentally stepped outside the box, what happens next? The space outside the box is very expansive—infinitely so—and there can be no guarantee that you will find a solution to your problem. So the answer is that you need to find a *new* box. And you must consciously build or choose that box yourself; if you do not, an unconscious process will do it for you.

The way we think means that we cannot be creative in a constructive way without inventing models or boxes. Ideally, you need to develop a *number* of new boxes—new models, new scenarios, new ways of approaching a problem—to structure your thinking. The challenge—and the real art of creativity—is to know how to build those new boxes and, in the process, provide the framework for fresh imaginative effort.

More than half a century ago, Bic, a French stationery company, brought to market the idea of making low-cost pens. Some creative brainstorming produced a series of variations on the theme: two colors, three colors, gold trim, advertising logos, erasers, and so forth. But who would have thought of making a razor? Or a lighter? Bic could come up with those ideas only by adopting a radical change of perspective. Instead of viewing itself simply as a pen company, Bic started to think of itself as a disposable objects company—that is, as a mass producer of inexpensive plastic implements. In making this transition, Bic had, in effect, created a new box.

Business offers a number of other examples.

- Apple, originally a manufacturer of popular personal computers, used its expertise to expand into the multimedia business. Initially, there was no logical reason for it to contemplate taking on Sony and its ubiquitous Walkman. But once Apple had created a new box and viewed itself through a different lens—specifically, as a multimedia company that knows circuits and bytes—the notion of developing a digital "walkman" became obvious.
- Google's original aspiration was to build the best search engine ever. Arguably, the company eventually achieved that. But for Google to enter a new era of growth, it needed to perceive itself differently. The creation of a new "we want to know everything" box sparked projects such as Google Earth, Google Book Search, and Google Labs, as well as further improvements to the company's search engine.
- Philips, a high-tech company, had concentrated its efforts on product-oriented ventures ranging from semiconductors to domestic appliances. Then it started to shift its strategic emphasis and endeavored to identify and exploit global trends in health care and consumer markets. In doing so, it has become a world leader in several new

categories, including home health care systems. By thinking in a new box, Philips has used its core skills in different ways—and has fundamentally changed its business as a result.

- Michelin and IBM illustrate how some companies have successfully moved from a product or technology orientation to a solutions or results orientation—without necessarily abandoning their core products or technologies. Michelin, the tire manufacturer, is now a road safety specialist, and IBM, the computer giant, has entered the consulting business.

## How to Create New Boxes

If the theory makes sense, how does it work in practice? Here is one example. Like many companies, Champagne de Castellane, a French champagne manufacturer, was committed to growing its sales. To develop ways of achieving this goal, it held workshops on three days over a two-week period. Senior executives were asked to build a new box that would foster some innovative business ideas.

To start with, the executives were asked to think about their business without mentioning the words they most often used to describe it—for instance, *liquor, drink, champagne, alcohol, bottle*, and so on. As a result of this exercise, the team came to the conclusion that the company's business was fundamentally about *contributing to the success of parties and celebrations*.

Once that insight had emerged—and a new box had been formed—the executives had a framework within which they could think about the company and its future. Many ideas flowed—a number of which enabled Champagne de Castellane to become more appealing to consumers and to grow sales. For instance:

- In the summer, champagne is often not cold enough, especially if it is brought to a party as a gift. The company found that it could solve the problem by making a plastic bag that was sturdy enough to carry not only the bottle but also a few pounds of ice.
- At many parties and celebrations, someone is called on to give a speech. The company determined that it could put together a self-help booklet titled "How to Write a Speech" and attach it to the bottle.

- Parties thrive on games and entertainment. The company resolved to modify the wooden crates that contain its champagne bottles so that they could be recycled as game boards for chess, checkers, and backgammon.

It is worth noting that during the three-day brainstorming process, about 80 percent of the executives' energy was devoted to the identification of a new box (the party). Once that was done, the ideas came relatively easily. Indeed, coming up with the right new box is *always* the tough part, regardless of whether the underlying challenge is scenario planning, business development, or the design of a new strategic vision. So it is critical that companies understand this—and adopt a process that allows them to create the new box.

The brain is like a two-stroke engine. We are well aware of the value of the second stroke, when the brain selects, compares, sorts, plans, and decides. But the first stroke—when the brain imagines, dreams, suggests, and opens horizons—is the one that really matters. This process, however, needs organization—hence the need for a new box. And in times of crisis, when companies everywhere are concerned about their future, the importance of being able to think in new boxes is greater than ever.

# 39

# Rethinking Scenarios: What a Difference a Day Makes

## Luc de Brabandere and Alan Iny

**W**hat is the probability that, five years from now, you will have to pay for a Google search? Today, most people would find this scenario unlikely, perhaps even impossible. Now consider a different question: suppose that five years from now, you *do* have to pay. How did it happen? The same people would offer up a range of possibilities: cash-starved governments are compelled to seek new tax sources; stratospheric energy prices, driven by a global fuel shortage, force Google, with its massive server farms, to start charging for its services; or a game-changing algorithm enables Google to charge for premium search results. In an instant, the impossible has become the plausible.

The "what if?" school of thinking clearly has a place in the business world. For a host of reasons, however, classic scenario planning of the sort pioneered by the legendary Pierre Wack at Shell in the 1970s has fallen out of fashion. Some executives believe that it is too time consuming and resource intensive. Others feel that markets are too changeable for scenarios to be of much help. And to a degree, they're right. Traditional scenario planning can be hard work that demands a dedicated staff and months of quantitative study. It is best suited to exploring a limited set of key issues that drive the fundamental economics of a business.

But Wack's approach to scenarios is not the only one. Many of the benefits of scenario analysis—for example, enhanced strategic creativity, greater preparedness, and superior risk awareness—can be achieved more rapidly. The scenarios that emerge are provocative but believable, if improbable. Their value comes not from any explicit predictions but from what the executive team learns during their development and how these lessons are applied.

## A New Box for Scenarios

As we discussed in Chapter 38, "Thinking in New Boxes," thinking outside the box is neither as desirable nor as liberating as it sounds, because the space outside the box is infinite. Faced with limitless possibilities, the human mind feels adrift and tends to fall back into the familiarity of the box. People cannot help using mental models, frameworks, and theories—or, as we call them, boxes—to organize their thinking. Thus, a far more powerful approach to spurring creativity is for companies to develop a new set of boxes that free the mind to think the unthinkable—and to do so proactively, before their competitors force them into an inhospitable box by outmaneuvering them.

A well-crafted scenario is, in essence, a new box—it can help a company look at its future from an entirely new perspective. But new-box thinking is relevant to scenarios in a more fundamental way. It can help redefine scenario planning for our more turbulent world. Ask most CEOs if strategically valuable scenarios can be created—and important insights captured and communicated throughout the organization—within a matter of several weeks, and nearly all would say no. But let's assume—as we did with the Google search example—that it *is* possible. This is the very challenge that we set for ourselves.

We had two hypotheses. First, we believed that the necessary level of engagement and insight could not quickly be achieved without involving the senior management team—under the guidance of an expert facilitator—in both shaping and exploring the scenarios. Second, we believed that by tapping the knowledge of the executives and then combining it with select data on critical megatrends likely to affect the company, its competitors, and its customers, we could rapidly craft scenarios that were at once believable enough to be embraced and radical enough to spur powerful ideas. Our experience has borne out these hypotheses.

# From Fact to (Near) Fiction

In 2009, UNIFE, the association of the European rail industry, felt certain that the future would not be a linear projection of the past. The financial crisis and subsequent recession were putting unprecedented stress on customers. Trade patterns were shifting. New competitors were emerging. UNIFE's members needed to think both more expansively and more creatively. They needed scenarios.

They convened a small working group of executives from major rail companies. This group took four weeks to prepare for a one-day scenarios workshop. They explored data on a carefully selected set of megatrends—such as urbanization, the rise of China, sustainability, terrorism, the increasing scarcity of fossil fuels, and increasing bandwidth and other technology trends—that had some bearing on the future of the rail industry. Eventually, they settled on four 2025 variables that would be the starting point for the workshop:

- Shipping bananas from Harare to Barcelona
- Preparing a tender for bids to supply trains for a new rail project
- Arriving at New York's Pennsylvania Station on a Monday morning
- Reading the cover of the 2025 year-end holiday double issue of the *Economist*

On the day of the scenarios exercise, a broader group of senior executives brainstormed a set of hypotheses for each variable. Their hypotheses had to be plausible and supported by specific industry, macroeconomic, or social trends—yet also improbable, as in the Google example. When imagining possibilities for the 2025 rail tender, for example, UNIFE generated a range of hypotheses, including one in which a winner-take-all tender would be conducted every 10 years for the whole of Europe and another in which customers bought trains through online catalogues without tenders or bids.

They then grouped some of the hypotheses into coherent clusters that could serve as the basis for specific scenarios, ultimately settling on four such clusters. But the four were not yet scenarios. They needed color. Much as in a novel, play, or film, a strong storyline is essential to fostering real intellectual and emotional engagement. By the end of the day, the group had outlined four scenarios:

- *World@Home.* Urbanization and advances in communication enable people to work from home, giving rise to increased productivity. Environmental and nutritional concerns have increased the demand for locally sourced products. People mobility is secondary to the movement of goods.
- *Mission mobility.* A revolution in energy science spawns new modes of low-cost green transport, leading to the increased movement of both people and goods—and putting greater pressure on the rail industry to differentiate itself in terms of speed, service quality, and price. End customers come to expect seamless intermodal shipping solutions.
- *Divided nations.* The world economy remains in poor shape. The European Union, World Trade Organization, and other regional trade blocs are breaking down. Protectionism is on the rise, and transport is mostly local as a result of rising barriers between regions.
- *Dragon corporation.* The world has bifurcated into two main regions. The West has become poorer, and China, now an industrial and financial powerhouse, dominates the global economy. Chinese rail enterprises lead the world with cutting-edge technology and low costs.

Clearly, none of the four scenarios is likely to unfold in its entirety, but each presented an engaging box within which UNIFE members could evaluate existing strategies and imagine radical new ones. After the one-day workshop, communication materials were developed to support the scenarios, enabling the people who were not directly involved in the exercise to understand the rationale and implications of each one. This created a common language that contributed to strategic planning and decision making within and across UNIFE's member companies.

Members have found these scenarios both provocative and practical as they grapple with how to plan for a changing world. A senior strategy executive at Alstom stated that the scenario-planning day was "intellectually challenging and very refreshing," and that it also "forced our group to think beyond conventional wisdom and in uncharted territory.... The resulting scenarios became a valuable basis for building our long-term strategy." Another participant, a former international manager of the French railway system, stated that the scenarios, although extreme, were far from academic.

"We are already beginning to see that our industry is evolving and facing a mix of the scenarios," he remarked. The experience has helped member companies to be more attuned to weak signals and thus more prepared to adapt to shifts in their markets.

## Rethinking Scenarios

The increase in uncertainty and the accelerating clock speed of many markets, rather than rendering scenarios impractical, is perhaps the strongest argument for embracing them. This new approach to scenarios is not about precision but is instead about expanding the perception of the possible—and breaking an executive team out of a tunneled managerial perspective and into a creative, entrepreneurial, and strategic one. With turbulence on the rise, the value of low-cost ways to envision and seize emerging opportunities while planning for potential threats has never been higher.

What a difference a day makes.

# 40 Business Model Innovation: When the Game Gets Tough, Change the Game

Zhenya Lindgardt,
Martin Reeves,
George Stalk, Jr.,
and Michael Deimler

**B**y the late 1990s, Apple's initial pathway to growth had hit a wall. The company's proprietary approach to designing both hardware and software limited Apple to being a niche player in the personal computer market and hampered its ability to compete on price. All that changed in 2001, when Apple launched the first in a series of networked products and services. The iPod and the iTunes online music service—followed by the iPhone, the iPad, and other connected devices and software—propelled Apple to the top of a redefined industry. But the shift represented by the iPod wasn't a matter of simple product innovation. Apple's success resulted from its ability to define a workable business model for downloading music—something that had eluded the music industry.

This combination of product innovation and business model innovation (BMI) also helped expand the company's share of the traditional computer market as new customers took another look at Apple computers.

Challenging environments require businesses to bolster and accelerate innovation. The discipline of BMI offers a fresh way to think about renewing competitive advantage and reigniting growth. But BMI means more than a brilliant insight coming at the right place and the right time. To confer a reliable competitive advantage, BMI must be systematically cultivated, sufficiently supported, and explicitly managed. In this chapter, we will describe circumstances in which it has proved valuable, identify common pitfalls, and discuss how companies can develop a competitive capability in BMI.

## What Is BMI?

A business model consists of two essential elements—the *value proposition* and the *operating model*—each of which has three subelements (Figure 40.1).

The value proposition answers the question: What are we offering to whom? It reflects explicit choices in the following three dimensions:

- *Target segment(s).* Which customers do we choose to serve? Which needs do we seek to address?
- *Product or service offering.* What are we offering customers to satisfy their needs?
- *Revenue model.* How are we compensated for our offering?

The operating model answers the question: How do we profitably deliver the offering? It captures the business's choices in the following three critical areas:

- *Value chain.* How are we configured to deliver on customer demand? What do we do in-house? What do we outsource?
- *Cost model.* How do we configure our assets and costs to deliver on our value proposition profitably?
- *Organization.* How do we deploy and develop our people to sustain and enhance our competitive advantage?

Innovation in a business model is more than mere product, service, or technological innovation. It goes beyond single-function strategies, such as enhancing the sourcing approach or the sales model. Innovation becomes BMI when two or more elements of a business model are reinvented to deliver value in a new way. Because it involves a multidimensional and orchestrated set of activities, BMI is both challenging to execute and difficult to imitate.

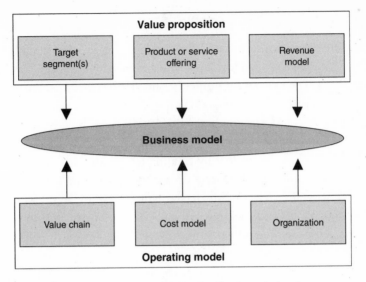

**FIGURE 40.1** A Business Model Typically Consists of Six Components
Source: BCG analysis.

Distinguishing BMI from product, service, or technology innovations is important. Companies that confuse the latter for the former risk underestimating the requirements for success.

## BMI's Potential to Change the Game

BMI is especially valuable in times of instability, disruption, and intense competition. In our experience, the companies that flourish in downturns frequently do so by leveraging the crisis to reinvent themselves—rather than by simply deploying defensive financial and operational tactics.

Many companies pursue BMI as a defensive move to protect a dying core business or defend against aggressive competitors. But we are convinced that BMI can be most powerful when it is approached proactively to explore new avenues of growth.

How a company goes about developing a new business model will depend on its industry and circumstances. Consider the different contexts in which BMI has played a decisive role in a company's success.

## Beating Back Intense Competition

In 2001, the Virgin Group entered the Australian airline market with Virgin Blue, an airline that offered low fares with a premium coach experience and a fresh brand. The new entrant quickly gained a 30 percent share, severely disrupting the primary incumbent, Qantas. Given its cost structure, Qantas realized that it could not compete with Virgin Blue directly, so it set up a new low-cost business model. Rather than simply copying Virgin Blue's model, Qantas chose to outdo it by creating Jetstar Airways—an ultra-low-cost airline operating as a separate division and designed from the outset to be lower cost than Virgin Blue. Jetstar launched in the first half of 2004, offering new planes and rock-bottom fares. It also boasted the lowest cost structure in the market and has since lowered costs further.

Jetstar's business model evolution continued when it initiated international service in 2006, making Jetstar the world's first low-cost, long-haul airline. It pioneered a revolutionary pricing approach by offering traditionally bundled services à la carte, enabling consumers to customize the onboard experience with different options for food, comfort, and entertainment. Although Jetstar has replaced Qantas on some leisure routes, its launch has been particularly effective in slowing Virgin Blue's growth plans. Virgin Blue found itself squeezed in a pincer, facing strong competition from Qantas in the leisure and business markets. In 2007, Virgin Blue abandoned its discount positioning and shifted its focus to target business travelers.

## Extending a Business Model with Current Customers

JCDecaux is a world leader in outdoor advertising and street furnishings such as kiosks and public restrooms. The company earns a large part of its revenues by securing exclusive rights to billboards and other public advertising. In exchange, it either returns some ad revenue to municipalities or covers the capital costs of public facilities. In 2006, JCDecaux's 10-year billboard advertising contract with the city of Paris was up for review. The company offered a compelling new value proposition: JCDecaux would build and maintain a citywide network of shared bicycles and bicycle racks that residents and tourists alike could rent for point-to-point transit, with the first half-hour of each trip at no cost. The city would keep the bike rental revenues, and JCDecaux would renew its billboard contract.

This system—named Vélib', a contraction of the French words for *bike* and *freedom*—was launched in 2007, deploying more than 16,000 bikes. Vélib' quickly became a high-value asset in a world where urban roads and public transit are increasingly congested and cities need to reduce carbon footprints. The network is expansive—with stations every 300 meters in the city. It is also popular: tens of thousands use the system daily. Other cities have adopted similar networks. The new value proposition, delivered with a new operating model, enabled JCDecaux to retain its billboard revenue and its market leadership.

## Extracting Brand Value by Extending the Business Model

When IKEA entered Russia, the home furnishings retailer noticed that every time it opened a store, the value of nearby real estate increased dramatically. So IKEA decided to explore two business models simultaneously: selling through the stores and capturing the appreciation in real estate values through mall development. A new IKEA division, Mega Mall, made more profit on developing and running malls in Russia than IKEA did on its traditional, stand-alone retail business. IKEA is a good example of how a company can exploit its existing assets and capabilities to experiment with new business models.

# What Can Go Wrong?

The short answer is plenty. Remember, we're not talking about simple product innovation but innovating simultaneously—and in a coherent and orchestrated manner—across several elements of the business. Managers should therefore be on the lookout for common pitfalls that include the following:

- *Portfolio bloat.* This can happen when a company has become bogged down in too many uncoordinated, bottom-up innovations. The result is a bloated, unbalanced, and overlapping portfolio of experiments, none of which has enough resources or support to win the favor of senior management.
- *Failure to scale up.* Once a project has been piloted and the initial excitement dies down, a lack of attention and resources can keep it from being scaled up successfully.

- *Pet ideas.* Every industry has its zombies—projects that don't go anywhere but refuse to die. Schemes whose time has come and gone need to be put away so that more promising ideas can gain traction.
- *Isolated efforts.* The downside of autonomous skunk works teams is that they can be too distant from the business to influence or benefit it. Companies should carefully consider the advantages and disadvantages before isolating BMI efforts from the mainstream business.
- *Fixation on ideation.* Some organizations churn out ideas endlessly but are unable to pilot and scale them up. To assume that creativity is the main or only bottleneck to BMI is to underestimate the task.
- *Internal focus.* A common problem is nearsighted attention to the organization's internal needs at the expense of customer needs. BMI that takes an inside-out approach frequently results in too little change too late.
- *Historical bias.* Organizations must resist the temptation to overvalue past models and undervalue forward-looking, disruptive ideas. Courageous and visible leadership is required to overcome this natural and powerful tendency.

# Establishing a Capability for BMI

Becoming good at BMI is much like developing other competitive capabilities. Companies must assess opportunities, identify promising projects, pilot the projects, select the most successful projects, and scale them up. Within these steps, however, a few activities are particularly important.

## Uncovering Opportunities

Before looking for new opportunities, it's important to diagnose the current model to understand its limitations. Look closely at each element of the business model and test how the choice aligns with industry trends, evolving customer preferences, and relative advantage or disadvantage over competitors. Valuable insights are often generated by dissatisfied customers.

Once a company understands its current choices, it is better positioned to brainstorm new opportunities. To give momentum to this exercise, it is useful to apply three types of successful BMI patterns from various industries: innovations to the value proposition, to the operating model, and to the business system architecture—that is, how the innovation integrates with the surrounding business network.

## Implementing the New Model

The winners in BMI aren't necessarily the originators of new models; more often they are simply the first to successfully roll out others' ideas. Therefore, scaling up can be the most critical step for BMI. When U.S. government regulation allowed generic parts to be sold, it wiped out the profits of branded engines and parts. GE Aircraft Engines wasn't the first in its industry to conceive of, or even implement, the idea of pay per use. But the company was the first to reinvent many of the elements in the business model that allowed it to be profitable with a pay-per-use value proposition.

An important choice that incumbent companies must make is whether to embed a new business model in the core business or establish it separately. The benefits of common assets, customers, and capabilities argue in favor of integration. But a significant disruption to the current model argues for a separate approach.

The most difficult cases are those in which management comes to realize that a successful business model has become obsolete and the alternatives are in direct opposition. In such cases, either very decisive leadership or competing structures are required to resolve the conflict.

## Building the Platform and Skills

The third and final step is to build a platform for systematically managing the BMI process, capabilities, and portfolio of experiments. Most new business models are inherently disruptive and can incur significant internal resistance. BMI requires a distinct set of processes and capabilities to overcome an organization's short-term focus and also to sustain a BMI advantage continuously.

# Questions for Mobilizing the Organization

BMI begins by assessing the company's current context, the needs of its customers, and the models of its competitors. These steps should be completed with sufficient clarity and honesty to reveal what is currently working, what is not, and what might constitute a better value proposition. Executives seeking to create a shared awareness of the threats and opportunities involved should ask themselves the following questions:

- What compromises does our current business model force customers to make?
- Why are nonusers or defectors dissatisfied with our offering?
- Do we offer customers a better value proposition than the competition?
- What alternative models are gaining share at the edges of our industry?
- If we were an industry outsider, what would we do to take advantage of the gaps or weaknesses in our business model?
- Do we have a plan for identifying potential business models, implementing them, and embedding BMI capabilities within the organization?
- What do we need to change in our organization and operations to implement a new business model?
- What information would we need to make a commitment to a new model?
- How urgent is the perceived need for change in our organization?
- How should our ideas be championed?

For companies that have yet to achieve the performance they are looking for, there may be no better time than now to launch new business models or transform old ones. Consider the state of your business today. Could you not only change your company's game plan but also change the game itself?

# 41

# The Deconstruction of Value Chains

## Carl W. Stern

*This chapter was first published in 1998. At the time the Internet was in its infancy—Google was founded the same year—but its implications for the economics of information were already becoming clear and remain true today.*

The end of the nineteenth century saw the construction of the vertically integrated value chains that came to define modern business. The end of the twentieth century witnessed their deconstruction. Markets intruded on the web of proprietary arrangements that held these chains together. As they did so, the boundaries defining businesses, companies, and industries came under attack—radically transforming the nature of competition. New concepts of strategy and organization are required in order to cope.

## The Logic of Value Chains—Undermined

Integrated value chains served business well. They enabled the sophisticated coordination that growing technical complexity required. They organized the dedicated assets, both human and physical, necessary for achieving economies of scale and scope. Expensive to create, they were a formidable barrier to competition once established. The vertically integrated value chain was a potent competitive machine.

Not anymore. Powerful forces have undermined the logic and practice of traditional vertical integration. Eroding trade barriers and the resulting globalization of markets give businesses worldwide access to world-class capabilities. Modern manufacturing and distribution technologies make global sourcing and selling increasingly low cost. Deregulation and increasingly sophisticated capital markets allow the laws of economics to prevail at every step of the value chain.

But the most powerful force subverting conventional value chains—partly because it acts as a catalyst and accelerator for all the others—is the revolution in the economics of information. Information has always been the glue that held value chains together. The cost of getting sufficiently rich information to suppliers, channels, and customers made proprietary information systems and dedicated assets a necessity and gave vertical integration its economic rationale.

That glue has now melted. Universal connectivity and common communications standards enable the open and virtually cost-free exchange of information of all kinds. Companies share product designs, logistics information, and financial data with equal ease both inside and outside the corporation. New intermediaries are emerging to support interconnection, facilitate comparison, guarantee performance, and make markets. Searching and switching are vastly simpler and cheaper than ever.

These trends have two simultaneous effects. On one hand, proprietary links give way to markets. Witness the outsourcing trend: companies make use of key activities in the value chain without owning them. On the other hand, opportunities for rich communication and collaboration between customers and suppliers are greater than ever. Both these developments undermine vertical integration, replacing it with a highly flexible mix of new coordination mechanisms, ranging from the ruthlessness of the spot market at one extreme to the most strategic of partnerships at the other.

## Patterns of Deconstruction

As traditional value chains deconstruct, fundamentally new business models begin to appear. In some cases, a start-up mounts a direct attack on the established business model by splitting information flows from physical flows. This was the essence of Amazon.com's challenge to conventional book selling.

A more common pattern begins when a vertically integrated incumbent recognizes the opportunity to outsource nonstrategic or particularly capital-intensive parts of the value chain—even as it continues to dominate the whole. In these cases, integration gives way to *orchestration*. Successful orchestrators possess powerful brands and use them to retain control of the lion's share of an industry's value added while minimizing their own assets.

But maintaining control of the value chain is not easy. The orchestrated—those that focus on a specific value-added step, or *layer*—have every incentive to drive for scale and scope themselves. If they succeed, they wrest control of the value chain from the orchestrator, as Intel and Microsoft did from IBM. The business then deconstructs entirely. Each layer becomes a distinct business with its own economics. Some of these layer businesses are highly scale sensitive; dominating them can be extraordinarily profitable. Others are naturally fragmented; after deconstruction, profits are hard to come by. The onset of fragmentation can, however, create opportunities for a new sort of player—*navigators* that help participants cope with the complexity of doing business in a deconstructed world.

# The Implications of Deconstruction

The competitive implications of deconstruction are profound and wide ranging:

- The traditional definition of businesses and industries—and, therefore, the reference set of competitors, suppliers, and customers—becomes obsolete.
- Competitive advantage is de-averaged. Businesses in which the economics of one activity are compromised for the sake of the whole will be especially vulnerable.
- Advantage across the entire value chain no longer matters; it's the advantage in each layer that counts. As a result, the new unit of strategic analysis is the layer.
- Horizontal strategies—those that apply layer capabilities across previously distinct businesses—become serious alternatives to traditional

strategies of vertical integration and customer franchise in a single industry.

- Managing resource allocation at the layer level requires new ways to evaluate investments and gives birth to a whole new concept of the portfolio. The finer parsing of risk permits imaginative new financial strategies.
- The boundaries of the corporation become fluid and permeable. Ownership is no longer a condition for effective coordination or control.
- Customers are empowered; brands become vulnerable. Traditional asymmetries of information are challenged by the rise of navigators that search and switch on the customer's behalf.
- Intermediaries that extract value from controlling a chokepoint in the flow of information are vulnerable to disintermediation.

In a competitive environment characterized by deconstruction, commitment to existing business models, however rational they may appear, becomes a liability. The attacker has the advantage. Incumbents are under threat from increasingly unfamiliar intruders—but they also have unprecedented opportunities to exploit their capabilities in new ways.

# 42

# Time-Based Management

## Thomas M. Hout
## and George Stalk, Jr.

*This chapter was first published in 1993, a time when the concept of time-based competition had taken hold and companies were moving beyond cost-based competition through an understanding of the strategic value of time and of the importance of focusing on business processes.*

We first spoke of time-based competition in the 1980s. The concept was simple: companies that meet the needs of their customers faster than competitors grow faster and are more profitable than others in their industries. We argued that time could be the next decade's most powerful competitive weapon and management tool for U.S. companies.

We were right. Companies of all sorts and sizes became time-based competitors. By inspecting their processes and organizations through the lens of time these companies have found new ways to operate, satisfy their customers, compete, grow, and invigorate themselves. Consider the results of three very different companies.

## Time and Innovation

Chrysler entered the 1990s with only two profitable product lines—minivans and Jeeps—and several outdated lines of cars and trucks. It needed a new winner soon and made the do-or-die decision to reinvent its new car development process and cut the old time of four to six years to 39 months.

In the company's traditional process, a new car concept moved sequentially from styling to engineering, to parts procurement, to manufacturing, with each step carefully planned and scheduled. Under a time-based approach, each new-car platform had a team of several hundred people working together on everything from the start. Everyone, including vendors, accessed the same information. All functions on the team were housed on one floor of the development building, breaking up the old departmental offices and enabling more face-to-face communication. Each new car team had a vice president in charge—many with no previous experience managing development on this scale—to make sure old habits and turf issues did not get in the way.

Chrysler made its first move with the LH large-car platform team—nicknamed by the skeptical press the Last Hope. In 1992, the LH models—Intrepid, Vision, New Yorker, and Concorde—were introduced. The team took 25 percent of the time out, cut the dollar investment to 30 percent below that in any previous program, and brought out a car to rave reviews and more orders than any new Chrysler model since the minivan.

## Time and Service

Because time-based competition started in manufacturing companies, large service organizations initially questioned whether its principles applied to them. Experience in industries ranging from insurance to package delivery to health care proved that these principles do. Take, for example, the case of Karolinska Hospital in Stockholm, Sweden.

Sweden has provided superior health care for its entire population since World War II. But by the early 1990s, rising costs and a weakened economy were forcing the government to reassess and reduce health care expenditures. In the face of expected cost cuts, Karolinska, one of the country's leading teaching hospitals, wondered if quality care could survive.

Karolinska turned to time-based competition. At first, the doctors were skeptical. How could they save time without imperiling patient care? In fact, they found that poor coordination and scheduling problems were not only reducing efficiency and inflating costs but also causing unnecessary delay, inconvenience, and anxiety for patients.

By redesigning operating procedures and staffing patterns, Karolinska was able to cut the time required for preoperative testing from months to days. It was able to close 2 of 15 operating rooms and still increase the number of operations per day by 30 percent. Doctors could schedule operations in weeks rather than months. The result: better service for patients, with no loss of quality, and less overhead.

## Time and Integration

Time-based competition may be at its most powerful when suppliers and customers use it to redefine how they do business. That is what happened when textile manufacturer Milliken & Company joined with the Warren Featherbone Company, a children's apparel maker, and Mercantile Stores, a large retail chain, to compete through what they called Quick Response.

In the mid-1980s, it took 66 weeks for the apparel industry to go from yarn at the manufacturer to clothing on the rack. But since no one in the chain knew what would be selling in a month, much less a year, the cost of that lengthy supply cycle was devastating. The industry as a whole lost billions of dollars each year through markdowns on what customers didn't want and by not having enough of what they did want.

The three companies were gaming each other every time they did business. Each level—fabric, garment, retail—carried redundant buffer inventory to protect against shortages caused by others. When demand turned down, each scrambled to avoid holding inventory by slashing orders to its supplier. Long lead times and slow communications between layers made things worse. The result was heavy markdowns at retail that sent cost pressure back through the system.

With Quick Response, the companies got together and reengineered their forecasting, production, reordering, and logistics systems, and in doing so, they created a new short-cycle replenishment system. Mercantile shared its point-of-sale (POS) information with Warren Featherbone and Milliken. Orders down the chain became more frequent and smaller. Inventories carried at each level shrank, eliminating the need to shift them. Any surprises or problems anywhere were communicated along the chain quickly. The result: retail inventory turns went from three times to five times a year, and markdowns dropped to one-third of the industry average.

Reaching this level of integration was difficult, because it required each company to make itself more vulnerable to the rest of the chain. Here, time was a unique catalyst. It was the one metric all the partners could easily understand and use that did not pit one against the other. By setting radical time compression goals, everyone was forced to change old assumptions.

# Time and Business Process Reengineering

Time-based competition begins with strategy and ends with process reengineering. Chrysler, Karolinska, and Milliken were all looking for higher revenues, not just lower costs. They focused their thinking first on getting to the customer faster, then reengineered the processes that could help them do this. They engaged the organization in a positive building effort, not a contraction.

For every dollar that can be removed by reengineering cost and reducing the consumption of time, several more can be saved by rethinking how to use speed to serve customers better and competitively reposition the company. Chrysler offered fresh, not old, product. Karolinska avoided cuts in service by increasing throughput. Milliken and its apparel partners raised price realization by eliminating markdowns.

Time-based competition is a reality, not just a concept. It has rapidly become the base line, not the exception.

# 43

# The New "Low Cost"

## Nicolas Kachaner, Zhenya Lindgardt, and David C. Michael

Low-cost offerings are not new. But there is a new wave of low-cost business models, and they are taking share from traditional players in many industry sectors and locations.

This new wave first appeared in rapidly developing economies (RDEs) where both local and multinational companies have had to design new models to serve a large segment of customers with limited financial means. These new models also have important strategic implications for the developed world. RDE-based market leaders are leveraging their home-market success to pursue global ambitions. And multinationals are disrupting competitors and pioneering new price points and applications in the developed world with low-cost offerings created for RDEs.

Although some traditional firms are riding this wave, too many are at risk of missing it.

## History and the Golden Rules of Low Cost

In 1436, Johann Gutenberg invented the printing press. Until then, books had been laboriously and exquisitely hand produced by monks. Gutenberg's invention dramatically reduced production costs and time, and by 1500, nearly 20 million books had been printed—more than had been produced in the whole of human history before Gutenberg's invention.

In 1869, John Sainsbury opened his first self-service supermarket in London. Until then, grocers had competed on the basis of location and sales staff. Sainsbury decided to locate his stores outside city centers and let customers serve themselves. Some of the money he saved by reducing staff and choosing less expensive locations was returned to customers in lower prices. Success came quickly.

A low-cost approach is more than merely an opportunity for current customers to buy the same goods for less. Most important, it is a truly new value proposition that addresses both existing and new customers and is supported by a novel operating model. Consider this: 55 percent of the first-time flyers on Ryanair, a low-cost airline, had never before traveled by plane.

Almost a century after Sainsbury's innovation, Theo and Karl Albrecht reimagined the grocery store once more, in Germany. Supermarkets had become hypermarkets, and, with ever-increasing store sizes, real estate and personnel costs had again become significant factors. The Albrecht brothers realized that by focusing on a restricted assortment of about 600 products and concentrating on private-label goods, they could offer low prices plus the convenience of city center locations. Their company, Aldi, became an international grocery empire.

Offering a limited range of products without compromising on quality is another critical pillar of many low-cost business models. Henry Ford employed this principle in 1908, when he introduced the Model T automobile and put America behind the wheel. With the introduction of the moving assembly line in 1913, he traded variety for cost, decreeing that the car could be manufactured in any color—"so long as it's black." Black, it should be noted, was the fastest-drying paint.

In 1948, Dick and Mac McDonald reinvented the restaurant: No more printed menus—only a limited set of choices. No waiters—customers would place orders directly at a counter separating the dining room from the kitchen. No more forks and knives—customers would eat with their hands. Perhaps they would even wipe their table before leaving. What a revolution. There would be no compromise on the quality of the food. Cost savings were achieved by range simplification and, as in a supermarket, by having customers perform part of the work traditionally done by employees.

These examples illustrate the four golden rules of low-cost business models:

- Low cost is not low margin. It can be highly profitable. Ryanair and McDonald's, for example, have been among the most profitable companies in their industries.
- Low cost is not low quality. It is, usually, narrower range.
- Low cost is not cheap imitation. It is true innovation.
- Low cost is not unbranded. It frequently supports potent brands.

Although not all successful low-cost business models are alike, many have characteristics in common and rely on a carefully selected set of radical and mutually supportive choices across all dimensions of the business model (Figure 43.1).

# The New Wave of Low-Cost Business Models

By the beginning of the twenty-first century, most multinationals had realized that to achieve their growth ambitions they would need to win in the so-called BRIC markets: Brazil, Russia, India, and China.

Most companies simply transplanted their traditional developed world business models to these markets. Serving higher-income customers in the major urban centers, these companies achieved double-digit growth with only a small revenue base. This kind of growth is nice, but it's unlikely to have a material impact on a company's global results or long-term leadership. In most sectors, achieving strategically significant revenues in RDEs requires going beyond the top of the pyramid and developing business models and offerings that address the broader market. A low-cost business model is a critical element of any RDE strategy.

Low cost is a necessity in emerging markets and often also a source of inspiration in mature markets. In 2002, General Electric (GE) was having only limited success selling ultrasound devices priced at $100,000 and higher to sophisticated Chinese hospitals. It was clear that capturing the heart of the market would require a dramatically different business model. GE chose to pursue a value proposition focused on low cost and portability. It made significant changes to its operating model—in R&D as well as sales

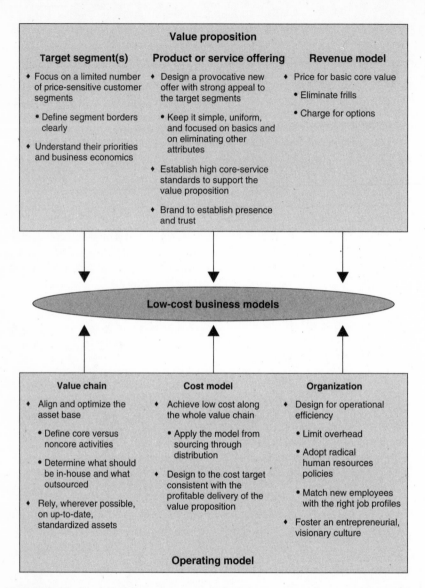

**FIGURE 43.1** Low-Cost Business Models Are Based on an Integrated Model with Radical Choices

Source: BCG analysis.

and service—to rapidly develop and launch a portable product. At an initial selling price of $30,000, since lowered to $15,000, the product was a success.

Sales took off in China. Moreover, GE discovered that this new product opened numerous new applications for ultrasound in the developed world where its traditional products were either too large or too expensive to be considered. By 2008, revenues from portable ultrasound equipment had grown to nearly $300 million. GE has reaped similar "two-way" benefits not only in other health care lines but also in other businesses such as aircraft engines. Jeff Immelt, GE's chairman and CEO, refers to this phenomenon as "reverse innovation."

Low-cost business model innovators are not all from the developed world. Taiwan's ASUSTeK Computer pioneered the low-cost market for netbooks with a *profitable* Linux-based machine priced only slightly higher than the computers from the nonprofit One Laptop per Child initiative.

# How Should Traditional Companies React?

Too often, when it comes to low cost, companies get caught in two traps: a denial trap and an innovation trap.

We all know the denial trap. Business leaders underestimate the power of low-cost models to affect their business. They think that low-cost options are not serious rivals. They presume that their customers value their company's service and brand too much to defect. When they start to see movement toward a low-cost player, they make some minor adjustments or efforts at imitation. When that approach eventually fails, they retreat to the premium segment.

This was exactly how traditional pharmaceutical companies reacted to the growth of generic drugs in the mid-1990s. Having considered generics to be negligible, they tried to cover the low-end market with older, off-patent products. Some launched generics divisions but closed them down because volumes were low and margins thin. But then Teva Pharmaceutical Industries, a leader in generics, achieved top-quartile profitability while growing at three times the rate of the pharmaceutical market overall. Then it turned the tables and diversified into patent-protected drugs.

The innovation trap is familiar too. Development teams typically think that new products should always be better, more sophisticated, *and, thus, more expensive than the models they replace.* When new high-end products are launched, the previous generations are discounted, becoming the midrange and bottom-of-the-line products.

Meanwhile, smart low-cost players invest in true innovation targeted at the bottom of the pyramid. Deploying new technologies and frequently new business models, these low-cost players compete and win against yesterday's products. In fact, a leading manufacturer of medical devices, recognizing this syndrome, recently decided to refocus some of its R&D activities to renew its low-end range.

For companies that have avoided the denial and innovation traps and have decided to participate in the low-cost game, there are still hard choices:

- Should the low-cost business model be operated within the core business?
- Should it share the same brand as the parent?
- Should it try to maximize synergies with the parent or favor autonomy?
- Should the low-cost business grow organically or by acquisition?

There are no one-size-fits-all answers to these questions, but experience suggests some general rules:

- Low-cost offerings cannot flourish within a traditional "high-cost" environment.
- Brands can stretch only so far. Thus, a secondary brand is often advisable.
- The first priority for a low-cost model is that it must win on its own merits. Synergies should be a secondary concern.
- There are some brilliant organic development successes in low cost. But, if good options exist, there is no shame in acquiring leading low-cost players in their infancy—and then giving them autonomy.

Jetstar Airways, the low-cost airline launched by the Qantas Group in 2004, is a great example of organic development. Jetstar was given a great deal of autonomy. It could buy its own planes, recruit staff under its own contract, and operate under its own brand. Jetstar became profitable in its first year of operation, and in 2009, Qantas announced that its own solid financial performance was principally due to Jetstar's strong profitability. Most other traditional airlines that launched low-cost offerings chose to closely link operations, undermining results because of the mismatch between their low-cost value proposition and a hybrid operating model that combined some low-cost elements with largely major-carrier economics.

Essilor International, a world leader in ophthalmic lenses, illustrates the role of acquisitions. The company has countered the rise of Asian imports in its core Western markets by systematically acquiring profitable, low-cost companies on all continents—among them a leading Korean manufacturer, Indian laboratories, and leading stock houses in Italy, the United Kingdom, and the United States. Essilor has let them run fairly independently with a focus on top-line success, an approach it calls "organic acquisition."

## A Call to Action

Multinational companies cannot avoid having a robust low-cost strategy. Without one, it would be impossible to compete in emerging markets and to prevail over innovative low-cost challengers in developed ones. Low-cost attackers often hit where it hurts, rapidly crippling the economics of more traditional business models.

So take a moment to dream: get your management team together and imagine your worst nightmare. Then ask yourselves what it would take to be the initiator rather than the victim. This might cannibalize some of your current profit, but most likely it will also expand your market scope in a significant way.

Are you like the monks of the fifteenth century, trying to illuminate manuscripts faster and better? Or do you envision creating the new printing press and vaulting to the top of the industry—and delivering a true revolution for the benefit of humankind?

# 44

# The Hardball Manifesto

## George Stalk, Jr. and Rob Lachenauer

The winners in business have always played hardball. When companies play hardball, they use every legitimate resource and strategy available to them to gain advantage over their competitors. When they achieve competitive advantage, they attract more customers, gain market share, boost profits, reward their employees, and weaken their competitors' positions. Then they reinvest their gains in their businesses to improve product quality, expand their offerings, and sharpen their processes to further strengthen their competitive advantage.

When they can continue this virtuous cycle of activity for a prolonged period, companies can transform their competitive advantage into a position even more powerful and desirable: they can achieve decisive advantage. With that, they put themselves into a far more powerful and influential position than just that of the market leader. They can use their decisive advantage to bring about fundamental change in an entire industry, put their competitors into a reactive position, cause their partners and suppliers to make adjustments, and deliver so much value to their customers that their market share grows larger still.

Winning through competitive advantage may sound like nothing more than good, serious, and sensible business practice. But hardball companies

This chapter is based on the authors' 2004 book, *Hardball: Are You Playing to Win or Playing to Play?*, published by Harvard Business School Press.

are further distinguished by their attitude and behavior. They play with such a commitment to the game, such fierceness of execution, and such relentless drive to maximize their strengths that they look very different from other companies that have admirable performance and sound business skills. Hardball players always play to win, in every aspect of the game. They always seek decisive victory. They don't want to win a 2–1 squeaker. They would prefer a 9–2 rout.

Softball players have no competitive advantage or, if they have one, may not know what it is or may be unable to exploit it. Some softballers can drift along for years, finding ways to stay afloat from quarter to quarter—through trade loading, for example, or cost cutting. A few may seek to disguise their poor performance through activities that are questionable, if not illegal, such as creating shell customers. In the parlance of pitching, such companies are throwing junk.

## Fundamental Corporate Purpose

We believe that the fundamental purpose of companies in our society is to compete as hard as they can against one another. In the September 13, 1970, issue of the *New York Times* magazine, Nobel laureate Milton Friedman quoted from his book *Capitalism and Freedom*: "There is one and only one social responsibility of business—to use its resources and engage in activities designed to increase its profits so long as it stays within the rules of the game, which is to say, engages in open and free competition without deception or fraud."

Friedman's comments sparked a debate about corporate purpose that raged in corporate suites across the United States and around the world, in the halls of academe, and in the influential "chat societies" of Washington and other power centers. The debate continues to this day.

Bruce Henderson, the founder of BCG, fundamentally agreed with Friedman but placed even greater emphasis on the importance of competition. In 1973, troubled by the antitrust actions taken against IBM and AT&T in the name of competitive "fairness," Henderson wrote: "The dominant producer in every business should increase his market share steadily. Failure to do so is prima facie evidence of failure to compete."

Henderson went on to describe the virtuous cycle that creates decisive advantage: "Competitors' market shares should be unstable. Low-cost competitors should displace higher-cost competitors. Customers should share the benefits of lower cost with those suppliers who make it possible. Any failure to gain market share even with lower cost is self-evident restraint of trade."

In Henderson's view, a failure by companies to strive for decisive advantage would lead to a failure of their industry to "concentrate"—that is, consolidate and improve. This would create an even larger shortcoming—"a failure of the national economy to optimize productivity and reduce inflation." In other words, as self-centered as playing hardball and seeking to win may appear to be, they are, in fact, essential to the health and strength of the larger economy and society.

We concur with Milton Friedman, Bruce Henderson, and many others who believe that it is the function of companies to compete as hard as they can to gain customers and profits, with the goal of achieving the maximum advantage over their competitors.

# A Never-Ending Cycle

From our experience working with clients over many years, in many industries, and in many countries, we know that the leaders of the world's most successful companies—the hardball winners—believe it is their obligation to their shareholders, customers, employees, and society to seek and exploit their competitive advantage to the fullest. When possible, the hardball leaders will push that advantage to the point where competitors are squeezed and even feel pain.

If competitors find themselves in this position, they have two choices. They can play softball, using nonstrategic means to get society to bend its rules to hobble their hardball opponents, or they can look for the chinks in the armor of the hardball players to change the rules of the game in their favor. We advocate the second approach. Business, like life, goes on as a never-ending cycle of achieving advantage, facing threats from bold and innovative competitors, and adjusting to or succumbing to those challenges.

But when an organization achieves advantage, it develops a tendency to continue operating with the same strategy or model that produced the advantage. The leader's main role, then, is to keep alive the quest for advantage. As Roger Enrico, former chairman and CEO of PepsiCo, said to us, it's impossible for an organization to "shadowbox" its way to continued advantage building. The leader's task is to make his or her people understand that their company's advantage is always in peril and, if necessary, to create an opponent against which the organization can focus its efforts.

In addition to having strong leaders, hardball competitors also have what is generally called good management. Indeed, the importance of "soft" issues, such as culture and employee relations, should not be downplayed but rather understood in the context of strategy.

Good management is a necessary but insufficient condition of business success. Differences in profitability correlate very strongly with differences in competitive advantage. We believe that a management team that can provide a hardball strategy and push the organization to use it to gain competitive advantage is the most likely to deliver benefits—emotional, intellectual, social, financial, and professional—to its people.

By championing hardball, we are not advocating that everything learned about how to create good relationships with people both inside and outside the organization should be discarded or ignored. On the contrary, we believe that people who work for and with hardball players are exceptionally well rewarded and among the most fulfilled you will find in business.

# 45 Leading Transformation

## Andrew Dyer, Grant Freeland, Steve Gunby, and Cynthia Blendu

*In this chapter we break from the format of the rest of the book and hand the microphone to nine CEOs who have successfully driven and sustained fundamental change in their organizations.[1] They run organizations headquartered in North America, Europe, Asia, and Australia in fields ranging from manufacturing and finance to the Internet, consumer, retail, and nonprofit sectors.*

Most CEOs, especially new ones, must fundamentally transform their enterprise at some time during their tenure. Boards are increasingly appointing CEOs with that explicit charter, and almost all CEOs recognize the need to take even successful enterprises to new levels of performance.

The CEOs we spoke with have relied on many of the same leadership tools. In fact, the similarities across their approaches far outweigh the differences. In particular, almost all the leaders discussed the three core elements of transformation: winning in the medium term, funding the journey, and building the right team, organization, and culture.

---

[1] A fuller version of this chapter featuring 11 CEOs is available at bcgperspectives.com. Videos and transcripts of the interviews are also available there.

# Winning in the Medium Term

The ultimate goal of any organizational transformation should be to create a vibrant and exciting future—and greater value. Transformations therefore generally require a fundamental rethinking of the organization and strategy, as well as a shift in direction. They cannot succeed in business-as-usual environments; rather, they need to be built on a bedrock of bold moves.

This does not take one masterstroke but many jumps. Most of the leaders we interviewed undertook several stark and ambitious steps to position their organizations on stronger footing; such moves have ranged from geographic expansion and product development to an emphasis on growth.

At Hilton Worldwide, for example, company president and CEO Christopher J. Nassetta has embarked on a massive expansion of Hilton's global footprint, focusing on the fast-growing developing markets. Similarly, after Irene Rosenfeld returned to Kraft Foods in 2006, the CEO recognized that her company needed greater exposure in developing markets. She spent $27 billion buying LU and Cadbury, increasing Kraft's presence in India and China.

Louis Vachon, president and CEO of National Bank Financial Group, shifted his organization's focus from cost control to growth—during the turbulence of the financial crisis. "It was a fair amount of work moving from optimization, efficiency, and cost management to growth, new products, new markets, and new customers," he says. "When you have an optimization strategy, you focus on minimizing cost in the branch structure. When you move to growth, you make sure you have more people in your branches. We hired 300 people in our branches."

But transformations are not just about bold moves and new directions. Many are also about fortifying traditional approaches that are fundamentally important, as Rosenfeld discovered upon her return to Kraft Foods. She says that the company had been "maniacally focused on cost" and had lost sight of growth opportunities. "It very quickly became clear that our issue was not our categories. It was our participation within those categories," Rosenfeld says. "Consumers were eating cheese, they were eating meat, and they were drinking coffee. They just were not eating and drinking our brands in those categories. So the idea was really to take a look at what we needed to do to look for the growth opportunities within those categories."

When Brian Gallagher took over as president and CEO of United Way of America in 2002, the main focus at about half of the local United Way affiliates was fund-raising, while the other half was focused on community impact. "We were completely divided, but my sense was that almost everybody wanted to get back to community and social change," Gallagher says. "So the first thing we did was drive toward that mission and get agreement. And it came incredibly quickly."

Communication is a tool to ensure that people are focusing on the things that matter most. At Hilton Worldwide, Nassetta wants his 135,000 employees to concentrate on culture, performance, brands, and global expansion. "When I talk about our four key priorities, I sing it from the mountaintops—all the time, everywhere I go—so that people will know that what we want to do as an organization is channel our energies more to get those things done over other extraneous things that might be good but are not going to be as helpful in the long term," he says.

Likewise, David Brennan, executive director and CEO of AstraZeneca, sees as one of the main roles of a CEO the channeling of conversation and communication around the key topics. "If we are discussing things that are off the subject or are not really on that list of priorities, I think it is important as the CEO to raise your hand and say, 'That may be important, but we have said we want to do three or four things here. Let's make the best use of our time together to be focused on those things.' So R&D productivity, commercial excellence in the marketplace, operating an ethical business: those are things that you cannot delegate."

## Funding the Journey

Transformations may take years, but senior leaders do not have the luxury of many years to demonstrate results. They face pressures from their boards, investors, and employees to show tangible progress quickly. Many of them must free up resources to fund the strategic shifts that are needed to transform the organization. Although this phase is not the ultimate goal of any transformation, it is imperative.

This is not just about fighting fires, although it may seem that way to outsiders. In conversations, the leaders talk about the need, in the early days, to operate at two speeds. While they have taken immediate and urgent steps to extinguish the flames of short-term crises, they have simultaneously built a foundation for the future. One of the supreme challenges of transformation is managing these two distinct work streams with very different paces but complementary goals.

"You also have to make short-term changes in order to make sure you get some improvement in returns almost immediately," says Ian McLeod, the managing director of Coles, an Australian supermarket chain and retailer, speaking in the midst of a five-year transformation. Early success helps build confidence among employees that they can "do even better in the future."

When the global financial crisis hit, Chanda Kochhar, managing director and CEO of ICICI Bank, shifted the orientation of India's second-largest bank away from growth and expansion to focus on reducing risk and costs. But she did not want employees to be discouraged by this lull in the bank's ambitions, so she spent a fair share of her time talking directly to employees about the bank's short-term needs and medium-term goals. "Putting the strategy in perspective helped a lot . . . . I think people saw that medium-term picture, rather than just the one-year picture, and that helped to keep morale stable," Kochhar recalls.

Among the many potential levers leaders can pull to effect change, delayering—removing unnecessary layers in the organization—has emerged as one of the most popular short-term instruments that the leaders discussed. It has been used as a way to both save money and create greater clarity. Facing a 50 percent drop in market volumes during the recession, Martin Daum, the president and CEO of Daimler Trucks North America, was able to generate nearly $1 billion in extra cash flow through delayering and other restructuring moves. "Big organizations grow organically," Daum says. "It is a good exercise, from time to time, to question every single position."

In 2007, when Nassetta took the helm at Hilton Worldwide, an organization that had been created largely through acquisitions, he removed layers of management and inefficiencies that had built up over the years. "We had layer upon layer of duplication in all sorts of roles—and many more layers of decision making than we needed. It just slowed us down," Nassetta says. "We had a cost structure that was bloated, and we needed to do something about it. But we had the added benefit of becoming a lot more effective."

Other approaches to funding the journey include reevaluating sourcing, pricing, and asset strategies. But no matter which levers they have pulled, the leaders have needed to track progress rigorously against established goals, especially in complex restructurings that involved many initiatives. "You need a kind of IT tool that helps you track those thousand different measures and then rolls them up comprehensively," Daum says.

# Building the Right Team, Organization, and Culture

All discussions about transformations culminate in an exploration of people, organization, and culture. Transformations require focus, commitment, and engagement throughout the organization; even the best-laid plans will fail unless the people are on board.

Archie Norman, speaking while nonexecutive chairman of ITV and who has been involved in several transformations since his days at Asda, posits, "Behind all financial failures is organizational failure." Although that may be a blunt assessment, all the leaders recognized the need to give top priority to people and to organizational and cultural issues.

In 2010, Jasmine Whitbread was appointed the first international CEO of Save the Children, a loose federation of 29 organizations—whose leaders do not report to her directly. She has sought to create a global organization that takes advantage of scale but also recognizes the importance of collaboration throughout the global enterprise.

"Even if people report to you—which, in my case, the chief executives do not—you have to . . . go and get the buy-in," Whitbread says. "Make sure that you do have a core group—and it need not be that large—of key players who are totally up for going on that journey with you. Really nurture and do not underestimate the value of that group."

Many leaders describe how they needed to make changes at the top of the organization in order to build a united purpose. "It's pretty clear who gets it and who does not," Rosenfeld explains. "The key is whether the leaders are on the bus. What I have come to understand is that if they're not on the bus pretty quickly, they are never coming."

Greater accountability has generally accompanied these changes in senior leadership. "When I took this job, one of the things I tried to do was to begin to push accountability and responsibility down throughout the organization," Brennan says. "I had people—my direct reports, people I pay a lot of money to—coming and asking me to help them decide on things that I thought they should be deciding on for themselves, and I told them that."

Change needs to percolate to the far reaches of the empire. In our conversations, the leaders talked about their travels to the front line and all the efforts to engage with employees and to monitor and improve culture and morale.

"Everybody in the company was involved in one of our work streams or initiatives," explains Daum. "Employees always knew they were part of a greater effort—one important part. They knew that if they failed, we might not reach our target."

At Coles, McLeod has been careful to praise employees for what has been accomplished so far rather than simply looking ahead at what needs to be done in the transformation. "Sometimes, in that environment, you are so focused on improvement and doing better that you forget to give people the acknowledgment they deserve for the efforts they have made," he says.

Rakuten, Japan's largest Internet company, has been in a steady state of transformation since its founding in 1997. Its chairman and CEO, Hiroshi Mikitani, says that the development of a corporate philosophy has helped create alignment as the company has expanded into strikingly new businesses and markets. "We tell managers to follow the basic framework and the foundation of our corporate practice." As long as his executives adhere to the fundamentals, Mikitani gives them free rein to manage their businesses.

CEOs should also actively monitor employee engagement at all times—but especially during a transformation. "At Asda, I could typically tell how sales would be going by looking at the morale and attitude surveys. If I see bad attitude, high turnover, and absenteeism, I know I have a problem with sales," Norman says. "People's motivation is the input; sales and financial performance are the output."

Changing a culture is hard, and it takes time; this type of change requires a deliberate plan and a set of actions that support a longer-term strategy. "The culture you forge—and the way you express it—that is phase two, not phase one," Norman says. "If you start talking about new values, missions, and all these things in the middle of making people redundant, and all you are doing is branding your new values as having to do with misery and making people redundant, it will not work."

■ ■ ■

"There is not a magic formula," says Norman. "If there were, we probably would not be having this conversation."

But the foundations of success are consistent—winning in the medium term, funding the journey, and building the right team, organization, and culture. A CEO who finds his or her formula to do this can succeed in transforming the organization and creating an enduring legacy.

# Inspiring

Today's successful leaders do not bark orders. Instead, they strive to create conditions that allow their teams to succeed. They aim to *inspire* their organizations rather than intimidate or instruct them.

John Clarkeson, a former CEO of BCG, foresaw this evolution two decades ago. His chapter, "Jazz vs. Symphony," written in 1990, posited that tomorrow's winning company would be more flexible and place a greater premium on creating synergies across the organization, operating "more like a collection of jazz ensembles than a symphony orchestra." The leader of such an organization would have the ability to inspire people to put their best abilities forward in the service of the team. In doing so the leader must ask penetrating "why" questions to better understand the environment and to help his or her team to do likewise. Chapter 47, "Probing," explains how current and budding leaders can do this effectively.

Inspiring organizations, we have found, are not simply better directed than other companies. They are broadly more capable, in part as a result of employees' willingness and ability to self-direct. Chapter 48, "Smart Simplicity," describes six ways—smart rules—in which leaders can foster this orientation and aptitude by building an environment conducive to collaboration and the development of creative solutions. By implementing the six smart rules, leaders can promote more effective, less complicated, faster decision making—and ultimately a smarter, more streamlined organization.

Companies that are inspiring are also often better able to handle change. The final two chapters in this section discuss how leaders can build and strengthen this capability.

Chapter 49, "Strategic Optimism: How to Shape the Future in Times of Crisis," argues that leaders must take a proactive stance during difficult times and create a compelling vision of the future for internal and external stakeholders, one that reframes challenges as opportunities. The chapter focuses on the specific challenges posed by the global financial crisis of 2008 and beyond but its insights are evergreen.

Change is hard, and often fails. Chapter 50, "Lessons from My Three Decades with the Change Monster," distills into 10 lessons Jeanie Daniel Duck's many years of experience helping companies in transition, with a particular focus on the soft side of change. Most of the lessons are common sense, she explains, but leaders frequently do not follow them.

# 46 Jazz vs. Symphony

## John S. Clarkeson

*This chapter was first published in 1990. It remains one of our most popular Perspectives to this day.*

Is there a leadership crisis? Are we really lacking executives to inspire and lead our organizations into the twenty-first century? Or are the specifications for the job changing? Should we reexamine what kinds of leaders our organizations need?

The critical function in today's organization is the creative function. As change accelerates, organizations that are not continually recreating their reason for existence will not survive for very long. Business leaders must inspire this ongoing creativity by harnessing the knowledge and thinking abilities of many people with different and highly specialized skills.

Whether a business is driven by the need to increase variety, segment the market more finely, cope with shortening life cycles, harness the possibilities of new process technologies, or reposition against new competitors, the key task is to lead the organization to create products, processes, and services that have not existed before.

Routine work can eventually be broken down into individual, repetitive, and ultimately unchallenging tasks. In fact, most of our companies derive from a model whose original purpose was to control creativity. The key advantage of Ford's assembly line was that each man did one job the same way every time without distractions, interactions, or self-expression.

Today's organization follows a similar blueprint in maintaining walls between its specialized functions: marketing, manufacturing, engineering, and finance.

This suits many employees just fine. Professionals of all types share a number of preferences: commitment to their specialty, insistence on autonomy and the right to choose their work methods, and resistance to direction and evaluation by anyone other than their professional peers. Our modern organizations often encourage specialists to pursue the goals of their specialties at the expense of the other functions, the company, and the customer.

As a result, the biggest leadership challenge in business today may be leading specialized professionals from various functions to achieve the overall aims of the company in a rapidly changing environment.

What kind of leaders are able inspire their people to do this? Where might we look for examples?

In the world of classical music, the symphony is regarded by many as its most complex creation, requiring the integration of a large assembly of highly talented individuals for its performance. It has been suggested that the CEOs of the future may resemble the great conductors.

There is one major flaw in this analogy: no one gives a CEO the music he should play. But American music suggests another possible answer.

Duke Ellington was not an unusually gifted individual or musical theorist. It is disputed how well he could read musical notation. But measured by his output of original compositions, he may be the dominant figure in twentieth century music.

How is his prodigious creativity to be explained? From people who worked with him it appears he learned how to forge the divergent personalities of his jazz group into a single, highly creative instrument.

Members of his band have described how he learned to create on the run: he would offer up a scrap of an idea, suggest in general what he wanted, and then rely on his players to take cues from one another and to fill in their parts as they thought best.

His players were good but not without equal. He knew their quirks, their gifts, and their problems, and he encouraged them to learn to do things they didn't think they could do. Some players came and went, but many stayed for years. They developed through their membership in the group, and they learned from one another. Most of all, their capacity for innovation grew as they built on their cumulative experience.

Finally, by performing live in the close atmosphere of a jazz club, audience reaction was immediately visible to all, and refinement of new ideas came fast. On piano, Ellington was in the middle of the process, and communication was instantaneous. The results were astonishing.

The winning organization of the future will look more like a collection of jazz ensembles than a symphony orchestra. Functional barriers will be reduced. Different specialties will work in more permanent teams around specific customer opportunities. Customer contact will be continuous. Information will be current, rich, and available to all.

Leaders will be in the flow, not remote. Teamwork and cooperation will increase at the expense of individual competition. Cooperative support will moderate anxiety and encourage risk taking. Talented people will be attracted by the ability to see and influence the whole process, to learn from other knowledgeable people, and by the opportunity to create and grow.

The leaders who emerge from this environment will not look exactly like the old models. They will not necessarily excel at any one specialty. They will not have all the ideas. They will not be able to rely on exclusive decision-making authority, nor on the overwhelming force of personality, nor on a monopoly of information.

Leadership will flow to those whose vision can inspire the members of the team to put their best abilities at the service of the team. These leaders will create rather than demand loyalty; the best people will want to work with them. They will communicate effectively with a variety of people and use the conflict among diverse points of view to reach new insights. They will exert influence by the values they choose to reinforce. They will make leaders of their team members.

There are no set pieces anymore. The distinctions between composer/conductor/performer are eroding. The new leaders are all around us.

# 47 Probing

## Jonathan L. Isaacs

*This chapter was first published in 1985 and describes the importance of avoiding a very human bias, a bias as prevalent today as it was then.*

The single most important word in strategy formulation is *why*.

*Asking why* is the basic act of probing. Searching for root causes takes strategy formulation away from the unconscious repetition of past patterns and mimicry of competitors. *Asking why* leads to new insights and innovations that sometimes yield important competitive advantages.

*Asking why* repeatedly is a source of continual self-renewal, but the act of inquiry itself is an art. It can evoke strong reactions from the questioned. It is only rarely welcomed. It is sometimes met with defensiveness and hostility, on one hand, or, on the other, the patronizing patience reserved by the knowledgeable for the uninformed.

To ask why—and why not—about basics is to violate the social convention that expertise is to be respected, not challenged. Functional organizations in mature industries have a particular problem in this regard. One risks a lot to challenge the lord in his fiefdom.

Questioning the basics—the assumptions that "knowledgeable" people don't question—is disruptive. Probing slows things down, but often to good effect. It can yield revolutionary new thoughts in quite unexpected places.

Few new thoughts have been as revolutionary as the so-called Japanese manufacturing technique. Toyota was a leader in its development and, over more than 20 years, slowly learned to turn upside down the most basic assumptions about how manufacturing must be conceived and organized. Central to this rethinking was tireless probing. In his book on the Toyota Production System, Taiichi Ohno, vice president of manufacturing for Toyota, cites the practice of the five whys. He gives an example of how asking why five times (or more) led him through all the explanations to find the most important root cause.

## CAN YOU REPEAT "WHY" FIVE TIMES?

It's easy to say, but difficult to practice.
Suppose a machine stopped functioning.

1. "Why did the machine stop functioning?"
   *"There was an overload, and the fuse blew."*
2. "Why was there an overload?"
   *"It was because lubrication of the bearing was not sufficient."*
3. "Why was the lubrication not sufficient?"
   *"Because the lubrication pump was not pumping sufficiently."*
4. "Why was it not pumping sufficiently?"
   *"The shaft of the pump was worn, and it was rattling."*
5. "Why was the shaft worn out?"
   *"There was no strainer attached, and this caused metal scrap to get in."*

To have stopped anywhere along the way would have ended the search before the root cause was found. To probe to the limits is to simplify the problem to its essentials and solve one problem rather than five.

To pursue such probing takes a special, strongly motivated person, unless one makes it the norm for the organization. Asking why five times is easy to say, but hard to do. It challenges people's knowledge and even self-respect. It can call into question their diligence and the basis of their expertise. It requires fresh thinking on all sides. Yet it's so basic to learning, to seeing new things from the familiar. In the early nineteenth century, doctors routinely went, without washing, from autopsies to the treatment of patients—with disastrous results. Ignaz Semmelweis is the man who first hypothesized the basic relationship and proposed and tested a change to clean hands—yet in his own time he had to struggle with his peers because he questioned the accepted practice.

## Probing Takes Us beyond Data Analysis

Good strategy depends critically on knowing the root causes. Finding them is often a task beyond quantitative analysis. One must look to broader frames of reference and bring basic judgment and common sense to bear. Probing—asking why—is the often intuitive search for the logic that heavy data analysis can miss or bury.

*Asking why* is a *qualitative* act. It is different from quantitative analysis, but the one gains power from the other. It propels analysis forward by raising new questions to be subjected to rigorous analysis. It takes us beyond the numbers to new answers, new solutions, and new opportunities. Quantitative analysis should not become both the means and the end.

*Asking why* can raise the questions that are fundamental, but not necessarily answerable through rigorous analysis itself. These are the basic questions of leadership and common sense. They are the search for the "point." For example:

- Why do we continue in this business?
- Why should anyone buy this product?
- What will prevent competitors from matching us? What will we do then?
- Why are we making so much money? Why won't it eventually come to an end? What must we do now to prepare for or moderate that change?

These sorts of probes search for the bedrock reasons for value and advantages to test how enduring they may be. They ask whether the shape and character of the business and its strategy make sense.

*Asking why* five times is easy in concept but more difficult in practice. It can be very rewarding. *Why not do it?*

# 48 Smart Simplicity

## Yves Morieux

Companies face an increasingly complex world. Globalization and technology have opened up new markets and enabled new competitors. With an abundance of options to choose from, customers are harder to please—and more fickle—than ever. Each day, competitive advantage seems more elusive and fleeting.

In and of itself, this complexity is not a bad thing—it brings opportunities as well as challenges. The problem is the way companies respond to it. Managers redesign the organization's structure, performance measures, and incentives. More layers get added, more procedures imposed. To smooth the implementation of those "hard" changes, companies introduce "soft" initiatives designed to infuse work with positive emotions and a sense of collaboration. Such initiatives are well intentioned, but they are no match for the problems that arise when an organization becomes overly complicated.

In some of the most complicated organizations, managers spend 40 percent of their time writing reports and 30 to 60 percent of it in coordination meetings. That doesn't leave much time for them to work with their teams. As a result, employees are often misdirected and expend a lot of effort in vain. Invariably, employee satisfaction and productivity end up suffering.

---

We've found a different and far more effective approach for managing complexity. It does not involve formal guidelines and processes; rather, it entails creating an environment in which employees can work with one another to develop creative solutions to complex challenges. The approach incorporates a set of simple yet powerful principles. We call them smart rules. Using the rules—all of them, or sometimes just one or two—enables a complicated company to transform itself into a smarter, more streamlined organization.

# Rule 1: Improve Understanding of What Coworkers Do

To respond to complexity intelligently, people have to really understand one another's work: the goals and challenges others have to meet, the resources they can draw on, and the constraints under which they operate. Without this shared understanding, people will blame problems on other people's lack of intelligence or skills, not on the resources and constraints of the organization.

This was the case at a hotel group that was struggling with falling occupancy rates, declining prices, and poor customer satisfaction. Many of the hotel managers blamed the "detached mentality" and weak customer-facing skills of the reception employees, who were young and inexperienced—and never stayed long enough to learn better. The chain therefore decided to set up an incentive based on occupancy rates and sales for the receptionists and to train them in customer service.

Despite all the energy devoted to these initiatives, the performance did not improve. Eventually, a team of salespeople decided to spend one month with the receptionists to see what was *really* going on. The team discovered that the receptionists' most pressing challenge was handling unhappy customers. Their constraint was a lack of cooperation from the support functions, including housekeeping, room service, and maintenance. Housekeeping, for instance, regularly failed to inform maintenance about broken appliances in rooms.

The new incentives were useless, because they had no impact on the lack of cooperation from the support functions. Exhausted and discouraged, the young clerks would often quit after a few weeks. Their high turnover rate didn't stem from a lack of commitment. On the contrary, the receptionists who cared the least were the ones who stayed the longest.

Exploring the real context of employees' work helps managers discover when people need to cooperate and how well they're doing it. Although you can measure the combined output of a group, it is difficult to measure the input of each member, and the more cooperation there is, the harder it gets. Indeed, when managers rely on traditional metrics and peer feedback, they may end up rewarding people who actually avoid cooperation.

# Rule 2: Reinforce the People Who Are Integrators

Conflicts between front and back offices are often inherent. Back offices typically need to standardize processes and work, and front offices have to accommodate the needs of individual customers.

A common organizational response is to create some sort of coordinating unit—a middle office. But that just turns one problem into two: between the back and middle offices and between the middle and front offices. The same thing happens vertically in organizations: coordination problems between the corporate center and country operations trigger the creation of regional layers in between.

A better response is to empower line individuals—or groups—to play that integrative role. If you've followed the first rule and observed people at work, it will probably be fairly obvious to you who these individuals or groups are. Once you've identified the integrators, you should reinforce their power by increasing their responsibilities and giving them a greater say on issues that matter to others. Removing some formal rules and procedures also helps increase the discretionary power of integrators.

At the struggling hotel group, the managers realized that the receptionists could play a key integrative role among the hotel staff and the customers. But rather than coordinating those interactions through a formal process, the company gave the reception staff a stronger voice in the promotions of people in support functions—particularly the housekeepers and the maintenance crew. The housekeepers soon started to cooperate by checking all equipment and appliances as they were cleaning rooms; maintenance would then readily intervene.

# Rule 3: Expand the Amount of Power Available

Usually, the people with the least power in an organization shoulder most of the burden of cooperation and get the least credit. When they realize this, they often withdraw from cooperation and hide in their silos. Companies that want to increase cooperation need to give these people more power so that they can take the risk of trusting others, showing initiative, and being transparent about performance.

However, firms have to do this without taking power away from others. The answer is to create new power bases, by giving individuals new responsibilities for issues that matter to others and to the firm's performance.

The experiences of a large retailer illustrate how this works. The retailer had decided to lower costs and enhance professionalization by centralizing the procurement and human resources functions. Store managers lost a lot of power in the process. Yet the store managers were supposed to play a strong role in making sure employees were responsive to customer needs. They were also a primary source of innovations for store layouts and shop floor operations. Without organizational clout, how were they to do this?

Senior managers addressed the problem by announcing to customers that the lines in front of cashiers would not exceed a certain length in their stores. The store managers were given responsibility for assembling the teams—from any section in the stores—that would help the cashiers if the lines were about to exceed the limit. The ability to decide who would be picked for these teams gave the store managers the power to foster cooperation and diligence in store operations and innovations.

# Rule 4: Increase the Need for Reciprocity

A good way to spur productive cooperation is to expand the responsibilities of integrators. Making their goals richer and more complex will drive them to resolve trade-offs rather than avoid them. But if you measure people only on what they can control, they will shy away from helping with many other problems you need their input on.

Consider the case of an airline that competes on asset utilization (having planes full and in the air rather than waiting on the ground) but doesn't want to compromise customer satisfaction. To achieve high utilization and satisfaction, the company makes aircraft crew members accountable for overseeing both cabin cleaning and ground service. The trade-off they are impelled to achieve—reconciling cabin cleanliness, customer experience, and speed of turnaround between flights—would be out of reach if people were forced to follow predefined procedures rather than decide what works best in each situation.

It might seem that you will multiply the number of goals and targets by applying this rule. Actually, this is not the case. What you will do is drive goals back to the employees who have to achieve them, so the people who are best positioned to resolve trade-offs are the ones handling them.

## Rule 5: Make Employees Feel the Shadow of the Future

Many of the decision makers who are involved at the launch of a three-year project will no longer be around when it's completed—they will have been moved to another job or location or have been promoted. They won't be affected by the consequences of the actions they take, the trade-offs they make, or how well they cooperate. To paraphrase game theorist Robert Axelrod, the "shadow" of the future does not reach them.

People are more likely to feel the shadow of the future if you bring the future closer. Companies can do this by shortening the lead times on projects or work processes or by assigning managers to downstream work. Consider the case of an industrial goods company that needed to lengthen the warranty period on certain products to fend off new competition. To do this cost-effectively, its engineering division had to make the product easier to repair.

Management established a new function that would coordinate all the decisions that affected repairability with all the engineering specialties—notably the mechanical and electrical groups. The coordinators, however, could not get the electrical and mechanical engineers to cooperate on repairability. Numerous "soft" initiatives had made them even more reluctant to negotiate tough trade-offs between electrical and mechanical constraints.

Then the company tried a new approach: moving some of the engineers to the after-sales network and making them responsible for the warranty budget. This meant that they would experience firsthand the effects of their design on that budget. The touchy-feely approach to collaboration stopped, and engineers quickly started to address the tough trade-offs. The solutions they developed enabled the company to meet both its repairability goals and the other requirements. Soon it extended the warranty period and did away with the coordination function and its processes, scorecards, and incentives.

# Rule 6: Put the Blame on the Uncooperative

Some activities involve such a long time lag between cause and effect that it's impossible to set up direct feedback loops that expose people to the consequences of their actions. There are also situations where jobs are so remote that it's difficult to have a direct feedback loop that makes the people who perform them feel interdependent with others. In those cases, managers have to close the feedback loop by introducing a penalty for any people or units that fail to cooperate on solving a problem and increasing the payoff when units cooperate in a beneficial way.

This was the approach taken by one railway company that was struggling to boost its on-time record. Applying Rule 1, the company focused on cooperation between the units whose performance affected timeliness. It became clear that each unit could, by cooperating, anticipate, absorb, and compensate for the delays or problems occurring in other units. But the company also realized that the people working in the various units were more concerned with not getting blamed for delays than with reducing them. That situation was the result of rules that assigned blame for a delay only on the unit responsible for its root cause. So, when Unit A had a problem, Units B and C did not feel impelled to help solve it.

The company modified the reward criteria. Once a unit told others it had a problem, the units that *failed to cooperate* in solving the problem would be held responsible for the delay. The station managers, who would be present in the necessary moments of cooperation, would judge which units had contributed to solving problems. In just four months, on-time performance jumped up to 95 percent on the major lines where the change was implemented.

## Why Not Aim for Smart Simplicity?

Smart rules allow companies to manage complexity not by prescribing specific behaviors but by creating a context within which optimal behaviors occur. This approach leads to greater organizational diversity, because frontline cooperation breeds creative solutions to problems. Yet despite this diversity, companies following smart rules are highly efficient, because problems are solved entirely by leveraging the skills and ingenuity of employees. Any costs generated by the diversity are more than offset by being able to ditch all the coordination and collaboration programs favored by many organizational experts. Employee satisfaction rises along with performance, as companies remove the complicatedness that causes both frustration and ineffectiveness. So rather than overload your org chart with a lot of arrows and layers, why not aim for the kind of smart simplicity you'll get from applying the six rules described in this chapter?

# Strategic Optimism: How to Shape the Future in Times of Crisis

## Hans-Paul Bürkner

For a while, during the height of the financial crisis, the world stared into the abyss. But in the end, there was no repeat of the Great Depression. Instead, there was what has become known as the Great Recession.

The concerted efforts of governments and central banks played a critical role in staving off a 1930s-style depression. But the actions of individuals and companies will shape the next phase of the recovery.

## The Glass Half Full: Optimism in Times of Crisis

It is all too easy to take a dark view of the decade to 2020. After all, there are several reasons to believe that growth in the global economy will remain sluggish for some time—even the once fast-growing developing markets such as China and India have slowed.

Companies and households are facing years—and governments are probably facing decades—of deleveraging; this bitter medicine will depress consumption and investment. Countries, in their efforts to prevent unemployment from rising ever higher and to champion the cause of local businesses, are engaging in protectionist measures; these moves could slow globalization. And regulators are clamping down on banks in ways that will constrain credit and investment.

We should be clear-eyed about these challenges and their implications. But we should also recognize that the world today is primed for change and filled with opportunity.

The fundamental drivers of growth are stronger than they have been at any point in human history. These include the increasing number of highly educated and capable people in the world, the breathtaking speed of technological breakthroughs, the onward march of globalization, the inclusion of the next billion into the world economy, and relative political stability.

Given this platform for growth, leaders have both an obligation and an imperative to move forward—with strategic optimism—to seek and to create growth, value, and opportunity for their countries and companies.

If this appears to be a tough assignment, that's because it is. But there will be support for this approach. Crisis and upheaval have historically unleashed enormous levels of pent-up creative energy, innovation, and fundamental change. When times are tough, we learn to make the difficult decisions that we should have made a long time ago. We cut back on waste and use scarce resources more efficiently. We come up with new solutions—and are willing to accept them. We step outside our comfort zone and go beyond our previous boundaries.

After the two oil shocks and the deindustrialization in major economies in the 1970s and early 1980s, the future looked bleak too. But technological advances, the fall of the Iron Curtain, and economic liberalization helped initiate nearly 30 years of unprecedented growth. Along the way, there were downturns and instances of greed, fraud, and irrational exuberance. But despite these detours, the world made progress. Many of the United Nations' much-heralded Millennium Development Goals—such as reducing hunger and child mortality and expanding education—are now closer to being realized than ever before.

Today's crisis could very well spur the next big wave of growth. In the aftermath of the Great Recession, we all have a rare opportunity to reinvent ourselves, to start afresh, to make things better than they were before.

# Carpe Diem: Turning Optimism into Action

What does this mean in practice?

For countries with bloated bureaucracies, aging populations, and rising health care and pension costs, it will require radically restructuring government programs, raising the retirement age, opening labor markets, and, of course, investing heavily in education. Greece, for example, would probably never have implemented its austerity program without the push of crisis. The undertaking will be a painful process, of course. But in a best-case scenario, Greece's moves will help return the country's people to a path of progress and prosperity.

For companies, it means making major changes that address the deep structural problems plaguing many industries. Pharmaceutical companies, for example, are facing a devastating double whammy: their labs are not developing the kind of breakthrough drugs they need to replace the blockbusters that are losing patent protection. Automotive manufacturers in Europe are still maintaining too much capacity and, in North America, they are producing too many of the wrong kind of cars—oversized gas-guzzlers. Media companies are struggling to persuade consumers to pay for news, music, and videos in the age of the Internet.

In the years before the crisis, companies were able to tinker with reform, safe in the knowledge that the rising tide of the global economy would help them in their efforts to survive and succeed. But today, these companies can no longer simply fine-tune their business model or fiddle with their cost base: the structural defects in their industries and in their business models are just too great to ignore.

Some companies have already accepted that they cannot go back. Faced with extinction and aided by government subsidies, General Motors has made painful but overdue decisions to sell money-losing divisions, close underutilized plants, and focus on energy-efficient cars.

But bold moves will not be enough. Companies also need to be quick, because time is not on their side. As the recovery takes hold, they will find it harder to make the tough decisions that were postponed during the boom years. With every passing year, they will also face growing global competition as companies from China, India, Brazil, and other emerging economies climb to the top of their industries. Unencumbered by legacy systems and cultures, these "global challenger" companies can move fast and aggressively.

So it is now time to stand up and be counted, take the future into your hands, grasp the opportunity presented by the worst economic crisis since the 1930s, and do things in a new and different way.

# 10 Steps to a New Way of Doing Business

Of course, this is easier said than done. But there are steps you can take to ensure that you become the master rather than the prisoner of circumstance—and that your organization returns to a strong growth trajectory.

1. Be frank about your company's current performance, your competitive threats, and why the crisis hit you so hard. Instill into your organization the courage to change, overturn the status quo, remove cumbersome legacy structures, and dispense with sacred cows.

2. Take a long-term view of value creation for your various stakeholders. Quick wins are nice to have, but sustainable success is nonnegotiable.

3. Move with deliberate speed to make the required transformation. Pace really matters: the ability to recognize and adapt swiftly to change will be a hallmark of the winners.

4. Help your organization see opportunity in the market changes. To be among the first to benefit from these changes, make use of shifting customer behaviors and attitudes and unleash the power of marketing.

5. Focus on innovation by investing in R&D, accelerating the introduction of new products and services, and redesigning processes.

6. Develop new business models: pilot low-cost approaches, experiment with high-value offerings, shift from products to services, or fundamentally restructure your portfolio of activities.

7. Embrace globalization and use fast-growing emerging markets not only as a supply base or as additional consumer markets but as a strong business base in their own right.

8. Play an active role in the consolidation of your industry through divestments and through mergers and acquisitions.

9. Take an agile and flexible approach. Experiment and transform yourself continually.

10. Build the strongest team you can. You should lead from the front and by example, but you should not expect to do it all on your own.

Future growth depends on our willingness to change the way we do things. This will not be easy. It will call for vision, courage, determination, and persistent execution. Above all, it calls for a resolute belief that we—each of us—can shape our destiny. As a guiding philosophy, optimism trumps pessimism. By acting with a positive outlook, we can succeed—individually and collectively.

After all, the future does not just happen. We make it happen.

# 50

# Lessons from My Three Decades with the Change Monster

## Jeanie Daniel Duck

Let me share with you 10 points that cover the majority of what leaders need to know, but don't often hear, about how to lead a major organizational transformation. Most of these lessons are common sense, but leaders frequently don't follow them.

## Be Bold

Any change effort requires resources and management attention. Why waste them on timid initiatives? Bold moves send a strong signal to the organization and build confidence. Confidence is central to change management. Do people believe that your plan is achievable and will make a substantial difference? Is it fact-based and strategically significant? If employees believe that management has the right plan and the skill, guts, and perseverance to go the distance, they will be willing to hang in there.

Too many companies start and abandon "projects du jour," declaring premature victory long before completion. This pattern sends employees the message either that their leaders are stupid or that they think the company's

---

This chapter is based on Jeanie Daniel Duck's 2001 book, *The Change Monster: The Human Forces That Fuel or Foil Corporate Transformation and Change*, published by Crown Business.

employees are. It teaches people to avoid changing and to dismiss what they hear from company leaders. Conversely, I've often worked with people who are near burnout but who keep going because they have confidence in the plan and in their managers.

## Be Utterly Obvious

Subtlety doesn't work. Even if you think that a message is obvious and that everybody ought to be able to connect the dots, they won't. As I've often said, people will connect the dots in the most pathological way possible. Therefore, you need to spell out your message, expectations, and reasoning as bluntly, clearly, and frequently as possible, showing the links between rhetoric and action, values and decisions, goals and metrics.

## Be Careful What You Promise

Always do what you say you're going to do. If you are going through a layoff, a restructuring, or a postmerger integration, everybody wants to know what's going to happen and when. If you promise an update by April 1, fulfill your promise—or else. Give yourself more time than you think you'll need. You can always be early, but being late is very costly.

## Make Commitments Stick

Let's talk about retroactive resistance. At the start of a project, everybody agrees about the need to change. Typically, they agree because they think it's someone else who needs to change. Then, when they get the detailed plan and discover that they themselves will have to change, they lose enthusiasm.

I believe in carrots and sticks. I don't believe there's one single way to motivate hundreds or thousands of people, and I'm convinced that some people will change only when they absolutely have to. I want to be able to use every possible lever available. I want to close all escape hatches. I want clear rewards, and I want clear negative consequences. If the initiative is working, the rewards will become far more frequent and punishments less necessary.

## Forget Happy

Some organizations think that if they change incrementally nobody will notice. But if nobody notices, then the change will not make a difference. If it doesn't hurt at some point, you're not changing. Trying to make people happy during a transformation is tough, if not impossible. Focus on what employees are doing rather than thinking or feeling. Coaches often talk about a winning attitude. I say, "You help me win a few times, and you'll be amazed at what happens to my attitude." At work, we rent behavior. Figure out what behaviors will create the win and then require those behaviors. Feelings follow behavior.

## Take Culture Seriously and Work On It Explicitly

Degrading a corporate culture is fairly easy to do and can happen amazingly quickly, but improving a culture takes time and consistency. You need to translate a new vision and new values into specific behaviors and actions using many different tools—job design, compensation, metrics, rewards, and evaluations, just to name a few. These tools must reinforce one another to reach a tipping point.

One company changed its compensation system so that financial performance made up only 25 percent of a senior manager's bonus, rather than 100 percent. For the first time, customer satisfaction, employee development, and process compliance weighed equally. At midyear, human resources showed managers what their bonuses would be based on their current performance. When people realized that ignoring employee development would cost them 25 percent of their bonus, they were blown away. The shock was equally strong when they saw the importance of customer satisfaction and process compliance. Suddenly managers started attending process-training sessions, truly paying attention to customers, and complying with established governance.

# Be Responsible and Stay Responsible

The kiss of death is the belief that implementation is somebody else's responsibility. Many corporate change initiatives follow a familiar pattern. Top executives decide on a new course and delegate implementation to line managers, who then delegate to their subordinates, and so on. This handoff almost always kills any meaningful possibility of change.

People need to be accountable. They need to know that the proposed changes will become permanent changes. Top executives need to visibly follow up, monitor, and step in to help, prod, and support. Top leaders need to receive monthly or quarterly scorecards or some other form of feedback to give them a sense of whether the initiative is steaming ahead or has fallen off the rails.

# Stay Connected

It's hard to be a leader if you don't know where the followers are. Many organizations are too big for top executives to talk to everyone, but it's usually possible to connect with the critical 10 percent. I would often ask leaders to name their 20 most critical people—those who shape the opinions of others and whom they count on to make things happen. You need to be engaged with these employees, and they need to be informed, involved, and heard. One way to achieve this is to send out a survey to these opinion leaders with a handful of questions: Is your boss clearly committed to making this change successful? Do you know what is expected of you? Do you think the change initiative will work? What three things could your boss do to become a more effective leader? Executives need this feedback, and they need to know what their star performers are thinking, doing, and telling others.

The first time I introduced this approach, one executive gave me a look that said, "You really are stupid. All I have to do is make sure that my 20 most important people are always up to date." My silent response was, "Yes, and if I have to do a survey every quarter to make sure you keep those 20 people well informed, I'll do it."

## Provide Interpretation and Meaning

Organizations look to their leaders to interpret events. People want to know what today's headlines, corporate moves, and failed projects mean and how they are supposed to react. If their leaders fail to provide this context, employees will quickly fill the vacuum with speculation and doomsday proclamations that would make Chicken Little jealous.

## Celebrate the Accomplishments Along the Way

Transforming an organization takes energy. Winning creates energy. Look for opportunities to create early wins—they build confidence and motivate the troops. During the early days of a massive transformation at an industrial goods company, employees were deeply cynical and short of hope. To change that dynamic, we identified the 20 most pressing quality problems and began to fix them. As those problems disappeared, people began to believe that change was possible. They started to contribute their ideas and volunteer their help. When employees see the power of energy, persistence, and engagement, they begin to have confidence in their ability to wrestle the change monster to the ground.

# Contributors

**Marcos Aguiar** is a senior partner and managing director in BCG's São Paulo and Rio de Janeiro offices.

**Lionel Aré** is a senior partner and managing director in BCG's Paris office and global leader of the firm's Financial Institutions practice.

**Gaby Barrios** is a project leader in BCG's Boston office and a member of BCG's Center for Consumer and Customer Insight.

**Cynthia M. Beath** is a professor emerita of information systems at the McCombs School of Business, University of Texas at Austin.

**Alex Bernhardt** is a principal in BCG's Atlanta office and a topic leader for Adaptive Advantage.

**Vikram Bhalla** is a senior partner and managing director in BCG's Mumbai office, a BCG Fellow, and the Asia-Pacific leader of the firm's People and Organization practice.

**Arindam K. Bhattacharya** is a partner and managing director in BCG's New Delhi office and a topic leader for the firm's Global Advantage practice. He coauthored *Globality—Competing with Everyone from Everywhere for Everything* in 2008.

**Cynthia Blendu** is a principal in BCG's Washington, D.C., office and previously the global manager for the firm's Transformation topic area.

**Alain Bloch** is a professor at CNAM and HEC Paris, the academic director of HEC Entrepreneurs, and a cofounder of HEC Paris Family Business.

**Dylan Bolden** is a partner and managing director in BCG's Dallas office and a global topic leader for Branding.

**Luc de Brabandere** is a senior advisor to BCG's Strategy practice. He was formerly a partner and managing director in the firm's Paris office and a BCG Fellow in Corporate Creativity. He wrote *The Forgotten Half of Change: Achieving Greater Creativity through Changes in Perception* in

2005 and is coauthor of *Thinking in New Boxes*, to be published by Random House in 2013.

**Thomas Bradtke** is a partner and managing director in BCG's Dubai office and the Middle East leader of the firm's Industrial Goods, Operations, and Global Advantage practices.

**John Budd** is a partner and managing director in BCG's Dallas office and the global topic leader for Retail Pricing.

**Hans-Paul Bürkner** is BCG's chairman. He is a senior partner and managing director in the firm's Frankfurt office and was president and chief executive officer of BCG from 2004 through 2012.

**Benjamin Burnett** is a former partner and managing director in BCG's Chicago office.

**Jean-Michel Caye** is a senior partner and managing director in BCG's Paris office, a BCG Fellow, and a topic leader in the firm's People and Organization practice.

**Sami Chabenne** is a partner and managing director in BCG's Casablanca office.

**Ted Chan** is a partner and managing director in BCG's Hong Kong office and the global topic leader for New Market Entry. He leads the firm's Corporate Development practice in Greater China.

**John S. Clarkeson** served as chief executive officer of BCG from 1986 through 1997 and as chairman from 1998 through 2007; he is chairman emeritus today.

**Pascal Cotte** is a senior partner and managing director in BCG's Paris office and leader of BCG's supply chain work in the energy industry.

**David Dean** is a senior partner and managing director in BCG's Munich office and is a former global leader of the firm's Technology, Media, and Telecommunications practice.

**Michael Deimler** is a senior partner and managing director in BCG's Atlanta office and was the global leader of the firm's Strategy practice from 2005 through 2012. He coedited *The Boston Consulting Group on Strategy*, published in 2006.

**Sebastian DiGrande** is a senior partner and managing director in BCG's San Francisco office and the Americas' leader of the firm's Technology, Media, and Telecommunications practice.

**Jeanie Daniel Duck** was a senior partner and managing director in BCG's Atlanta office from 1988 through 2008. She is the author of the best-selling 2002 book *The Change Monster: The Human Forces That Fuel or Foil Corporate Transformation and Change.*

**Patrick Dupoux** is a partner and managing director in BCG's Casablanca office and a topic leader for Global Advantage.

**Sylvain Duranton** is a senior partner and managing director in BCG's Paris office and the global topic coleader for Pricing.

**Andrew Dyer** is a senior partner and managing director in BCG's Sydney office and was previously global leader of the firm's People and Organization practice from 2006 through 2012.

**Lisa Dymond** is a topic specialist in organization and people issues in BCG's Toronto office.

**Tenbite Ermias** is the managing partner of BCG's Johannesburg office and is the sub-Saharan Africa topic leader for BCG's Energy and Global Advantage practices. He is actively involved with BCG's Economic Development topic area.

**Philip Evans** is a senior partner and managing director in BCG's Boston office and a BCG Fellow. He founded the firm's Media and Internet practices. He coauthored the bestselling book *Blown to Bits* in 2000.

**Hady Farag** is a principal in BCG's Hamburg office.

**Adam Farber** is a senior partner and managing director in BCG's Boston office and the Americas' leader of the firm's Health Care practice.

**Dominic Field** is a partner and managing director in BCG's London office and is the global leader of the firm's Digital Economy initiative.

**Paul Foo** was a principal in BCG's Shanghai office until 2012.

**Grant Freeland** is a senior partner and managing director in BCG's Boston office and is the global leader of the firm's People and Organization practice.

**Daniel Friedman** is a senior partner and managing director in BCG's Los Angeles office and has also worked in the firm's Chicago office. He leads BCG's Corporate Development and Post Merger Integration practices for the Americas.

**Erin George** is a principal in BCG's Dallas office.

**Eugene Goh** is a principal in BCG's Oslo office and the firm's topic leader for Social Advantage.

**José Guevara** is a partner and managing director in BCG's Monterrey office and a topic leader for Biopharma in emerging markets.

**Steve Gunby** is a senior partner and managing director in BCG's Washington, D.C., office and the global leader for Transformation/Accelerated Change.

**Knut Haanaes** is the global leader of BCG's Strategy practice. He is a partner and managing director in BCG's Geneva office.

**Gerry Hansell** is a senior partner and managing director in the BCG's Chicago office and a BCG Fellow.

**Whitney Haring-Smith** is a project leader in BCG's San Francisco office.

**Jim Hemerling** is a senior partner and managing director in BCG's San Francisco office. He is the leader of the firm's Behavior & Culture topic and coauthor of the 2008 book *Globality—Competing with Everyone from Everywhere for Everything*.

**Bruce Henderson** founded BCG in 1963. He is most famous for discovering the experience curve and inventing the growth-share ("Boston") matrix. He served as chairman and chief executive officer of the firm until 1985. He died in 1992.

**Dieter Heuskel** is a senior partner and managing director in BCG's Düsseldorf office and is the chairman of BCG Germany. He previously headed the firm's Global Strategy Practice Initiative.

**Thomas M. Hout** is a former BCG partner and managing director. He has held an adjunct appointment as faculty associate at Harvard University's Center for International Affairs.

**Rich Hutchinson** is a senior partner and managing director in BCG's Atlanta office and the coleader of the firm's Enablement initiative.

**Alan Iny** is a senior topic specialist for Creativity and Scenarios in the Strategy practice, based in BCG's New York office. He is coauthor of *Thinking in New Boxes*, to be published by Random House in 2013.

**Jonathan L. Isaacs** was a senior partner and managing director in BGC's Boston office. He died in 2003.

**Lisa Ivers** is a principal in BCG's Casablanca office.

**Jean-Manuel Izaret** is a partner and managing director in BCG's San Francisco office and the global topic coleader for Pricing.

**Dan Jansen** is a former partner and managing director in BCG's Los Angeles office and was the firm's global practice leader for Media and Entertainment.

**David Jin** is a partner and managing director in BCG's Shanghai office and a topic leader in the firm's Global Advantage practice.

**Jeremy Jurgens** is a senior director and the head of membership at the World Economic Forum.

**Nicolas Kachaner** is a senior partner and managing director in BCG's Paris office and a BCG Fellow on Business Model Innovation. He is the global topic leader for Strategic Planning and Family Business and leads the firm's Strategy practice in Western Europe and South America.

**Simon Kennedy** is a senior partner and managing director in BCG's Boston office and the global leader of the firm's Health Care IT practice.

**David Kiron** is the executive editor of *MIT Sloan Management Review*'s Innovation Hubs.

**Claudio Knizek** is a partner and managing director in BCG's Washington, D.C. office.

**Jeffrey Kotzen** is a senior partner and managing director in BCG's New York office and the firm's global topic leader for Shareholder Value Strategy.

**Nina Kruschwitz** is the sustainability editor for *MIT Sloan Management Review*. She coauthored *The Necessary Revolution* in 2010.

**Rob Lachenauer** is a former partner and managing director in BCG's Chicago office and coauthor of the 2004 book *Hardball: Are You Playing to Play or Playing to Win?*

**David Lee** is a partner and managing director in BCG's Shanghai office and leads the firm's Operations practice in Greater China.

**Richard Lesser** became president and chief executive officer of BCG in January 2013. Before that, he was the firm's regional chairman in North and South America. He is based in New York and also has an office in Beijing.

**Thomas Lewis** is a senior advisor based in BCG's Rome office and is a leader of the firm's Social Impact practice.

**Zhenya Lindgardt** is a partner and managing director in BCG's New York office and is the firm's Business Model Innovation topic leader.

**Claire Love** is a project leader in BCG's New York office and was an Ambassador to the BCG Strategy Institute from 2010 to 2011.

**Joe Manget** is a former senior partner and managing director in BCG's Toronto office and was the global leader of the firm's Operations practice.

**David Matheson** is a former senior partner and is currently a senior advisor to BCG. He was one of the founders of the firm's Health Care practice and led BCG's Boston office.

**Antonella Mei-Pochtler** is a senior partner and managing director in BCG's Vienna office. She leads the firm's Marketing and Sales practice in Europe and is the worldwide topic leader for Branding.

**Keith Melker** is a principal in BCG's Dallas office.

**Amyn Merchant** leads BCG's Northeast U.S. system and the firm's New York office and is a senior partner and managing director of BCG.

**Michael Meyer** is a partner and managing director in BCG's Singapore office and leads the firm's Global Advantage practice in Southeast Asia.

**David C. Michael** leads BCG's Global Advantage practice. He is a senior partner and managing director in the firm's San Francisco office, having also served in BCG's Beijing office. He coauthored the 2012 book *The $10 Trillion Prize: Captivating the Newly Affluent in China and India.*

**Yves Morieux** is a senior partner and managing director in BCG's Mumbai office and a BCG Fellow. He leads the firm's Institute for Organization.

**Lyuba Nazaruk** is an associate director at the World Economic Forum.

**Christoph Nettesheim** is a senior partner and managing director of BCG and led the firm's business in Greater China until 2013.

**Ron Nicol** is a senior partner and managing director in BCG's Dallas office and previously was the global leader of the firm's Technology, Media, and Telecommunications practice and its Organization practice.

**Eric Olsen** is a senior advisor to BCG. He served as a senior partner and managing director in the firm's Chicago office and as the global leader for Shareholder Value Management.

**Paul Orlander** was BCG's global topic leader for Engagement and Culture. He is a former partner and managing director in the firm's Toronto office, where he worked with many leading financial institutions.

**Petros Paranikas** is a partner and managing director in BCG's Chicago office and the firm's Americas' topic leader for Procurement.

**David K. Pecaut** is a former senior partner and managing director in BCG's Toronto office. He died in 2009. Pecaut Square in Toronto is named after him.

**Ignacio Peña** is a former partner and managing director in BCG's São Paulo office and was the Latin America leader of the firm's Strategy practice.

**Frank Plaschke** is a partner and managing director in BCG's Munich office and the global topic leader for Office of the CFO and the European topic leader for Shareholder Value Strategy.

**Martin Reeves** leads the BCG Strategy Institute. He is a senior partner and managing director in the firm's New York office and is a BCG Fellow.

**David Rhodes** is the chairman of BCG's Global Practices. These are 16 centers of expertise devoted to particular industries and functions; together they cover all of the firm's business. He is a senior partner and managing director in BCG's London office and coauthor of *Accelerating out of the Great Recession: How to Win in a Slow-Growth Economy*, published in 2010.

**Catherine Roche** is a partner and managing director in BCG's Toronto office and the worldwide topic leader for the firm's Center for Consumer and Customer Insight.

**Alexander Roos** is a senior partner and managing director in BCG's Berlin office. He leads the firm's Corporate Development practice and its Global Mergers and Acquisitions team.

**Jeanne W. Ross** is director and principal research scientist at MIT Sloan School's Center for Information Systems Research. She coauthored *IT Savvy: What Top Executives Must Know to Go from Pain to Gain* in 2009, *Enterprise Architecture as Strategy: Creating a Foundation for Business Execution* in 2006, and *IT Governance: How Top Performers Manage IT Decision Rights for Superior Results* in 2004.

**Rohan Sajdeh** is a senior partner and managing director in BCG's Chicago office.

**Stuart Scantlebury** is a senior advisor in BCG's Boston office. He served as a partner and managing director until 2006 and was the founder and global leader of the firm's IT Organization topic area.

**Filippo L. Scognamiglio Pasini** is a project leader in BCG's New York office and an ambassador to the firm's Strategy Institute.

**Jonathan Sharp** is a partner and managing director in BCG's Melbourne office and is a global topic leader in the firm's Consumer practice.

**Lawrence E. Shulman** is a senior partner and managing director in BCG's Chicago office and was previously the global leader of the Strategy practice.

**Michael J. Silverstein** is a senior partner and managing director in BCG's Chicago office. He coauthored *Treasure Hunt: Inside the Mind of the New Consumer; Trading Up: Why Consumers Want New Luxury Goods-and How Companies Create Them; The $10 Trillion Prize: Captivating the Newly Affluent in China and India;* and *Women Want More: How to Capture Your Share of the World's Largest, Fastest-Growing Market.* He led the firm's Consumer practice from 1995 to 2003.

**Janmejaya Sinha** is a senior partner and managing director in BCG's Mumbai office. He is currently chairman of the Asia Pacific region for the firm.

**Harold L. Sirkin** is a senior partner and managing director in BCG's Chicago office and formerly the global leader of the firm's E-commerce practice, its Operations practice, and its IT practice. He coauthored *The US Manufacturing Renaissance: How Shifting Global Economics Are Creating an American Comeback* in 2012, *Globality—Competing with Everyone from Everywhere* in 2008, and *Payback: Reaping the Rewards of Innovation* in 2006. He writes a weekly column for Businessweek.com.

**Marty Smits** is a partner and managing director in BCG's Amsterdam office and leads the consumer goods sector in the Strategy and Sustainability practice.

**George Stalk Jr.,** is a BCG senior adviser and a BCG Fellow. He serves as an adjunct professor of strategic management for the Rotman School of Management at the University of Toronto and is a Fellow of the Strategic Management Society. He is the coauthor of *Competing against Time, Kaisha: The Japanese Corporation,* as well as *Hardball: Are You Playing to Play or Playing to Win?* He is the coeditor of *Perspectives on Strategy from The Boston Consulting Group* and a frequent contributor to *Harvard Business Review* and other major business periodicals.

**Daniel Stelter** is a senior partner and managing director in BCG's Berlin office and a BCG Fellow. He was formerly the global leader of the firm's Corporate Development practice and coauthored *Accelerating out of the Great Recession: How to Win in a Slow Growth Economy* in 2010.

**Carl W. Stern** served as president and chief executive officer of BCG from 1987 through 2003 and as chairman until 2011. He coedited *The Boston Consulting Group on Strategy*.

**Peter Strüven** is a senior advisor in BCG's Munich office and was the Post Merger Integration global topic leader from 2005 to 2010. He was a senior partner and managing director at the firm from 1978 to 2010. He coauthored *Gebt uns das Risiko zurück* in 1998 and wrote *Der Befreiungsschlag* in 2003.

**Deran Taskiran** is a partner and managing director in BCG's Istanbul office.

**Bob Tevelson** is a senior partner and managing director in BCG's Philadelphia office and the firm's global topic leader for Procurement.

**Philipp Tillmanns** is a consultant in BCG's Hamburg office and a Ph.D. candidate at RTWH Aachen University in Germany.

**Roselinde Torres** is a senior partner and managing director in BCG's New York office and is the firm's global topic leader for Leadership. She was named a BCG Fellow in 2009.

**Andrew Tratz** is the global manager for BCG's Global Advantage practice.

**Masao Ukon** is a partner and managing director in BCG's São Paulo office and the Brazil leader of the Global Advantage practice.

**Sharad Verma** is a partner and managing director in BCG's New Delhi office.

**Diederik Vismans** is a project leader in BCG's Geneva office.

**Kim Wagner** is a senior partner and managing director in BCG's New York office and a topic leader for Agribusiness and Research & Product Development.

**Bernd Waltermann** is a senior partner and managing director in BCG's Singapore office and is head of BCG in Southeast Asia.

**Stephanie L. Woerner** is a research scientist at MIT Sloan Center for Information Systems Research, with focus in the areas of digitization investment and governance and digital business models.

**Bob Wolf** is a former manager in BCG's Boston office and founded the firm's Network Advantage practice.

**Yvonne Zhou** is a principal in BCG's Beijing office.

**Michael Zinser** is a partner and managing director in BCG's Chicago office and is the firm's Americas' Manufacturing topic leader. He coauthored *The U.S. Manufacturing Renaissance: How Shifting Global Economics Are Creating an American Comeback* in 2012.

**Paul Zwillenberg** is a partner and managing director in BCG's London office.

# Index